TRACTs

Trauma Recovery Activities

Over 130 Activities, Ideas and Forms to
Encourage Healing after Trauma

By Becca C. Johnson, Ph.D.

Graphics used in this book were developed by the author, used by permission or copyright free from websites or document program files.

Published by Rescue: Freedom International

ISBN:

9780998980027

The information contained herein is not intended to be psychotherapy or to substitute for consultation with a licensed health or mental health professional. Application of the contents is at the reader's sole discretion.

DEDICATION

To the amazing, resilient trauma survivors I have had the privilege to meet or serve. Your strength amidst the grief and horrors of your traumas is inspirational. And, to those who assist the traumatized on their healing journey, may this book help you help others.

ACKNOWLEDGEMENTS

Thank you to those who have allowed me to use many of these activities with them in the course of their healing journey. As always, my prayer is to help facilitate the healing process. Thank you also to those service providers who shared about activities they have found helpful.

Table Of Contents

NUMERICAL LIST OF ACTIVITIES

To make a difference in someone's life you just need to care.

Whoever is kind to the needy honors God.

PROVERBS 14:31

OVERVIEW

WHY THIS BOOK?

This book has been twenty-five years in the making. I first started compiling these helpful counseling activities after seeing first-hand how beneficial they are to the people I have the privilege of serving. Many people I've worked with, whether in the privacy of the office or at a seminar or retreat, have shared with me how helpful and effective these activities have been for them. This encouraged me to begin gathering these practices together for others to use.

Now, years later, I return to this project because it is still needed. While other books provide activities that aid in the counseling and healing process, I have yet to find any that *compartmentalize the activities according to components of trauma treatment* or that adequately categorize activities by numerous helpful criteria.

The activities included in this workbook are intended to assist the individual serving in the counselor role as they seek to help victims of trauma, whatever the gender preference, age, whether victims of one or multiple traumas, or whether the trauma is recent or from years ago.

WHY THESE ACTIVITIES?

This book could easily have twice as many pages. The Trauma Recovery Activities (TRACTs) chosen to be included represent a variety of possible exercises for each trauma recovery stage or category, but they are by no means exhaustive. Instead, there is a section entitled Variations, which encourages creativity in adapting or developing new activities based on the need or the situation. Many of the activities can be adapted for use with different age groups or by simply switching from written worksheets to verbal questioning. This, of course, also works with the pre-literate or illiterate. Like reading a recipe, some will follow the exact directions in the exact order while others will glance at the overall recipe and create their own adaptation. Both are welcomed here.

Our primary goal is to foster personal growth and healing with those we serve. My deepest desire is that these activities help both the person in the counseling role as well as the individual on their journey of restoration.

FEATURES OF THIS BOOK

Whether you're trying to find a helpful activity for dealing with feelings (emotional regulation) using little or no supplies, or you're looking for something to help an illiterate adult engage in and increase more positive thinking patterns (dealing with cognitive distortions), you'll be able to find what you're looking for in these pages.

Each Activity...

- **Is organized** by trauma recovery component category
- **Is clearly labeled** according to a variety of criteria
- **Is cross-referenced** by name, trauma target, format (individual-group-both), and preferred age group
- **Includes helpful information** regarding supplies and time needed
- **Provides a section on variations** with ways to adapt or use the activity differently
- **Includes reflection or debrief questions** to ask the client
- **Cites any concerns or limitations** to consider when using it

TERMINOLOGY

Because this workbook will be used by both professional therapists and lay-trained facilitators, as well as those from both high and low resource countries, the preferred terms chosen to refer to the therapist/counselor, the client/victim, and the helper/caregiver are explained here.

■ Those We Serve

Our focus is to serve, help, encourage, and guide. The terms *client, victim,* or *beneficiary* often seem clinical and impersonal. Instead, the words *person, individual,* and *participant* are used more frequently in these pages. Occasionally the word *survivor* may be used to convey that the person is no longer being victimized or that the person is healing and moving from *victim* to *survivor.*

■ Those On The Front Lines

To describe those who work directly with victims, the words *helpers* or *caregivers* are primarily used. While this may refer to parents, relatives, or foster care parents, it also includes resident managers, house moms, and house counselors in residential programs.

■ Those Providing Counseling Services

Whether social worker, psychologist, therapist, or professional or lay counselor, this is the person who incorporates the activities purposefully in an effort to assist the individuals (victims) toward healing. Primarily referred to as the *facilitator,* another term used is *counselor.*

■ Those Who Caused Harm

Most activities do not focus on the person who caused harm—the abuser, offender, perpetrator, trafficker—but those that do primarily use the terms *perpetrator* or *abuser.*

ACTIVITY FORMAT

Each activity is presented in a similar format to provide a quick and clear reference of the key features and purpose. Format components include:

■ Activity

The activity # reflects the ongoing number of activities (rather than re-numbering within each stage of the recovery process). This makes searching and cross-referencing more efficient.

■ Trauma Recovery Area

The third chapter explains the selection of the trauma recovery components, such as why the categories were chosen and how they were named. Activities are presented in the trauma recovery area that is the "best fit" though some can be used or adapted for use in other areas.

■ Setting: (Individual – Group – Both)

Some activities are most effective in a one-on-one setting while others are most beneficial in groups. Others, though intended for private sessions, can be adapted for groups. If the facilitator specifically needs a group or an individual activity within a trauma recovery target area, this information is quickly accessible in the top right corner of the page.

■ Age: (Children – Adults – Both)

TRACTs are included that focus on children, youth, and adults. While most tend to focus on youth or adults rather than children, many of the trauma recovery activities can easily be adapted for younger populations by using stories, pictures, illustrations, or games. Once the facilitator understands the underlying purpose of the activity, they are free to be creative in how they approach using the activities for the various age groups.

■ Name of Activity

Activities are given common-sense, easily understood names whenever possible to facilitate quick understanding.

■ Time

The approximate amount of time needed is very flexible and represents an estimate of the time needed to complete the activity. While the approximate time necessary for the activity is listed, it varies greatly depending on the amount of discussion, the number of reflection questions asked, whether done in individual or group settings (as well as the number of people in the group), and whether translation is needed.

■ Supplies Needed

If additional supplies are needed (markers, paper, or other materials), it is listed. An attempt has been made to focus on activities with little or no supplies required. Most often, the need for supplies is limited to the included worksheet which may be copied from the book or translated and placed in another document.

■ Reflection

Questions to ask participants before, during, or after the exercise are included in this section. Italics are used (instead of quotation marks) for statements or questions representing what the facilitator could ask directly to participants.

■ Variations

Other ways of conducting the activity are listed to foster flexibility, especially given different country and cultural contexts and issues. *Facilitators are encouraged to contextualize and individualize the activities for their setting and situation.* Creativity is also encouraged to adapt and develop additional activities. Most activities can be offered verbally as well as using the included worksheets. Explanations can be discussed directly with adults or adapted for young children in the form of stories.

■ Concerns

Our primary goal is to help, not harm. Limitations, concerns, and things to consider are listed in this section in order to provide the facilitator with additional insight into when and whether or not to use the activity with certain participants or in certain situations. Possible concerns are listed, but facilitators are encouraged to identify additional concerns specific to their clients, culture, and context.

TRAUMA RECOVERY COMPONENTS: SUMMARIES AND CHECKLISTS

Each trauma recovery area in this book begins with a summary overview of the goals and steps. This is not intended to provide extensive information on trauma recovery; just a review. The included Checklists are also only intended as a guide, not as an inflexible list of required tasks. The facilitator decides which activities to use and which tasks to complete based on the individual needs of the client and your cultural context. (The chapter on Understanding Trauma Recovery presents information on how the trauma treatment components used in this workbook were selected.)

GENERAL CONCERNS AND LIMITATIONS

While more specific concerns are listed for the various activities, general issues and concerns exist that apply to all.

■ Adequate Rapport

If a trusting, safe relationship has not been established between the facilitator and the individual, the activities become less effective. They are built on the foundation of a growing trust developing between the person in the therapist role and the individual in the client role. The person must feel emotionally safe, and that he or she is in a non-judgmental, accepting environment, for the activities to be most beneficial.

■ Mutual Understanding of Purpose

Both counselor and client must understand why they are meeting. The overall goal is for the person "to feel better," to recover from the aftermath of trauma, heal from emotional pain, develop healthy coping skills, and reduce negative beliefs and behaviors. This also encompasses safety planning and future goal setting.

■ Client-Centered

The client and his/her concerns are our focus. We allow the individual to help determine what, when, and how we proceed. The clients help establish the pace, communicate the direction (whether spoken or unspoken), and inform us by their reactions. Our therapeutic agenda is flexible and ever-adaptable according to the individual's needs. Illiteracy, health, disability, mental illness, memory deficits, developmental delays, learning challenges, etc., all require us to adjust what we do with the individual. One size does not fit all.

■ Appropriate Age, Gender, and Culture

As we provide opportunities for healing, we do so with a continual awareness of the need to ensure all activities are appropriate to the age, gender, and culture of the individuals we serve. We adapt, change, adjust, and modify in order to best help each individual.

■ Research-Supported

Provision of counseling services should be grounded in well-researched therapeutic treatment models. What we do is based upon the experience of those who have gone before us. We respect and rely on our predecessors who have painstakingly provided us with information on what does and doesn't work well when working with victims and survivors of extreme trauma. While much research has been conducted on trauma recovery, it is not yet available in many countries or to all those working with highly and multiple-traumatized victims—such as those who have suffered human trafficking. In these situations, we rely on what is available but remain aware of the need for flexibility and adaptation due to cultural and population differences.

■ Client Resistance

There are many reasons why the individual may be resistant to counseling and/or to doing the activities. The primary problem is generally a lack of therapeutic alliance with the counselor. That is, if the person doesn't feel comfortable, liked, and safe with the facilitator, he/she will resist interactions, questions, ideas and activities.

Here is a list of factors contributing to client resistance.

- Lack of a positive, safe relationship with the facilitator
- Embarrassment from not understanding, having poor grammar, spelling, and/or writing skills...
- Fear of wrong answers
- Fear of displeasing the facilitator
- Doesn't understand why counseling can be beneficial
- Doesn't believe in counseling or believes it to be meaningless
- Believes counseling is only for the seriously ill or "crazy" people

- Lacks understanding of what is being asked
- Hesitant to face the emotional pain
- Counseling isn't meeting individual needs and concerns
- Displays passive-aggressive behavior
- Feeling overwhelmed, depressed, hopeless
- Past failures and negative memories are triggered
- Lacks motivation
- In denial that anything is wrong or that they need help
- Demonstrates difficulties with people in authority

These are but some of the many challenges that we may face as we seek to help victims. Add to the list what you have experienced as hindrances or blocks to therapeutic success in your work as a counselor or service provider.

WORKBOOK CONCERNS AND LIMITATIONS

It is critical that users of this book understand that the content is designed to accompany and to assist those already familiar with and having education, training, and/or experience in trauma recovery. It is not intended to be an instructional tool or training manual on the *how-to* of trauma therapy, but to assist those already providing such services. And, this workbook was developed with lay service providers from low resource countries in mind. Thus, psychological terminology and constructs have been minimized or presented in a user-friendly approach.

For those wanting more, detailed training, a free online training of a recommended trauma recovery model is available on the TF-CBT website (accessed at https://tfcbt2.musc.edu). Trauma-Focused Cognitive Behavioral Therapy, developed by Drs. Cohen, Mannarino, and Deblinger, includes many of the common trauma treatment components used here. Also helpful is the extensive training and resource book, *Treating Traumatic Stress in Children and Adolescents* by Margaret E. Blaustein and Kristine M. Kinniburgh, (The Guilford Press, 2019) which conceptualizes a treatment framework using a series of building blocks related to attachment, self-regulation, and competency.

The first few chapters in this workbook, as well as each section's introduction, provide a brief overview of steps in the recovery process but do not provide the necessary education nor foundational understanding required. *This is not a training manual, but a resource meant to supplement the facilitator's provision of service.*

■ Benefits of This Workbook

Adaptable: Facilitators are encouraged to adapt the various activities considering their culture, context, setting (residential or non-residential), and the person's issues (abuse, exploitation, trafficking, violence, etc.). Adjust, adapt, revise, edit or add as deemed beneficial.

Facilitator-Chooses: Each section or trauma recovery component includes at least 10 activities, usually more. The facilitator chooses those activities determined most beneficial for those in their care, whether one activity or many. Activities are chosen according to the trauma recovery target area and the individual's age, issues, culture, setting, developmental level, literacy...

Why use these activities? How might they be beneficial? They can potentially:

- Save time
- Identify key concerns or problems more readily
- Focus in on key issues
- Help the unspeakable become 'speakable'

- Provide direction to sessions
- Foster helpful discussions
- Open up new possibilities for healing
- Identify patterns more quickly

May this book of counseling tools and activities be beneficial as you seek to help others.

To live is to suffer, to survive is to find some meaning in the suffering.

FRIEDRICH NIETZSCHE

UNDERSTANDING TRAUMA

As I have trained on trauma recovery around the world, I have met many people who don't fully understand what trauma is—even though they work directly with the traumatized. Many have not learned how to help people overcome the ongoing negative effects of their trauma. While numerous helpers initially think "I already know about trauma", I am regularly approached after a training and told, "I thought I knew about trauma but after this, I realize how much I don't know."

Just because we have experienced a trauma or helped someone in our past doesn't mean that we understand what it is or how it intrudes and affects our day-to-day lives. This chapter presents an overview of trauma and provides the foundation on how to assist victims and survivors in the recovery process.

TRAUMA DEFINITIONS

Those in the medical profession use the word "trauma" to refer predominately to a physical injury. Those in helping professions, such as counseling and therapy refer to the emotional or mental affects or aftermath. These helpers have described trauma as:

- a heart wound
- an emotional pain
- a bad experience
- an emotional response to a shocking or unexpected negative experience

DICTIONARIES DEFINE TRAUMA AS:

- a deeply distressing or disturbing experience
- emotional shock following a stressful event or a physical injury, which may be associated with physical shock and sometimes leads to long-term neurosis

(Merriam Webster Dictionary, 2018)

Other words used interchangeably might include shock, upheaval, distress, stress, pain, anguish, suffering, upset, agony, misery, sorrow, grief, heartache, heartbreak, torture; ordeal, trial, tribulation, or trouble.

Related terms might include crisis, abuse, complex trauma, and PTSD (Post-Traumatic Stress Disorder).

TYPES OF TRAUMA

While there are many causes of trauma, three types of trauma are identified here.

➤ Trauma

Trauma (direct or primary trauma) refers to the direct effect on an individual who has experienced a traumatic event.

➤ Secondary Trauma

Secondary Trauma refers to the effect on someone who is close to a trauma victim or who has observed a traumatic event, even though the trauma didn't happen directly to him/her.

➤ Vicarious Trauma

Vicarious Trauma, (sometimes referred to as Compassion Fatigue or Secondary Traumatic Stress), refers to the trauma experienced by those who work with the traumatized. It is the accumulation of being exposed to others' trauma stories.

TRAUMA EVENTS AND EXPERIENCES

Traumatic events are overwhelming, unexpected, and unwanted. They often bring up feelings of anger, frustration, regret, remorse, ridicule, sadness, and shame or self-blame. The response to trauma is specific to the individual's personality and may also be influenced by his/her family, ethnicity, religion, and culture.

Responses will also depend on age at the time of the traumatic event, the longevity of the trauma, the relationship with the offender, and the existence (or lack of) supportive caregivers (refer to list below). What is traumatizing to one person may not be to another, and vice-versa. Visiting a dentist, seeing a snake, being laughed off a stage, experiencing rejection or betrayal are but a few of the many possible events considered 'traumatic.'

I once gave this list to parents and their young adult daughter who had been adopted at age 9. They were frustrated at the relational challenges they were experiencing. As an exercise, I gave each a list of trauma events and asked them to indicate how many traumas they had experienced. The mother had 3, the father had 4 and the daughter had 16. This exercise alone increased the parents' understanding and empathy for their daughter and the traumas she had experienced before joining their family. Some of the traumas on the list include:

- ➲ Child Physical Abuse
- ➲ Child Neglect
- ➲ Emotional Abuse
- ➲ Child Sexual Abuse
- ➲ Satanic Ritual Abuse
- ➲ Being Prostituted
- ➲ Domestic Violence
- ➲ Assault: Physical
- ➲ Assault: Sexual (Rape)
- ➲ Serious Accident
- ➲ Violent death of loved one
- ➲ Witnessed violent death (anyone)
- ➲ Accidental Death (observed or close person)
- ➲ Exposed to War
- ➲ Exposed to Community or School Violence
- ➲ Exposed to Gang Violence
- ➲ Exposed to acts of Terrorism
- ➲ Deprivation
- ➲ Unjust Imprisonment
- ➲ Serious Physical Injury or illness

- ⮑ Risky or Unplanned medical procedure
- ⮑ Abortion (forced or not)
- ⮑ Forced Separation and/or Relocation
- ⮑ Drug Use
- ⮑ Divorce of parents
- ⮑ Divorce (self)
- ⮑ Adultery and/or Infidelity of Spouse

- ⮑ Suicide
- ⮑ Homicide/Murder
- ⮑ Natural Disaster (earthquake, tornado, fire)
- ⮑ Man-made Disaster
- ⮑ Torture (self)
- ⮑ Kidnapped (self or child)

One's reaction to trauma depends on a variety of factors such as:

- ⮑ Age at time of the trauma(s)
- ⮑ Gender – Race – Religion – Family Values - Culture
- ⮑ Existence of supportive caregivers

- ⮑ Longevity of the trauma
- ⮑ Relationship with the offender
- ⮑ Resiliency and personality of the victim

Whether one time or 100 time; whether an accident, assault, or abuse; whether domestic violence, divorce or death; all trauma can be traumatizing.

TRAUMA CONTINUUM

The Trauma Continuum was developed to help professionals and volunteer counselors better understand various experiences of trauma. We experience events in different ways and degrees regardless of where the traumatic experience falls (on which arrow). The longer the arrow, the trauma reactions are generally more severe, with trauma symptoms becoming more pronounced and recovery services and support requiring more time.

Multiple, Multiple Perpetrators and Events

Multiple, Multiple Perpetrators and Events refers to multiple types of traumatic events that happened to the person in addition to multiple traumas perpetrated by multiple perpetrators. Events may include exposure to death, drugs, violence, accidents, abortion, imprisonment and/or deprivation, as well as ongoing abuse or exploitation.

Multiple, Single Perpetrator

Multiple, Single Perpetrator refers to multiple traumatic events perpetrated on the victim by the same person. An example would be ongoing domestic violence or sexual or physical abuse.

Single Interpersonal

Single Interpersonal refers to a one-time trauma experienced by the victim, perpetrated by another person. Examples would include rape, molestation, or physical assault.

Single Impersonal

Single Impersonal refers to a one-time trauma experienced by the victim but not perpetrated by another person. An example would be a natural disaster such as a monsoon, earthquake, or tornado.

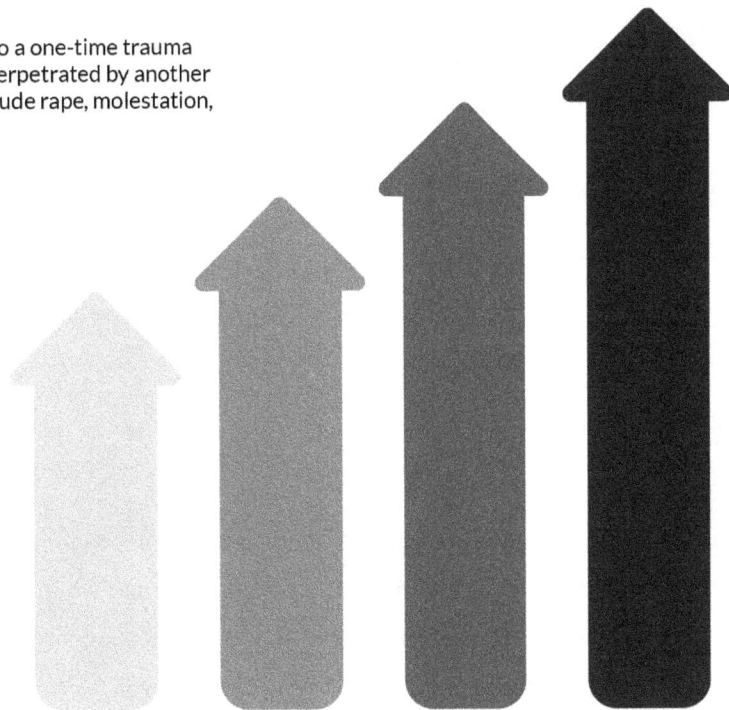

TRAUMA SYMPTOMS

Although symptoms of trauma are numerous, one research study placed them into the following seven categories:

■ *Attachment*

Difficulties with relationships, boundaries, trust, affect attunement (awareness of emotions).

■ *Biology*

Increased medical problems, somatization.

■ *Affect Or Emotional Regulation*

Difficulty identifying, expressing and/or controlling emotions

■ *Dissociation*

Altered states of consciousness, amnesia, depersonalization, and de-realization

■ *Behavioral Control*

Poor impulse control, eating and substance use problems, aggressiveness, oppositional, compliant, and other generally harmful or self-destructive behaviors

■ *Cognition*

Problems with perceptions, understanding, sustained attention

■ *Self-Concept*

Low self-esteem, guilt, and shame

(Cook, Blaustein, Spinazzola, and van der Kolk, 2003)

As we examine these seven categories, it becomes apparent that nearly all of the symptoms are psychologically based. Social, emotional, behavioral, and mental symptoms abound while only one of the categories addresses physiological concerns. This reiterates the importance of emotional healing after trauma. Trauma recovery methods must address these psychological issues in order to be most effective.

THE IMPORTANCE OF EMOTIONAL HEALING

The following illustration summarizes the importance of trauma-focused emotional healing. If a victim's practical needs of food, clothing, and shelter, as well as educational, vocational, financial, and legal opportunities are met, but he/she is not given opportunities for emotional healing after trauma, the person becomes more vulnerable to future victimization and the likelihood of living a shame-filled life. If, however, a victim's practical needs are met *and* he/she is given opportunities to address the psychological symptoms of the trauma, that person is more likely to experience emotional healing, restoration, and to live a hope-filled life.

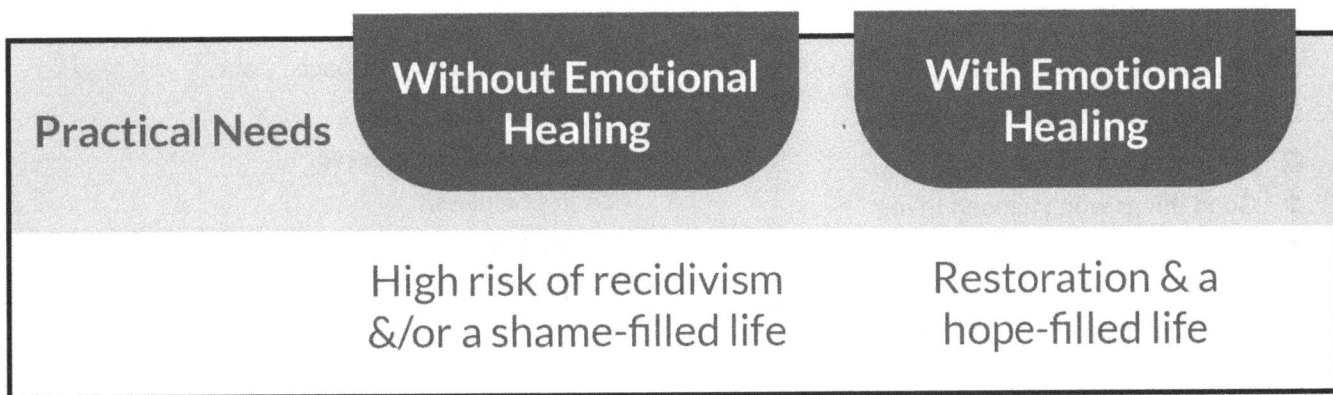

Practical Needs	Without Emotional Healing	With Emotional Healing
	High risk of recidivism &/or a shame-filled life	Restoration & a hope-filled life

Victims suffering from trauma often experience depression, anxiety, self-hatred, dissociation, substance abuse, despair, and somatic ailments. They are also at higher risk for self-destructive and risk-taking behaviors, re-victimization, and experience difficulties with interpersonal and intimate relationships.

(Courtois, 2004)

Without emotional healing, research overwhelmingly confirms that victims are much more likely to be re-victimized. Without help and healing, individuals are more prone to live a guilt-ridden, anger-controlled, shame-filled life.

THOUGHTS AND BELIEFS

To better understand trauma victims, we must understand what and how they think, what they believe, and what they tell themselves. The following list, compiled from years of working with trauma victims, provides insight into victim thinking. This list was given to a group of women survivors of sexual exploitation (prostitution) who were asked to check those thoughts and beliefs they had or still have. Everyone marked over 30 of these 41 statements, and most checked over 35.

- ○ I'm worthless.
- ○ I'm a nobody.
- ○ I'm a slut, ho, bitch, whore, prostitute
- ○ I don't deserve anything good to happen to me.
- ○ This is as good as it gets.
- ○ It's my fault.
- ○ I can't trust anyone.
- ○ No one will help
- ○ No one can help.
- ○ No one cares.
- ○ I can't do anything right.
- ○ I chose this life.
- ○ I can't make good decisions.
- ○ I'll never change.
- ○ Life won't or can't get any better.
- ○ My feelings don't matter.
- ○ Good things won't happen to me.
- ○ I am to blame.
- ○ God doesn't care (won't help).
- ○ God can't help.
- ○ God doesn't exist.

- ○ I should have tried harder.
- ○ I should have known better.
- ○ I'll never be good for anything.
- ○ All I'm good for is sex (or _____)
- ○ I must not let things bother me.
- ○ I must hide or ignore my feelings.
- ○ I can't trust myself.
- ○ Everyone thinks like the abuser/perpetrator does
- ○ I am a bad person (unworthy, shamed).
- ○ I'm so stupid.
- ○ People use and abuse me, even those who say they love or care about me.
- ○ I've got to be tough and not let things bother me.
- ○ I'm dirty, filthy, garbage.
- ○ Love hurts.
- ○ This is what I deserve.
- ○ It's helpless.
- ○ I'm helpless.
- ○ I'm hopeless.
- ○ This is as good as it gets.
- ○ This IS my life.

FEELINGS, REACTIONS AND RESPONSES

Healing from trauma includes facing painful memories, powerful feelings, and potentially harmful behaviors. Victims experience overwhelming feelings of powerlessness, scary fear, and depressive grief. Each of these feelings alone can be crushing, but when you experience a combination of them simultaneously, it can be overpowering and devastating

(Johnson, 2018, p. 96).

■ Common Feelings

- ○ Anger
- ○ Anxiousness, worry
- ○ Betrayal
- ○ Blame
- ○ Confusion (ambivalent)

- ○ Deceived
- ○ Dirty
- ○ Embarrassed
- ○ Guilty
- ○ Helpless

- ○ Hopeless
- ○ Lonely
- ○ Numb
- ○ Powerless
- ○ Responsible

- Scared, fearful
- Sad (depressed)

- Shame
- Stuck (trapped)

- Stupid

As we seek to understand the many and varied emotions experienced as the result of trauma, it is helpful to know more about both anger and fear. While *anger* may be directed at the offender, it is also directed at caregivers (who may have been unaware and un-protective), God (or a higher power or authority figure who didn't intervene), and another person, such as a neighbor or relative who "knew but said nothing".

Most anger, however, is directed at oneself. Time and time again victims have affirmed that they are most angry at themselves for not saying anything sooner, for not responding differently, for not fighting back, etc. It is important when working with victims of trauma, especially interpersonal trauma, that we understand the focus and direction of their anger. Without this understanding, the persons we are seeking to help might feel misunderstood, shame-filled or that you simply 'don't get it.'

Similarly, to be helpful, we must understand the nature of the *fear* experienced. While fear of bodily harm is often present through threats and physical abuse and assault, the fear of disclosure is often greater. *What will people say or think? Will people believe me if I tell? Will I be blamed for what happened?* The fear of shame, blame, and others' disbelief combined with the risk of negative consequences keeps most victims silent.

■ Reactions—Fight, Flight, or Freeze

When we are in unanticipated situations our responses are to fight, flee (run away), or freeze (to become immobile). Most people aren't aware that freezing is quite common during a traumatic event. It is an involuntary bodily response to a dangerous or shocking situation. The person does not choose it, but the body's built-in survival mechanism takes control and determines that becoming still is the best option.

> *When neither fight or flight will ensure safety, there is another line of defense: immobility (freezing) which is just as universal and basic to survival. This defense strategy is rarely given equal billing in texts... yet freezing... is an equally viable survival strategy in threatening situations. In many situations, it is the best choice... It is not a sign of inadequacy or weakness (Levine, 1997, p. 95-96).*

Unfortunately, those who experience this reaction often feel shame for not having fought back or run away. They do not view this 'freezing' option as admirable, but cowardly. We must help change that believe in order to remove unnecessary shame by teaching the physiological facts – freezing is common and is sometimes the best or only choice available to us.

■ Behavioral Responses – Coping Mechanisms

When trauma victims' heads and hearts are filled with negative and overwhelming thoughts and emotions, they seek ways to deaden the pain as a way to cope. Unfortunately, many of their coping mechanisms are unhealthy and harmful.

These coping mechanisms include, but are not limited to:

- Addictions
- Anger problems
- Bad habits
- Bullying
- Compulsive behavior
- Control
- Dependency
- Eating disorders
- Frequent illnesses

- Impulsiveness
- Lying, cheating
- Manipulation
- Extreme exercising
- Over-achieving
- Promiscuity
- Unhealthy relationships
- Rescuer
- School problems

- Self-harm
- Self-hatred
- Self-sabotage
- Stealing
- Substance abuse
- Suicidal thoughts
- Truancy
- Vandalism

■ Losses

What are the **losses** experienced as a result of a trauma? What events and relationships or what characteristics, emotions and beliefs do they not have the opportunity to develop? While some losses are obvious, others aren't. Trauma victims offer experience several or more losses in their lives.

- A sense of "Normal"
- A sense of belonging
- Boundaries
- Communication skills
- Confidence
- Contentment
- Control
- Dignity
- Dreams
- Education
- Enjoyment

- Faith
- Family
- Friends
- Future
- Healthy relationships
- Hope
- Identity
- Innocence
- Material possessions
- Meaning
- Morality

- Motivation
- Nurturing
- Respect
- Safety
- Security
- Sense of self
- Stability
- Support
- Treasures
- Trust
- Virginity

■ The Transition to Tragedy

The *Transition to Tragedy* (diagram) illustrates the downward movement common to many trauma victims. The trauma experience is followed by numerous negative and harmful thoughts and feelings. In response, victims employ various unhealthy behaviors or coping strategies to deaden the emotional pain. This, in turn, makes the person more vulnerable to further victimization—almost as if they are wearing an 'available' sign on their forehead. The self-blame, lowered self-worth, and confusion often provide an invitation to perpetrators. Then, the person is re-victimized, and the downward pattern continues. While this could be illustrated as a never-ending vicious circle, the descending steps on the following graphic were chosen to depict the sinking, negative, downward motion.

As we better understand victims' thoughts, feelings, reactions, behaviors, and losses, we become more knowledgeable and empathetic and therefore more effective in helping them on their healing journey.

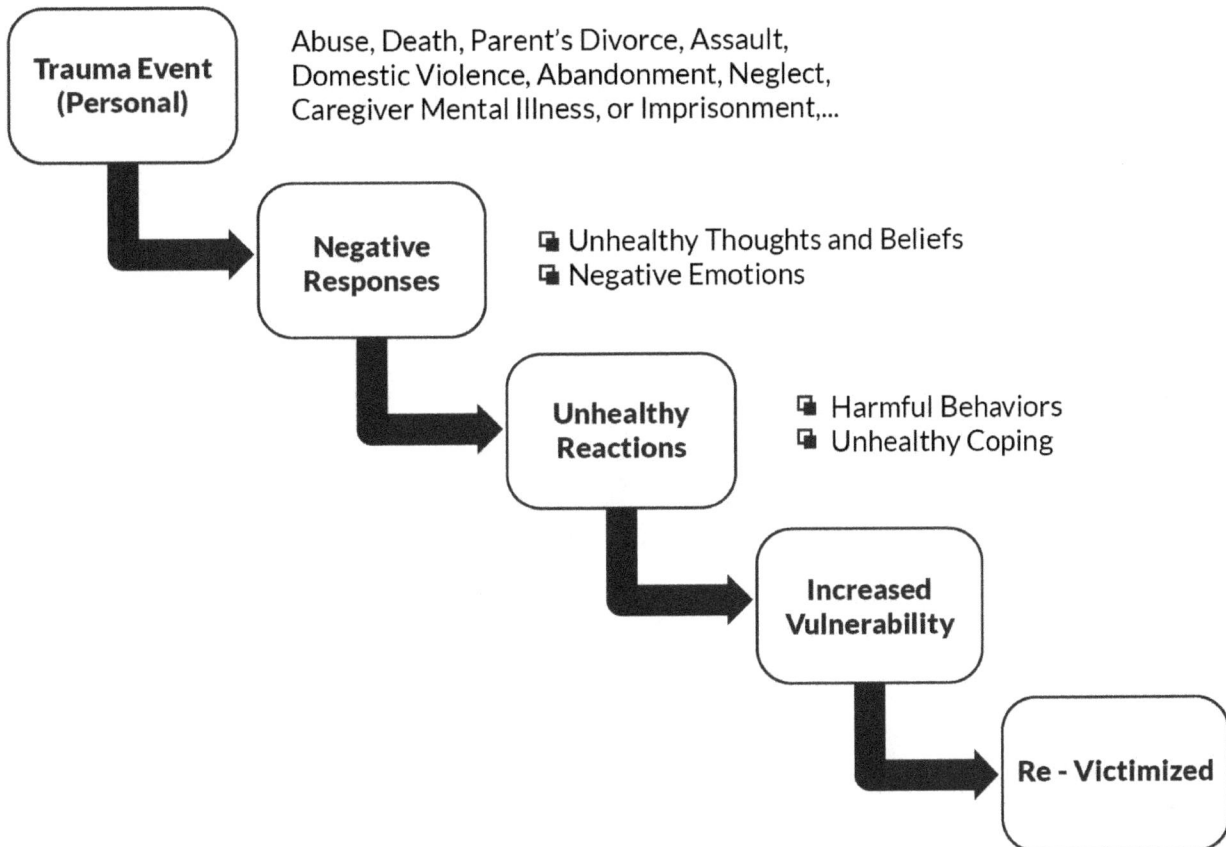

Trauma Event (Personal)

Abuse, Death, Parent's Divorce, Assault, Domestic Violence, Abandonment, Neglect, Caregiver Mental Illness, or Imprisonment,...

Negative Responses

- Unhealthy Thoughts and Beliefs
- Negative Emotions

Unhealthy Reactions

- Harmful Behaviors
- Unhealthy Coping

Increased Vulnerability

Re - Victimized

> Although the world is full of suffering, it is also full of the overcoming of it.

HELEN KELLER

UNDERSTANDING TRAUMA RECOVERY

Trauma recovery refers to efforts to specifically assist a victim in overcoming the negative effects of a traumatic event. The focus of the intervention is the trauma, not other life issues. The *Transition to Tragedy* (final diagram from the last chapter) illustrates the common negative journey taken by many victims after a trauma. As these steps are addressed with the help of a counselor or trained professional, a victim's negative thoughts and feelings will be challenged and changed, harmful behaviors will be altered, and the revealed trauma story will bring internal freedom and peace. The focus of the treatment is the *trauma*.

While providing trauma recovery training around the world, I've found far-too-many who are in the counselor role provide "general counseling." They meet with the trauma victims many of whom have been multiply traumatized by war, violence, abuse, and exploitation (trafficking)—to discuss their families or current issues. The counselors dance around the trauma, rather than facing it head on. And thoughts, feelings, and behaviors are addressed separately, rather than in the context of the trauma.

Addressing life issues rather than the trauma is like treating the symptoms and not the root cause. While "general counseling'" is beneficial for dealing with life issues, relationships, and emotions, and other concerns, it is not recommended until after specific trauma-focused therapy has been completed.

> *Interventions that undershoot the therapeutic window are those that either (a) completely and consistently avoid traumatic material, including any exploration of childhood abuse, or (b) are focused primarily on support and validation in a client who could, in fact, tolerate greater exposure and processing of traumatic material. Undershooting interventions are rarely dangerous; they can, however, waste time and resources at times when more effective therapeutic interventions might be possible.*

(Myers, Berliner, Briere, Hendrix, Reid, and Jenny, 2002, p. 10)

THE PHASES OF TRAUMA RECOVERY

Practitioners and researchers have reported that addressing trauma is best done in a specified progression of phases or stages[1][2]. Dr. Judith Herman presented a phased framework for trauma recovery in her influential work, *Trauma and Recovery (1992)*. These phases include:

- ⮑ Safety and Stabilization
- ⮑ Embracing and Mourning
- ⮑ Reconnection and Integration

---

[1] "There is consensus that treatment development should take a phase-based, or sequential approach. Research with traumatized adults indicates that treatments in which all aspects of work occur simultaneously tend to create "information overload" such that learning never fully occurs. This is likely to be especially true of children whose ability to attend to and process information is less well developed than adults.
The sequential order of the treatment is such that the lessons learned in one phase serve as a building block for those to come next. The process is not linear, however, so that it is often necessary to revisit earlier phases of treatment in order to remain on the overall trajectory." Complex Trauma in Children and Adolescents, National Child Traumatic Stress Network, www.NCTSNet.org

[2] "The recommended course of treatment from those experienced in treating CPTSD (Chu, 1998; Courtois, 1999, 2004; Courtois, Ford, and Cloitre, 2009; Ford, Courtois, Van der Hart, Nijenhuis, and Steele, 2005) involves the sequencing of healing tasks across several main stages of treatment." (Courtois, 2010)

Developers of Trauma-Focused Cognitive Behavioral Therapy (TF-CBT) recommend treatment components be delivered in three sequential phases of treatment:

1. **Stabilization**

   Psychoeducation, Relaxation, Affective Expression and Regulation, Cognitive Coping, and Caregiver/Parenting sessions

2. **Trauma Narrative**

   Trauma Narrative and Processing component

3. **Integration/Consolidation**

   Addressing residual fears (In Vivo Mastery), Enhancing Future Safety, and Parent-Child sessions

   (Cohen, Mannarino, and Deblinger, 2006, 2012)

The recommended course of treatment from those experienced in treating Complex PTSD involves the sequencing of healing tasks across four main stages of treatment. These stages include:

- Pre-treatment assessment
- Early stage of safety, education, stabilization, skill-building, and development of the treatment alliance
- Middle stage of trauma processing and resolution
- Late stage of self and relational development and life choice

(Courtois, 2010)

TRAUMA RECOVERY MODELS

Though many trauma recovery counseling models exist, they generally share several common components. All agree on the essential foundation of safety and trust. For a helping relationship to be effective, the victim must feel understood, valued and accepted—in other words, emotionally safe.

Other common components include psychoeducation, or the learning about trauma events and reactions, as well as relaxation (anxiety reduction), and emotional regulation skills. Unraveling how trauma has affected one's thoughts and emotions and the telling of one's story (the trauma narrative) are also essential parts of trauma treatments. Lastly, treatment includes opportunities to explore and enhance one's sense of safety and future.

One study on trauma recovery recommends that treatments for youth be conceptualized using four central goals:

- Safety in one's environment, including home, school, and community,
- Skills development in emotion regulation and interpersonal functioning,
- Meaning making about past traumatic events they have experienced so that youth can consider more positive, adaptive views about themselves in the present, and experience hope about their future, and
- Enhancing resiliency and integration into social network.

(Complex Trauma in Children and Adolescents, 2019)

John Briere, who developed the Self Trauma Model writes:

> *The self-trauma model suggests that, beyond its initial negative effects, early and severe child maltreatment interrupts normal child development, conditions negative affect to abuse-related stimuli, and interferes with the usual acquisition of self-capacities—perhaps especially the development of affect regulation skills. This reduced affect regulation places the individual at risk for being more easily overwhelmed by emotional distress associated with memories of the abuse/trauma, thereby motivating the use of dissociation and other methods of avoidance in adolescence and adulthood. In this way, impaired self-capacities lead to reliance on avoidance strategies, which, in turn, further preclude the development of self-capacities. This negative cycle is exacerbated by the concomitant need of the traumatized individual to process conditioned emotional responses and distorted cognitive schema by repetitively re-experiencing cognitive-emotional memories of the original traumatic event—a process that can further overwhelm self-capacities and produce distress.*

(Myers et al., 2002)

Briere states the need for affect regulation, addressing negatively conditioned emotional responses and distorted cognitions as well as the "methods of avoidance" (behavioral responses or coping strategies used).

Another study developed a set of criteria for working with those suffering from disorders of extreme stress. These included:

- Safety
- Self-regulation
- Self-reflective information processing
- Traumatic experiences integration
- Relational engagement
- Positive affect enhancement

(Pelcovitz, van der Kolk, Roth, Mandel, Kaplan, and Resick, 1997)

From these and other studies and models, the following list of common components of trauma recovery was compiled: Safety, Psychoeducation, Emotional Expression, Correct Maladaptive Thinking, Trauma Narrative, and Empowerment. These are listed here with some of the other terms used to explain and express similar content.

AREA	OTHER TERMS / TASKS
SAFETY *(Caring)*	Establishment of trust, physical and emotional safety, therapeutic alliance, relationship building, mutually understood goals.
PSYCHOEDUCATION *(Learning)* **(including Anxiety Reduction techniques)**	Teach on applicable topics such as abuse, trauma, victimization, exploitation, violence, dynamics of control, sex education, healthy relationships, etc. Teach: somatic responses, relaxation techniques, anxiety management, self-regulation skills (self-control), mindfulness.
EMOTIONAL EXPRESSION *(Feeling)*	Affect expression, emotional control, positive affect enhancement, emotional identification and processing.
CORRECT MALADAPTIVE THINKING *(Thinking)*	Cognitive distortions, wrong or false thinking, identification and alteration of maladaptive thinking.
TRAUMA NARRATIVE *(Sharing)*	Integration/sharing one's story, trauma processing.
EMPOWERMENT *(Living)*	Instilling hope, future plans pursued, re-establishing relationships and re-integration, life choice, self and relational development, problem-solving skills, foster resiliency.

When training on trauma and trauma recovery, I request that all staff and volunteers be present. The goal is to establish an environment of trauma-informed care, or as I prefer to say, trauma-sensitive care. Everyone who works directly or indirectly with victims should understand the nature of trauma in order to increase their empathy and effectiveness. Because most of the trauma recovery training I provide is international, the various components were given names using words common to all languages (italicized words in parentheses in the previous chart). Safety became **Caring** and Psychoeducation became **Learning**. Affective Expression became **Feeling**, while Correct Maladaptive Thinking became simply **Thinking**. The telling of one's story or the Trauma Narrative became **Sharing**, and lastly, Empowerment became **Living** (Free, Safe, and Well).

To facilitate understanding, these components then became part of the *Transition to Hope*, illustrated in the following diagram. The ascending steps demonstrate the healing process as one of upward movement and growth. The steps (Caring, Learning, Feeling, Thinking, Sharing, and Living) are the trauma recovery areas used for this book and are explained more fully in the following pages.

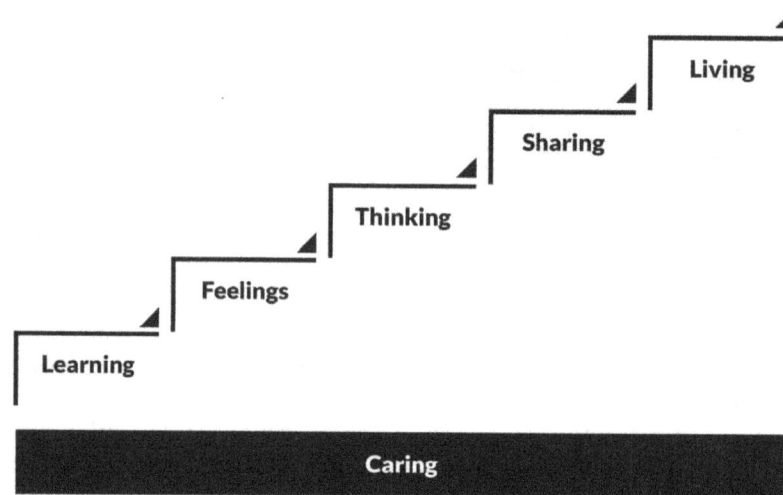

TRAUMA RECOVERY AREAS: OVERVIEW

■ Caring

Ensure emotional and physical safety with well-trained, supportive caregivers

- ➲ Foster a positive, trusting therapeutic alliance
- ➲ Collect information (intake, psychosocial history) and individual measures (tests) in order to develop a treatment plan

- ➲ Train all caregivers in trauma, trauma recovery, strengths-based approach, and behavioral management in order to create a trauma-sensitive (trauma-informed) environment

■ Learning

Provide psychoeducation on relevant topics in addition to self-regulation and relaxation techniques

- ➲ Teach about abuse, trauma, exploitation, coercion and control, human trafficking, sex education, and any other applicable topics

- ➲ Teach self-regulation, anxiety management, and relaxation skills

■ Feeling

Identify and express emotions appropriately

■ Thinking

Understand the difference between thoughts and feelings, and expose and address common unhealthy thoughts (cognitive distortions)

■ Sharing

Share one's trauma story(-ies) (the trauma narrative)

- ➲ Sharing: Client shares their trauma narrative

- ➲ Evaluating: Counselor helps client identify and

change harmful beliefs (correct)

⊃ Sharing Again: Client shares their corrected trauma story with another emotionally safe person

⊃ Sharing More: Client is encouraged to share any stories of trauma perpetrated on others

▊ Living

Live Free, Safe and Well (Empowerment)

⊃ Live Free of any avoidance areas, residual fears and harmful coping mechanisms

⊃ Live Safe with safety planning and the development

of problem-solving and decision-making skills

⊃ Live Well with resiliency building, future planning and goal setting

The *Transition to Hope* is a components-based framework developed to assist those in the counseling role, primarily in developing or low- to middle-resource countries where access to graduate studies, training, and licensed professionals is limited. It is not meant to replace the well-researched treatment models available, but rather draws upon them in selecting treatment components.

Each activity in this book is categorized according to its Trauma Recovery step. While some of the activities could be used in several areas, they are placed where they best fit in the recovery process.

TRAUMA RECOVERY ACTIVITIES

▊ Caring

Activities in this area serve as the foundation of the trauma recovery process and are divided into three categories: *Building Relationships, Helping the Helpers, and Collecting Information.*

Building Relationships

This first part of the foundation focuses on facilitating a sense of emotional safety and trust between the individual and the facilitator. Many of the activities aim at helping the individual identify and share about their family background, likes and dislikes, and other details that will allow the individual to get to know themselves better while, at the same time, sharing and opening up to the facilitator. The non-judgmental attitude, unconditional acceptance, and affirmative interactions of the counselor are critically important.

Helping the Helpers

The second part of the foundation focuses on helping Caregivers. They are taught about trauma in an effort to make sure there is a trauma-informed environment. I prefer the term *trauma sensitive* as it reflects a desire to engage the heart and not just the mind in understanding trauma's effect on individuals. The goal is to help caregivers be more sensitive and effective, whether parent, guardian, foster parent, house mom or other.

Collecting Information

The last part of the foundation includes collecting helpful information that will assist in developing a treatment plan and identifying needed resources for the victim. After collecting this helpful information, the facilitator will be able to select which of the subsequent Trauma Recovery Activities are best suited for the individual. Any pre-tests or measures are generally given in this step.

■ Learning

These activities are divided into two categories: *Trauma and Sex Education* and *Relaxation Exercises*.

Trauma and Sex Education:

Activities in this step concentrate on bringing awareness and increasing knowledge about abuse and trauma, as well as teaching relaxation, mindfulness, and self-regulation skills. The information on trauma includes types, causes, symptoms, feelings, thoughts, reactions, and other helpful topics (refer to the chapter "Understanding Trauma"). As the individual learns more about these topics, he/she usually experiences a sense of validation and normalization. "I'm not the only one!" (who has experienced this). "What I've thought or felt is NOT crazy!" (but 'normal'). "I'm not alone" (others have gone through this too). Information on sex education provides a common understanding of sex, sexual activities, sexual diseases, anatomy, reproduction, pregnancy, and more and is needed for those having experienced a sexual trauma.

Relaxation Exercises:

In the process of healing from trauma, research has shown that implementing relaxation exercises and identifying calming activities is important, especially as intrusive memories and intense emotions arise. Activities included in this section teach and encourage the use of various relaxation techniques as well as help the individual determine which interests or leisure pursuits help in their personal trauma recovery process.

■ Feeling

One of the areas most affected by traumatic events is emotions—how, what, why and how much one feels. Affect dysregulation is a term used to describe how emotions become short-circuited or "out of sync". Trauma victims' feelings are often stifled, stunted, numbed, or, heightened, overly sensitive, and reactionary. Sometimes the emotions displayed don't match the situation nor the intensity of what's going on. Victims need to expand their "feeling vocabulary," learn new emotional responses, and how to express feelings in healthy ways. There are numerous activities in this trauma recovery area that assist the person in identifying emotions, expressing emotions, and ultimately expressing emotions appropriately.

■ Thinking

Trauma experiences are accompanied by a multitude of thoughts and feelings, many centered upon self-blame and shame. The differences between thoughts and feelings is presented in this step. The activities in this section highlight the need to acknowledge and identify unhealthy thinking, also referred to as cognitive distortions, false thinking, or, as I say, *lies*.

■ Sharing

Sharing the stories of one's trauma is also referred to as the Trauma Narrative. Telling one's story is therapeutically beneficial—a bit like surgery to remove a malignant growth. It's deadly if kept inside. We wait until this healing step to ask for details about trauma experiences in order to minimize possible re-traumatization.

Before we ask the person to tell their trauma story (**SHARING**), it is helpful to first teach relaxation and calming/grounding activities in case the person becomes anxious, is triggered, or has a flashback (**LEARNING: Relaxation**). It is also beneficial that the person learns about trauma and learns that he/she is not alone nor crazy before telling their experiences (**LEARNING: Trauma**). As they examine feelings and expose negative thinking, the trauma story takes on new form as negative thoughts and emotions begin to fall away (**FEELING and THINKING**). Foundational to it all, it is crucial that the person feels emotionally safe (**CARING**).

Activities in this section now focus on the individual's experience. In previous steps we attempt to remain somewhat neutral, talking about what "'someone'" might do, think, or feel. These activities now ask about the individual's personal feelings and thoughts. Previously, the feelings and thoughts were presented as *what others have experienced* but are now personalized to what did you feel, think, or do? The foundational steps up until now have been preparing the person for this step— to share his/her trauma stories. *Activities in Sharing should be selected with care according to age, situation, and readiness.*

There are several components to this trauma recovery step:

Sharing

The person is asked to share his/her trauma story in a self-chosen format, whether through writing, art, drama, dance, music, the Book About Me, and/or dictation (the facilitator writes it down as the person tells their trauma story).

Evaluating

Outside the session, the story is evaluated by the facilitator who identifies lingering unhealthy thoughts, feelings, and coping patterns. The individual and facilitator then meet to review the story and the person is encouraged change or correct any unhealthy aspects (thoughts, feelings, plans...).

Sharing Again

The individual identifies an emotionally safe person (not the facilitator) to whom they will share their (corrected) trauma story again.

Sharing More

For this section, the facilitator explains how some victims victimize others due to their own hurt, pain, shame, and anger and then shares examples. Trauma recovery addresses the trauma that happened to the person, whereas, for some, there may also be trauma related to what they have *done or not done* that caused harm or trauma to someone else. This area often remains hidden deep inside in dark, shameful places. But, for trauma healing to be complete, these must also be spoken and shared. While the focus of counseling has been on what happened to the person, the focus now is on what the person may have done to someone else.

■ Living

Activities in this step are divided into three categories: *Living Free, Living Safe, and Living Well.*

Living Free

After sharing one's trauma story, some triggers may remain and should be addressed. Triggers, fears, and avoidance areas are exposed, plans are identified and implemented to decrease or eliminate them from reemerging.

Living Safe

In this section, the use of role plays, self-defense lessons, and safety planning is recommended. The overall goal is to increase one's sense of safety. Activities concentrate on empowering, self-esteem building, problem solving, and increasing self-efficacy. Activities focus on fostering personal safety and identifying what to do in various situations.

Living Well

As hope and healing grow, future dreams are re-kindled and self-made plans are put in motion. We celebrate the growth and the future. Activities in this section assist the individual in identifying goals, dreams, and future plans.

SUMMARY

The sequential phases of trauma recovery draw upon years of research. ***Transition to Hope*** is built on this suggested progression from *CARING to LIVING* and is offered as a components-based framework. We begin with a sense of physical and emotion safety between the individual and all staff and volunteers (*CARING*). We then provide validation and comfort through teaching about abuse, trauma, sex education, and exploitation, along with teaching anxiety reduction skills (*LEARNING*). The next step (*FEELING*) assists the individual in developing a healthy emotional understanding which will be needed later when sharing their trauma story. Exposing negative thoughts, beliefs, and patterns is also necessary before addressing the trauma narrative (*SHARING*) so that the person can identify hindrances to healing (*THINKING*).

Trauma stories shared (*SHARING*) prior to the completion of these first several steps may be incomplete, shared for shock value, and/or changed to minimize possible blame. Each of the prior steps enables *Sharing* to be a more cathartic and helpful step in the journey of healing. Once the pain and shame of the trauma has been exposed, future freedom, safety, and empowerment are reinforced, completing this part of the restorative process (*LIVING: Free, Safe, and Well*).

In each trauma recovery area numerous possible activities are given. You, the facilitator, must carefully choose which activities to use for each individual in your care. Choose, adapt, implement, debrief and evaluate. Our goal is to facilitate personal healing and growth for those we serve.

- ✓ **Building Relationships**
- ✓ **Collecting Information**
- ✓ **Helping Caregivers**

STEP 1

CARING

CARING

■ Overview

The foundation of any helping relationship is trust. Before any progress or healing can take place, the individual (client) must feel emotionally safe (heard, valued, and free from criticism and judgment). However, we also want to extend this to the client's caregivers. We meet with caregivers, seeking to increase their awareness of and empathy for the victims. We equip caregivers with practical skills so that they, too, can foster growth and healing.

In order to provide personalized and professional assistance, we also need to gather information about the client. This information helps the counselor develop a specific, individualized treatment plan.

■ Goals

- ⊃ To build a positive, emotionally safe relationship with the individual
- ⊃ To share and collect information helpful to the counseling process
- ⊃ To assist caregivers in dealing effectively with trauma victims

WITH THE CLIENT:

■ Develop

Develop a therapeutic relationship of emotional safety, rapport, and trust facilitated by using a variety of activities, games, stories, and questions.

■ Provide

Provide the person with information regarding the counseling process:

- ⊃ Explain what counseling is/isn't
- ⊃ Provide a brief overview of the *Transition to Hope* model
- ⊃ Inform about consent/client rights
- ⊃ Clarify expectations
- ⊃ Emphasize the importance of communicating if uncomfortable, confused, or angry

■ Collect information

- ⊃ Conduct a thorough Intake Assessment (including a Mental Status Exam and a comprehensive Psychosocial History) and administer any desired assessment measures for treatment planning, progress, treatment and program effectiveness, evaluation, and/or research

◼ Document A Treatment Plan

- ⊃ Write an individualized *Treatment Plan* based on information gathered and observed regarding the client's strengths, concerns, background (cultural, religious, ethnic), resistance, diagnosis, additional resources needed, and any other relevant information

- ⊃ Encourage the client to tell a story in detail (from a positive or neutral memory, *not* a negative one). This will serve as a baseline narrative (practice) for later, when asked to tell his/her own trauma narrative

◼ Begin

- ⊃ The personalized "book about me" (*optional but recommended*), and/or
- ⊃ Personal journaling (give the person a blank book/notebook), and/or
- ⊃ Responsive journaling between client and counselor (a back-and-forth journal where each person writes comments, thoughts, feelings and/or questions, and the other responds)

WITH THE CAREGIVER/HELPER:

◼ Provide

Provide an overview of the *Transition to Hope* trauma recovery plan and explain the key role caregivers play in the process of emotional healing.

◼ Help

Help caregivers understand the effects of abuse and trauma on victims and how to respond to the victims' trauma symptoms, reactions, and behaviors in ways that are helpful by providing psychoeducation, behavioral management, and positive reinforcement skills (strengths-based approach).

◼ Instill

Instill in caregivers the importance of clear, consistent boundaries and discipline for the victim's emotional healing.

◼ Encourage

Encourage caregivers to deal with their own abuse/trauma experiences and any dysfunctional parenting concerns (past and/or present).

◼ Prepare

Prepare caregivers by discussing (preparing for) times that might be more emotionally difficult for the victims.

TRACTs | TRAUMA RECOVERY ACTIVITIES

Name		Program Location	

Tasks *(Some Optional, Depending On Person/Situation)*	Date Completed	Notes
FOR THE CLIENT		
Build a safe, trusting relationship		
Complete thorough Intake Assessment		
Explain the purpose of counseling, confidentiality, client rights, give an overview of the *Transition to Hope*		
Complete initial symptoms and assessments: trauma, depression, anxiety, self-esteem, clinical concerns, etc.		
Develop list of client strengths, concerns, personal issues (cultural, religious, ethnic), resistance, needed interventions, diagnoses, etc.		
Write/document an individualized Treatment Plan		
Have client share a positive or neutral memory (story) in detail (baseline narrative)		
Begin *Book about Me*		
Begin personal journaling (or responsive journal between client and counselor) *Optional*		

Utilize a variety of activities, resources and/or games to develop and establish the therapeutic relationship.

Tasks (Some Optional, Depending On Person/Situation)	Date Completed	Notes
FOR THE CAREGIVER/ HELPER		
Educate about child development (*if needed*)		
Educate about abuse/trauma: common victim symptoms, thoughts, feelings, and behaviors		
Explain the *Transition to Hope* and Caregiver's key role in emotional healing.		
Encourage Caregivers to address their own trauma and to identify any of their own unhealthy parenting styles (past or present)		
Educate about discipline (behavioral management): clarity, consistency, consequences, etc.		
Teach affect attunement and regulation (skills in recognizing, responding, and controlling emotional reactions and behaviors)		
Teach behavioral management techniques: strengths-based practice, focused attention, time-outs, using charts..., etc.		
Help Caregivers anticipate client's emotionally difficult times		
Role play/practice real life scenarios		
Educate about sex education topics if caregiver has insufficient knowledge (*optional*)		

BUILDING RELATIONSHIPS

CARING

1 THIS IS ME

Age	All	Setting	Individual	Trauma Recovery	CARING-Building Relationships

Purpose	To create self-awareness and establish a relationship between the counselor and individual that will be needed later when sharing their trauma story.
Overview	The individual fills out a survey providing personal information, including physical features, where they live/were born, and information about their family to help them share the story of who they are.

Approximate Time	10-20 minutes

Supplies Needed	Worksheet and pen or pencil

■ Activity Explained

- ➲ The individual completes the survey.
- ➲ The facilitator asks questions about the information in order to learn more about the person.

■ Reflection

How do you feel about your name? What does it mean? Why did you choose these items for what you like about yourself? Were you mostly happy or scared as a child? Was there a question that was difficult to answer? Why?

■ Variations

Activity may be verbal or written. If verbal, ask the information directly. The survey may also be completed independently and brought to the session. This could also be used in a group setting.

■ Concerns

Answering questions about one's family might be especially distressing to some, depending on their circumstances. The individual might desire to be reunited with family or might come from an abusive, violent, or dysfunctional family. In these cases, the facilitator may choose to ask the questions verbally or may instruct the person saying, If there is anything you don't want to answer, just leave it blank.

THIS IS ME (Fill out as much as you like)

PERSONAL INFORMATION

Full Name	Nickname
Name's Meaning	Date of Birth
Eye Color	Hair Color

Hair Size	☐ Short	☐ Medium	☐ Long

Height	Weight
Birth City	Birth State / Province/Region
You Live With?	Current City

What you like about your self?

MY FAMILY

Mothor's Name	Father's Name

No. of Children in House Including Yourself

Name	Age	Name	Age

What you like about your family?

What you wish was different about your family:

List 2 - 3 Unique Things About You (or your friends/family)

2 MY FAVORITES

Age	All	Setting	Individual	Trauma Recovery	CARING-Building Relationships

Purpose	To gain information using a list of favorite items to build self-awareness and to continue building the therapeutic relationship.
Overview	The individual will complete a survey listing their favorite items including foods, activities, and people.

Approximate Time	10-20 minutes		Supplies Needed	Worksheet and pen or pencil

■ Activity Explained

- ➲ The individual completes the survey about their favorite things., If needed, keep a copy for your records.
- ➲ The facilitator asks questions in order to learn more about the person.

■ Reflection

Ask questions such as *Why is that one your favorite?* Whenever possible, add personal comments and favorites as well, especially if they are similar. Statements such as, *That's my favorite too. Or I've heard of that. Or I have a friend whose favorite is that too. What does that particular favorite remind you of? What is your memory of that favorite thing?*

■ Variations

Activity may be verbal or written. The worksheet can be completed independently and brought to the session.

■ Concerns

The list of favorites may need to be changed to be age and culturally appropriate for the individual.

MY FAVORITES - WHAT I LIKE

Food	
Color	
Subject in School/ Subject to Learn About	
Things to Do	
Tv Show	
Movie	
Place to Go	
Music	
Cloths	
Holiday	
Dance	
Toy	
Dessert	
Friends	
Book to Read	
Relative	
Teacher	
Drink	
Day of The Week	
Number	
Smell	
Fruit	
Other	

3 GET TO KNOW YOU QUESTIONS

Age	All	Setting	Individual	Trauma Recovery	CARING-Building Relationships

Purpose	To build a relationship with the individual through asking a variety of personal questions.
Overview	The facilitator will ask the individual a series of questions about themselves.

Approximate Time	10-25 minutes		**Supplies Needed**	List of questions (worksheet)

■ Activity Explained

- ⊃ The facilitator selects various questions from the following list.
- ⊃ The individual answers the questions orally.

■ Reflection

The facilitator should comment or ask further questions about the client's responses in order to build rapport and to learn more about the individual.

■ Variations

If needed, the facilitator can answer a few questions first to create a comfortable atmosphere.

■ Concerns

Be sure to use only those questions appropriate for the person's age, culture, and experiences. Avoid questions that might trigger negative trauma memories.

GET TO KNOW YOU QUESTIONS

- ➲ What are three things you like to do?
- ➲ Where do/did you live? What is/was your house like?
- ➲ What is something you have always wished for?
- ➲ What is something you like about school? Dislike?
- ➲ What was your family like when you were younger? What is your family like now?
- ➲ Do you like to sing?
- ➲ What music do you like?
- ➲ Do you like sports? What sports/teams do you like?
- ➲ Do you go to church/synagogue/mosque? Do you enjoy it? Why or why not?
- ➲ Do you believe in God?
- ➲ Do you believe that God loves you? Is it hard for you to believe?
- ➲ What makes you happy?
- ➲ What makes you sad?
- ➲ Is there a place where you go to be alone?
- ➲ What is your favorite place?
- ➲ What are you afraid of (people, places, things)?
- ➲ Are you good at keeping secrets?
- ➲ Have you ever told someone a secret?
- ➲ If you could have any job what would it be?
- ➲ What's your favorite food?
- ➲ What's your favorite color?
- ➲ What's your oldest memory?
- ➲ What's one place you have always wanted to visit?

4 "WOULD YOU RATHER"

Age	All	Setting	Individual	Trauma Recovery	CARING-Building Relationships

Purpose	To build a relationship by getting to know the individual through asking a series of questions about their preferences.
Overview	The facilitator asks the individual a series of questions regarding what they would prefer, given two or more options.

Approximate Time	10-20 minutes

Supplies Needed	Worksheet and pen or pencil

■ Activity Explained

➲ The facilitator asks the individual questions from the questionnaire, or the person circles their preferences on the given worksheet.

➲ The facilitator asks questions to elicit more information about the person.

➲ The facilitator acknowledges any similar preferences he/she may have with the person to help build rapport.

■ Reflection

Whenever possible, add personal comments and answers as well, especially if they are similar. Statements such as, *That's mine too.* Or *I prefer that as well.* The identification of similarities between the facilitator and the individual helps build their relationship.

Ask questions such as *Why did you choose that one? Why do you prefer that?*

■ Variations

The activity may be verbal or written.

Activity may be used individually or in groups. If done in a group setting, individuals should form groups of two to share their responses together. Once gathered back together as a larger group, participants can be asked to share something interesting they learned about the other person.

■ Concerns

Questions should be appropriate for the individual's age, developmental level, culture, and experiences.

"WOULD YOU RATHER" QUESTIONNAIRE

Write down or circle your answers to the following questions:

- ⊃ Would you rather be indoors or outside?
- ⊃ Would you rather swim in water, ride a bicycle, or go on a walk?
- ⊃ Would you rather make a meal or clean the dishes?
- ⊃ Would you rather wake up early or sleep in?
- ⊃ Would you rather have something sweet or salty?
- ⊃ Would you rather have a pet dog, cat, rabbit, pig, or goat?
- ⊃ Would you rather pick out your own present or have a surprise present?
- ⊃ Would you rather sing or play an instrument?
- ⊃ Would you rather go to the beach or to the mountains?
- ⊃ Would you rather go to the city or to the country?
- ⊃ Would you rather draw, read, or write?
- ⊃ Would you rather be a politician, a movie star, or a famous athlete?
- ⊃ Would you rather dust, clean the dishes, or wash clothes?
- ⊃ Would you rather it be winter, spring, summer, or fall all the time? Rainy season or dry?
- ⊃ Would you rather have a friend who is funny, kind, or smart?
- ⊃ Would you rather be known for being beautiful, smart, or strong?
- ⊃ Would you rather live alone or live with a lot of people?

5 ABOUT MY FAMILY

Age	Youth - Adults	Setting	Individual	Trauma Recovery	CARING- Building Relationships

Purpose	To gather helpful information about the individual's family.
Overview	The individual completes a worksheet asking information about their family. *Note: This is similar to an earlier activity but asks more information and is more suitable for youth to adults.*

Approximate Time	20-30 minutes

Supplies Needed	Worksheet and pen or pencil

■ Activity Explained

- ➲ The individual completes the worksheet for the facilitator to obtain relational and descriptive information about their family. This will include information about similarities, differences, celebrations, roles, perceptions, and relationships.

- ➲ After the individual finishes with the worksheet, the facilitator can collect it and then use additional questions from the reflection section to discuss their family.

■ Reflection

What are some of your best memories of your family? Which family member are you closest to?

■ Variations

Activity may be verbal or written.

Before debriefing the answers, the facilitator may want to review the answers in order to best select which questions to ask.

■ Concerns

Extra sensitivity is needed with those who come from an abusive, violent, or dysfunctional family. Remind the person that they do not have to answer all of the questions. If there is anything you don't want to answer, just leave it blank.

MY FAMILY

Name	Date

Describe your family (close, distant, co-existed, enmeshed, volatile, independent, isolated.):

1 - Who was around in your family while you were growing up?

2 - Who was closest to mom? To dad? Other?

3.- Did you have contact with extended family? If 'yes' who and how often?

Parent	Mother	Father	Step - Parent
Age			
Occupation			
Ethincity			
Relegion			

5 - Describe your father (For example: hard-working, likable, detached, quiet, strong, insecure, confident, angry, creative, practical, overweight, worrier, serious, moody, impatient, successful, workaholic, alcoholic, critical, perfectionist, gentle, forgiving, controlling, logical, etc.).

a - In what ways are you like your father?

b - In what ways are you different from your father?

6 - Describe your mother (for example: hard-working, likable, detached, quiet, strong, insecure, confident, angry, creative, practical, overweight, worrier, serious, moody, impatient, successful, workaholic, alcoholic, critical, perfectionist, gentle, forgiving, controlling, logical, etc.).

a.   In what ways are you like your mother?

b.   In what ways are you different from your mother?

7 - Describe your siblings, then indicate how you might label your sibling's roles in the family (For example: the athlete, the pleaser, the smart one, the problem child, the perfect child, etc.).

S.No.	Name	Age	Martial Status	Occupation Family Role
1				
2				
3				

In what ways are you and your siblings similar?

In what ways are you and your siblings different?

8 - How were holidays and special occasions acknowledged or celebrated in your family? (Examples: birthdays, holidays, festivals, etc..)

9 - How would others describe your family?

10 - Rate the following relationships 1–10. (1 representing terrible, sad, or dysfunctional and 10 representing great, happy, and/or healthy)

Your parents' relationship with each other (whether together or not)	
Your parents' relationships with other partners (either past or current)	
Your childhood	
Your family growing up	

6 DRAWING MY LIFE

Age	All	Setting	Individual	Trauma Recovery	CARING-Building Relationships

Purpose	To describe a person, place, or thing with a drawing and to build a relationship with the facilitator through sharing information.
Overview	The individual draws a picture of a person, place, or thing and shares it with the facilitator.

Approximate Time	10-20 minutes		Supplies Needed	Worksheet or blank paper, pencil and eraser, colored markers, crayons, paints, etc.

▪ Activity Explained

- ⮂ The individual is asked to draw a picture of one of the following (chosen by facilitator): a person, place, thing, or memory. This can include a drawing of their family or of himself/herself. The facilitator might ask the person to draw a picture that represents a word such as safe, happiness, or peace. The instructions should include something like: The purpose is to share a drawing, not to have a perfect picture.
- ⮂ The facilitator asks questions about the drawing.

▪ Reflection

What did you draw? Why did you choose this drawing? Who/what's in your picture? What happened before or after this moment? Tell me more about the drawing.

▪ Variations

Activity may be done individually or in groups. Drawing may be completed outside the session then brought in to discuss. The facilitator may also choose to draw a picture alongside the person in order to foster a sense of safety.

▪ Concerns

The individual should be reassured that the purpose of drawing is to share an experience or memory, not to judge artistic skill.

▪ Story

This activity can be helpful if a person struggles to describe things verbally or if they don't have the language ability to describe an experience or thing. Drawing pictures alongside the person can help make them feel more comfortable and create a safe space to share experiences.

DRAWING

Please mark which drawing you are doing:

☐	My Family	☐	Me	☐	My Home	☐	Safety
☐	Happiness	☐	Peace	☐	Sadness	☐	Other

7 IF... QUESTIONS

Age	All	Setting	Both	Trauma Recovery	CARING-Building Relationships

Purpose	To build the relationship between the individual and the facilitator.
Overview	The individual is asked a series of questions regarding what they would do or how they would feel given different *If you could...* scenarios.

Approximate Time	10-20 minutes	**Supplies Needed**	Worksheet and pen or pencil

■ Activity Explained

- ➲ The individual answers questions about various scenarios.
- ➲ The facilitator asks questions to elicit additional information about the person and to build the relationship.

■ Reflection

Reflection should focus on why the individual chose their answers. *Why? What else would you do/choose? Why did you choose that answer?*

The facilitator should look for commonalities and share them to build rapport, responding with such statements as, *I would choose that too. That's what I would say as well. We answered that the same way.*

■ Variations

Activity may be verbal or written. Activity may be used individually or in groups..

■ Concerns

Questions may need to be tailored appropriately for the person's developmental level, culture, and experiences.

IF... QUESTIONNAIRE

If you could...

➲   If you could fly, where would you fly?

_____

➲   If you could talk to your country's leader, what would you say?

_____

➲   Ifyou could help someone in the world, who would you help and what would you do?

_____

➲   If you could travel anywhere, where would you go?

_____

➲   If you had a lot of money, what would you do?

_____

If you were...

➲   If you were in charge of your country/school/family, what would you do and why?

_____

➲   If you were famous, what would it be for? (Examples: an invention, singing, art, dance, acting, sports, an ability, intelligence..., etc.)

_____

➲   If you were an animal, what would you be and why?

_____

➲   If you were a piece of furniture, what would you be and why?

_____

➲   If you were a musical instrument, what kind of music would you play?

_____

8 MY UNIQUENESS

Age	All	Setting	Both	Trauma Recovery	CARING- Building Relationships

Purpose	To continue to build a safe, helping relationship and to help the individual identify unique things about himself/herself.
Overview	The individual is given a survey to fill out about experiences they've had and is asked to list three unique things about themselves.

Approximate Time	10-15 minutes

Supplies Needed	Worksheet and pen or pencil

■ Activity Explained

- ⊃ The individual completes the worksheet (or is asked verbally)
- ⊃ The facilitator asks questions about marked items

■ Reflection

I see you checked _____, can you tell me about that experience? How did you choose the three items that make you unique? Are you proud of these attributes?

■ Variations

Activity may be verbal or written. Activity may be used individually or in groups.

■ Concerns

The list should be adjusted to be culturally and developmentally appropriate.

MY UNIQUENESS

Have You Ever...? (place a check next to those you have done)

	Had your ears pierced		Fixed something that was broken
	Played on a team sport		Played in the mud
	Played a musical instrument		Laughed uncontrollably
	Drawn a picture		Danced in the rain
	Watched a professional sports game		Written a letter to Santa Claus
	Broken a bone		Watched the sunrise or sunset
	Gone to the hospital		Seen a falling star
	Eaten a sweet (dessert) for dinner		Blown bubbles
	Done something you said you wouldn't		Caught a wild animal
	Jumped off a bridge into deep water		Seen snow
	Sang a song in front of a lot of people		Driven a car
	Recited a poem out loud to others		Won a race
	Ridden a horse, cow, or large animal		
	Ridden a bicycle		
	Played a game		

3 Unique Things About Me (Something you have done, seen, experienced, or about an ability you have.)

_____

_____

_____

9 COMPLETE THE SENTENCE

Age	All	Setting	Individual	Trauma Recovery	CARING- Building Relationships

Purpose	To build a relationship with the individual by having them complete sentences about themselves.
Overview	The individual is asked to complete a series of sentences regarding how they feel and what they would change.

Approximate Time	10-15 minutes

Supplies Needed	Worksheet and pen or pencil

■ Activity Explained

- ➲ The individual completes the sentences on the worksheet.
- ➲ The facilitator reviews and discusses the worksheet with the individual primarily for the purpose of developing the relationship. The information gathered may also provide insight useful for treatment planning and for future topics to discuss.

■ Reflection

Why did you write this? What makes you feel this way?

■ Variations

Activity may be verbal or written. If using with younger children, sentences can be adapted and given verbally. Worksheet may be completed independently and brought to the session.

Activity may be used individually or in groups.

■ Concerns

The individual may need assistance in writing out their answers. If the individual is unsure or doesn't want to complete one, they should not be forced to do so.

COMPLETE THE SENTENCE

- ➲ If I could do anything, I would _____
- ➲ I wish my family would _____
- ➲ I don't like it when _____
- ➲ I think it is important _____
- ➲ When I'm older _____
- ➲ I feel sad when _____
- ➲ Sometimes I feel like _____
- ➲ My family is _____
- ➲ I get scared when _____
- ➲ I want _____
- ➲ School/work is _____
- ➲ Friends are helpful when _____
- ➲ Friends let me down _____
- ➲ My family doesn't understand _____
- ➲ My mom is _____
- ➲ My dad is _____
- ➲ I get mad when _____
- ➲ God is _____
- ➲ I hate it when _____
- ➲ I love _____
- ➲ I wish life were _____
- ➲ I wish someone would ask me _____
- ➲ I need _____
- ➲ I'm happiest when _____

10 WHO I TALK TO

Age	All	Setting	Individual	Trauma Recovery	CARING- Building Relationships

Purpose	To learn about our different levels of vulnerability and sharing, with whom we share.
Overview	The individual is asked with whom they would share certain types of information. This aids in relationship building as well as learning about the individual's relationships, privacy, and boundaries.

Approximate Time	10-15 minutes

Supplies Needed	Worksheet and pen or pencil

■ Activity Explained

- ➲ The facilitator explains that there are different types of information we tell different people, such as strangers, friends, people close to you, and yourself. Often times, people choose to share certain things with specific people. For example, if I passed a test, I might tell close friends or even social friends but probably wouldn't tell casual acquaintances or strangers.
- ➲ The facilitator asks the individual if they can think of and name people in their life that are at different levels of sharing (vulnerability).
- ➲ The individual completes the questions either by telling the facilitator their response or writing their responses

■ Reflection

Why did you choose to tell only this person_____ happened? Why do you feel like you can't tell some things to certain people? Is there anyone you could tell anything to?

■ Variations

Activity may be verbal or written. The worksheet may be completed independently and brought to the session. For younger children, adapt the examples to be age appropriate.

■ Concerns

The individual should be reassured that there are no wrong or right answers, just their preferences. The purpose of the activity is to gain information about what and with whom they feel comfortable sharing different levels of information.

WHO I TALK TO

■ Who Knows the Most

This pyramid represents the amount of information known about me by people in each level. Those in the top, wider, bigger sections know more than those toward the bottom. That is, I know the most about myself (my inner thoughts and feelings, doubts and fears, hopes and dreams). My close friends know more than others, but strangers know very little about me except what they may gather from my outside appearance.

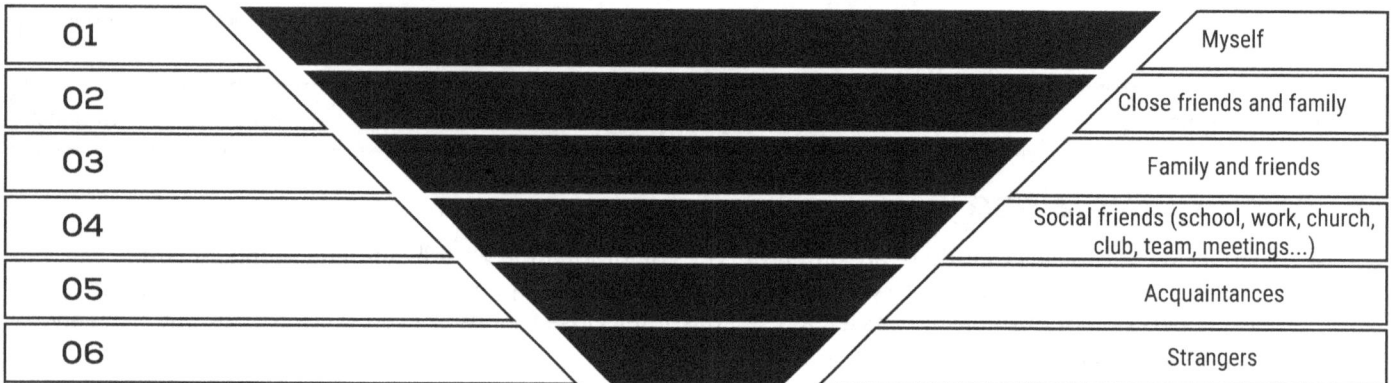

01		Myself
02		Close friends and family
03		Family and friends
04		Social friends (school, work, church, club, team, meetings...)
05		Acquaintances
06		Strangers

Who would you tell the following? (indicate which level 1-6)

When you're done with the list, make up your own situations then indicate Who you would talk to, 1-6).

	You're afraid of the dark		What happened to you
	You sometimes wet your bed (or used to)		Your feelings, doubts, and hurts
	You won an award at school/work		Whether or not you believe in God
	You got in trouble		You lied to an adult (teacher, parent, etc.)
	You stole something		You saw someone steal something
	Someone touched you inappropriately		You heard someone lie about something important
	It's your birthday		You've used drugs
	You've been sexually abused		You hate someone
	You saw someone hurt a child		
	Your deep secrets		
	You got bullied at school/work		

11 WHAT IS IMPORTANT TO ME

Age	Youth - Adults	Setting	Individual	Trauma Recovery	CARING-Building Relationships

Purpose	To bring awareness to priorities and how they shift throughout one's life.
Overview	The individual is asked to write, then rank, their priorities before evaluating how those would change if they have limited time left in their life.

Approximate Time	10-15 minutes

Supplies Needed	Worksheet and pen or pencil

◼ Activity Explained

- ⮂ The facilitator introduces the idea of priorities as things that are important or things that we spend the most time doing.
- ⮂ The individual uses the form to list five things that are important to them and then follows the prompts to make changes based on a proposed lifespan of one year or one month to live. The individual then writes how they would live (what they would do) if they only had a week to live.

◼ Reflection

Is there anything you would change about your current priorities? Anything you wish was higher or lower? What's preventing you from living according to your desired priorities?

◼ Variations

Activity may be verbal or written. Worksheet may be completed before and brought to the session.

Activity may be used individually or in groups.

◼ Concerns

The individual should be reassured that there are no right or wrong answers; these are their own opinions and preferences.

◼ Story

I always find it helpful to reflect on my priorities. Doing this activity has motivated me to spend more time on what is truly important to me.

WHAT'S IMPORTANT TO ME?

Make a list of five people, places, and things that are important to you—your priorities. These are the places where you spend most of your time and mental, emotional, and physical energy.

1	
2	
3	
4	
5	

Now, answer the following questions.

- ➲ If you only had one **YEAR** to live, would you remove anything from your list? Put an X next to it.
- ➲ If you only had one **MONTH** to live, what would you remove from the list? Put a circle around the number.
- ➲ If you only had one **WEEK** to live, what would you do? How would you spend your time? Write your answer here:

_____

_____

_____

_____

What have you learned about your priorities and what's important to you?

_____

_____

_____

_____

12 WHAT DO YOU DO WHEN?

Age	Youth - Adults	Setting	Individual	Trauma Recovery	CARING- Building Relationships

Purpose	To build a relationship between the facilitator and individual.
Overview	The individual is asked a series of questions regarding what they would do in a given situation.

Approximate Time	10-20 minutes		**Supplies Needed**	Worksheet and pen or pencil

■ Activity Explained

➲ The individual answers questions from the worksheet either by writing their answers or orally telling the facilitator.

■ Reflection

Why would you do, think, or feel that? Would it be different at a different time and place?

This is another opportunity for the facilitator to acknowledge any similarities as a way to build the therapeutic relationship. *That's what I would do too. We are similar on that one. I agree, that's a good thing to do.*

■ Variations

Activity may be verbal or written. Worksheet may be completed independently and brought to the session.

If the individual is unsure how to answer a question, they may take the worksheet home to observe their thoughts in certain situations and then complete the questionnaire.

■ Concerns

Questions may need to be appropriately tailored for the person's developmental level, culture, and experiences.

WHAT DO YOU DO WHEN? (Answer as many questions as you can)

When you wake up in the morning...

⮑ What do you think about?

_____

⮑ What do you think about?

_____

⮑ What do you think about?

_____

⮑ What do you think about?

When you go to bed at night...

⮑ What do you think about?

_____

⮑ What do you think about?

_____

⮑ What do you think about?

_____

⮑ What do you think about?

When you are alone...

⮑ What do you think about?

_____

⮑ What do you think about?

_____

⮑ What do you think about?

When you are here...

⮑ What do you think about?

_____

⮑ What do you think about?

_____

⮑ What do you think about?

_____

13 TELLING A STORY

Age	All	Setting	Individual	Trauma Recovery	CARING- Building Relationships

Purpose	To practice telling a story (not of a traumatic event) in detail as a way to build communication skills, to give the individual a voice, and to practice for sharing one's personal trauma story later in counseling.
Overview	The individual tells a story using a life event that is either happy or neutral while the facilitator asks questions to elicit details. This serves as the baseline narrative, a practice and example of what is to come when the person is asked to share about their personal trauma experiences.

Approximate Time	5-20 minutes

Supplies Needed	Worksheet and pen or pencil (if written)

■ Activity Explained

⮕ The facilitator asks the individual to tell a story about a happy or neutral event in their life (not a trauma memory) using as much detail as possible, including sights, sounds, smells, feelings, etc. It could be about a person, place, thing, event, or experience. (Example: last placement, family, cultural festival/holiday, birthday, game, etc.). The story should be told in as much detail as possible, and the facilitator should prompt for additional details throughout the storytelling process as needed.

⮕ The individual tells their story and the facilitator listens intently, asking prompting questions such as: Who was there? When did it happen? What happened before, during, and after? Who else was there with you? How did you feel? What did it sound, smell, taste, feel like? How old were you? What time of year was it? What were you wearing? What did you like about it? What do you wish was different? Thank the person when finished.

■ Reflection

If details are missing, the individual should be asked questions to elicit more information. The facilitator may also ask the individual what they would change if they told this story again.

■ Variations

Activity may be verbal or written. Story may be written before and brought to the session. If preferred, paper could be provided for the person to write their story down or to draw a picture— whatever he/she prefers and is age appropriate.

■ Concerns

Be sure that the story is a pleasant memory, without trauma triggers.

COLLECTING
INFORMATION

CARING

14 CHECKING IN

Age	All	Setting	Individual	Trauma Recovery	CARING-Collecting Information

Purpose	To quickly gather a self-report before each session on how the person is doing.
Overview	The individual is asked to rate themselves on a scale of 1-5, from not doing well to *doing really well* in five holistic areas – emotionally, socially, physically, mentally (school/work) and spiritually.

Approximate Time	5-10 minutes

Supplies Needed	Worksheet and pen or pencil

■ Activity Explained

- ➲ The individual is given the worksheet at the beginning or the end of each session. It is best to combine several of the weekly rating sections onto one page and make copies.
- ➲ Once a week, the individual rates (1–5) how they are doing emotionally, socially, physically, mentally (school/work), and spiritually.
- ➲ The facilitator may ask clarifying questions if appropriate.

■ Reflection

Reflection should focus on changes week-to-week. *Your Social rating went down this week- what happened? You rated yourself higher Emotionally this week, what changed?*

■ Variations

Activity may be used individually or in groups. Activity may be verbal or written. With children, adapt the activity by using drawings or illustrations of sad to happy smiley faces, different animals, or a variety of colors to indicate feeling terrible to very good.

■ Concerns

The individual may need assistance in completing the worksheet.one, they should not be forced to do so.

WEEKLY SELF RATING: HOW I'M DOING

Each week, before beginning, please circle a number that reflects how you're doing—physically, mentally, socially, emotionally and spiritually. Then, write a couple of words that describe what you're thinking and/or feeling (some examples are given but write words that reflect what you are thinking or feeling).

- ⮌ Emotionally = how you are feeling about life and yourself. (sad, happy, mad, scared, ashamed, shy, cautious, bored, hurt)
- ⮌ Socially = how you are feeling about relationships with family and friends. (sad, happy, mad, scared, ashamed, shy, cautious, hurt, strained, broke up, good friend)
- ⮌ Physically = how your body is feeling. (sick, weak, tense, tired, energetic, in shape, overweight, looking good)
- ⮌ Mentally (School/Work) = how you're doing in school or at work. (good student, flunking, studying hard, not getting it, bored, like/don't like teachers) or (hard-working, underpaid, under-appreciated, enjoyable, stimulating)
- ⮌ Spiritually = how you're feeling or what you're thinking about God (pray a lot, nothing, feel His presence, went to church, don't believe, unsure)

1 -	Not Doing Well At All Or Terrible	2 -	Not So Good	3 -	Fair Or Okay	4 -	Good	5 -	Really Good

WEEK:	TERRIBLE	NOT SO GOOD	FAIR	GOOD	REALLY GOOD	WORDS TO DESCRIBE
Emotionally	1	2	3	4	5	
Socially	1	2	3	4	5	
Physically	1	2	3	4	5	
School/Work	1	2	3	4	5	
Spiritually	1	2	3	4	5	
Socially	1	2	3	4	5	
Comments:						

WEEK:	TERRIBLE	NOT SO GOOD	FAIR	GOOD	REALLY GOOD	WORDS TO DESCRIBE
Emotionally	1	2	3	4	5	
Socially	1	2	3	4	5	
Physically	1	2	3	4	5	
School/Work	1	2	3	4	5	
Spiritually	1	2	3	4	5	
Socially	1	2	3	4	5	
Comments:						

15 MY LIFE: PAST, PRESENT, AND FUTURE

Age	Youth - Adults	Setting	Individual	Trauma Recovery	CARING-Collecting Information

Purpose	To create a timeline of the individual's life through recalling memories from each year of the individual's life.
Overview	The individual will be asked to recall memories, including transitions and emotions, based on their age.

Approximate Time	10-30 minutes

Supplies Needed	Worksheet and pen or pencil

■ Activity Explained

⮑ The individual completes the form by writing down memories/events from each year of their life that they can remember. Future years can be left blank or the person can indicate what they hope or plan to do.

⮑ The facilitator asks the person to share about the various memories but is careful not to trigger a traumatic reaction.

■ Reflection

Debrief should focus on clarifying questions, such as: *What happened when you were ten years old? Can you tell me more about this event? How did this effect you? What were you thinking or feeling when that happened? What did you do when it happened?* (ex. death, divorce, move, new school, broke an arm...

Regarding future years: *What do you hope will happen in the future?*

■ Variations

Activity may be verbal or written. Activity may be used individually or in groups, though debrief is best done individually. The worksheet may be completed independently and brought to the session to share.

■ Concerns

Certain events may trigger trauma reactions. The individual should be assured that they don't need to share details or answer questions if they do not want to or are not ready to discuss it.

MY LIFE: PAST, PRESENT, AND FUTURE

Write a few words about something you remember when you were each age. These can be happy or sad memories, family changes, things you're proud of, or things you wish were different. For the future, write what you would like to happen/do in the future. Then, put a few words to describe how you felt about what happened and/or what you did. It's okay to leave part blank if you can't think of anything.

	MEMORY (Event, Experience) OR FUTURE PLANS (Hopes, Dreams, Ideas)	HOW I FELT / WHAT I DID (Confused, Mad, Sad, Happy, Frustrated)
Birth - 2		
3		
4		
5		
6		
7		
8		
9		
10		
11		
12		
13		
14		
15		
16		
17		
18-19		
20-25		
26-30		
After 30		

16 TREATMENT PLANNING

Information for the Facilitator	Trauma Recovery	CARING- Collecting Information

Purpose	To provide a guide for the facilitator to use when developing the individual's treatment plan.
Overview	Specific lists are provided regarding what information the facilitator should gather, including the individual's strengths, concerns, needed referrals, goals, etc.

Approximate Time		Supplies Needed	Worksheet and pen

◼ Activity Explained

- ⊃ The facilitator uses the worksheet provided as a guide for general information to gather from the individual.
- ⊃ The facilitator documents client answers, as well as observed and gathered information.
- ⊃ The facilitator reviews all information and develops a specific, individualized treatment plan.

◼ Reflection

Questions to Consider when Setting Goals[3] (ask the person)

- ⊃ *What are your strengths? Weaknesses? Challenges?*
- ⊃ *What do you see as your biggest problem or concern right now?*
- ⊃ *What do you hope will happen as a result of our time together?*
- ⊃ *What will be different when you reach your goal?*
- ⊃ *Does the goal involve changing things about yourself? Other people?*
- ⊃ *Do you anticipate any problems in reaching that goal?*
- ⊃ *What will help you attain that goal?*

◼ Variations

The Treatment Plan can be developed directly with the individual or by the facilitator with information collected from the individual.

◼ Concerns

Those not trained in Treatment Planning should especially find this worksheet to be helpful, as it provides direction and guidelines.

---

3   Adapted from Essentials of Treatment Planning by M. Maruish, 2012, p 141.

DEVELOPING A TREATMENT PLAN

▮ 1 - Gather Information: Develop, List or Identify the following related to the client:

Strengths	(identified from the individual, other people, and observed.)
Problems/Concerns	(from the individual and other sources.)
Issues to Consider	(cultural, religious, ethnic, etc.
Potential Barriers to Treatment	(unsupportive or lack of family; lacks motivation/feels hopeless, resistant to change/counseling.)
Needed Resources/ Interventions	(Possible referrals: psychiatric, medical, social services, neurological, educational, vocational or career services, others (occupational therapists, speech therapists, pastoral counseling, nutritionist, lawyers...,etc.)
Diagnoses	(if needed or helpful for treatment. To be conducted by trained professional.)

■ 2 - Write an individualized Treatment Plan which includes:

Individual's Goals

Overall Therapeutic Goals

General Goals and Treatment Steps (example)

- ➲ Build Safety and Trust
- ➲ Teach about Trauma and other relevant topics
- ➲ Teach relaxation, mindfulness, and emotional regulation skills
- ➲ Teach about emotions, emotional identification, and expression
- ➲ Teach the difference between feelings and thoughts, recognizing inner thoughts, combatting false or harmful thinking
- ➲ Client shares their trauma story(-ies)
- ➲ Facilitator reviews the stories for negative beliefs and self-statements
- ➲ Client shares their trauma story(-ies) with another safe person
- ➲ Facilitator and client identify any trauma stories to share which might have been done by the client to others
- ➲ Facilitator and person identify any remaining fears or phobias related to the trauma(s) and make a specific plan for overcoming them
- ➲ Engage in safety planning and role plays which empower the client and increases his/her control, sense of safety, and problem-solving abilities
- ➲ Celebrate the positive decisions, changes, and growth accomplished

17 COLLECT HELPFUL INFO

Information for the Facilitator	Trauma Recovery	CARING- Collecting Information

Purpose	To create a timeline of the individual's life through recalling memories from each year of the individual's life.
Overview	The individual will be asked to recall memories, including transitions and emotions, based on their age.

Approximate Time	20-60 minutes

Supplies Needed	Worksheet and pen

■ Activity Explained

- ⮕ The facilitator decides which measures they are going to use to collect information on the individual they are helping.
- ⮕ The individual completes a series of worksheets or drawing activities.
- ⮕ The facilitator uses the information collected to determine how to best help the individual.

■ Reflection

How do you feel after filling out so much information about yourself?

Why do you think it helps for me to know more about you?

■ Variations

Activity may be used individually or in groups.

■ Concerns

The individual may need assistance in filling out forms

COLLECT INFORMATION

We do not want to be overly intrusive, pushy, re-triggering or re-traumatizing when we collect information from those we serve. We gather the information in ways that are sensitive, caring, and aware of the difficulty for many in sharing about their lives.

The following list highlights the information we need to gather in order to develop a treatment plan based on the specific needs of the individual. Generally, we want to conduct a thorough Intake Assessment (including a Mental Status Exam and a comprehensive Psychosocial History) and administer any desired assessment measures for treatment planning, treatment progress, treatment and program effectiveness, and treatment evaluation and research (if needed).

Information to gather should include:

■ Psychosocial History Intake

Information on family, health, prior counseling, education, substance use, job history, relationships.... An extensive example follows. Please adapt it as needed to reflect the nature of your country, culture, and clientele. This can be given to the client to complete (youth and adults), asked aloud with answers written down by the counselor, or a combination of both.

■ Mental Status Exam

Assessment of current mental/emotional/behavioral functioning. Is the client able to orient, focus, remember, attune, use motor skills, etc. An internet search for this should provide various examples in your preferred language. Note: some forms are extremely detailed while others are used more for screening purposes.

■ Assessment Measures

(Depression, anxiety, trauma, self-esteem, PTSD, clinical concerns): Some of these various measures can be accessed via internet and are free of cost. Make sure you use an instrument (test, measure, questionnaire) that has been well-researched, including norms and validity. If using a pre-printed Book About Me, these measures can be added to the booklet.

■ Drawings (optional but insightful)

Even if you are not familiar with projective measures or do not understand how to interpret their meaning, having the individual draw their experiences and emotions may be insightful. A colorful, well-drawn family with a dark and scribbled member can be revealing even to the untrained eye. A self-drawing without hands and feet helps us understand the depth of the person's feeling of powerlessness. A dark drawing of happiness, safety, or peace can reveal the lack of those experiences. Scribbles, erasures, or detailed drawings can help us understand more of the client's personality and/or fear of getting it wrong. Ask the individual to make several drawings during the initial sessions or incorporate them into the Book About Me (activity #19).

18 INTAKE FORM – PSYCHOSOCIAL HISTORY

Information for the Facilitator	Trauma Recovery	CARING-Collecting Information

Purpose	To provide facilitators a tool for gathering important information about the person.
Overview	The intake form, divided into four parts, gathers information helpful to the counseling and treatment planning process.

Approximate Time	60+ minutes

Supplies Needed	Intake Form and pen

■ Activity Explained

⊃ Depending on the age of the person, either he/she can complete the form or the facilitator can ask for the information, writing down the responses.

⊃ The facilitator reviews the information in formulating a treatment plan for the person, what activities to use, what resources to access, what areas to focus on, etc

■ Reflection

Debrief should focus on clarifying questions, such as: *Could you tell me more about this? Could you help me understand what you wrote/said about this?*

■ Variations

Activity may be verbal or written. If written, the form should be given and completed independently, then brought to the session. Since this extensive questionnaire is divided into four parts, it could be given at four different times. It could also be shortened and adapted as needed.

■ Concerns

The individual should be assured that they don't need to share details or answer any questions they do not want to.

The following Intake example is extensive and was compiled to gather facts and information on the individual, but also to gain additional insight specifically for those working with victims of sexual abuse and exploitation. Unlike most Intake forms, this example incorporates more subjective client input using sentence completions and asking questions about situations, thoughts, feelings, behaviors, preferences, and concerns, rather than focusing on facts and history.

LIFE HISTORY QUESTIONNAIRE (A)

The following information helps us help you. Please clearly print your response to each question. If you are unable to complete some items, leave them blank for now. Please use additional paper as needed.

Today's Day and Date	Location
Name	Nickname
Address	City
Zip	Home Phone
Cell	Birthdate / /
Age	Last Grade Completed in School
Email	Facebook Name
Emergancy Contact	
Relationship	Phone
Who do/did you live with?	

Name	Age	Relationship (Parent, Friend, Boyfriend)	Supportive? (Y/N)

■ Friends And Family

❑ **I have** family I can count on for support. Who?

❑ I have felt abandoned by friends.

❑ My friends would do almost anything for me.

❑ I have few friends I can really trust.

❑ My friends are my family.

❑ I have family / a friend **that I feel comfortable sharing my private thoughts and feelings with.**

Who? _____

If applicable, what is your boy/girl-friend's name: _____

Describe your relationship with your boy/girl-friend *(place a ✓ on the line below)*

☐ Major Problems   ☐ Minor problems   ☐ Good   ☐ Very good

How long have you known the person? _____

How long have you been with the person? _____

What do you like about the person? _____

▉ Education

Last Grade Completed _____   School name _____

School Location _____

What did you **like** about school? What did you **NOT like** about school?

_____

_____

Who was your favorite teacher _____   Grade _____

Why was he/she your favorite? _____

What were you good at and not so good at in school? _____

How would you describe your academic performance (how you are doing or did in school):

☐ Above Average   ☐ Average   ☐ Low Average   ☐ Poor

Did you date in middle school?   ☐ Yes   ☐ No

Did you date in high school?   ☐ Yes   ☐ No

▉ Religious Background

Religious Upbringing _____

❑ Christian   ❑ Buddhist   ❑ Muslim   ❑ Other

Other

Current Religious Affiliation   Attendance   / Month

Do you consider yourself a religious person?

| ❑ Yes | ❑ No | ❑ Unsure | ❑ Searching |

If yes, I consider myself to be

Strongly Committed   Somewhat Committed   Detached

Church involvement

| ❑ Very Active | ❑ Somewhat Regular | ❑ occasional | ❑ rarely involved |

■ Counseling Background

Have you ever seen a psychiatrist, psychologist, therapist, counselor, or pastor?

| ❑ Yes | ❑ No |

If 'yes', please complete the following chart:

❑ Reason	❑ Where	❑ Therapist	❑ When?	❑ Helpful? (Y/N)

| Have you ever had a severe emotional? | ❑ Yes | ❑ No | And, was hospitalized | ❑ Yes | ❑ No |

Have you ever been given a mental health diagnosis from a professional?   ❑ Yes   ❑ No

---

If yes, what is/was that diagnosis

■ Current Concerns or Problems

What are some of the main questions, concerns, and/or problems that you are currently dealing with?

How long has this been a significant problem for you? Please be specific (i.e., not "all my life").

How bad is your concern or problem right now

❏ Mild   ❏ Moderate   ❏ Serious   ❏ Severe

What have you done so far to help or to try and change the situation?

If applicable, please describe any incidents or problems that may have contributed to what you are currently experiencing (e.g., problems with relationships, past trauma, abuse, death, accident, etc.):

In the past, what has been helpful to you in dealing with problems?

How do you hope we can help? How can we be most helpful to you?

LIFE HISTORY (B): FAMILY AND GROWING UP

The following information helps us help you. Please clearly print your response to each question. If you are unable to complete some items, leave them blank. Please use additional paper as needed.

Name		Nickname	
Birthdate	/ /	Age	
Today's Date			

■ Family And Growing Up

	Age	Name	Occupation	Alive? (Yes/No)
Parent/Guardian				
Parent/Guardian				
Stepparent				
Stepparent				
Siblings				

Who can you count on for emotional support in your family?

Have any members of your family had problems with

❑ Drugs   ❑ Alcohol   ❑ Depression   ❑ Anxiety   ❑ Violence/ Abuse

❑ Other

Concern	Who: (Mom, Dad, brother, sister, aunt, uncle, grandparent...)	Now Y / N	Past Y / N

Circle any of the following that apply to your growing up:

☐ Happy Childhood   ☐ School Problems   ☐ Medical Problems   ☐ Unhappy childhood

☐ Family Problems	☐ Alcohol Abuse	☐ Emotional / Behavior	☐ Drub abuse
☐ Legal Problems	☐ Strong Religious Convictions	☐ Other	

Has any relative attempted or committed suicide?	☐ Yes	☐ No
Have you ever attempted suicide?	☐ Yes	☐ No

Have you thought about how you would commit suicide if you were to do it? How?

Have you thought about how you would commit suicide if you were to do it? How?

☐ Yes   ☐ No

Who?

■ Check all that apply.

- ☐ I don't remember being loved physically as a child (hugs, being held, etc.)
- ☐ My parents divorced when I was a child. I was _____ years old.
- ☐ I had no father growing up because of (circle): death / divorce / too busy / abandonment.
- ☐ One of my parents (or friends) committed suicide. I was _____ years old. who _____
- ☐ I was sexually abused as a child. By whom? _____
- ☐ I was put in foster care at age _____
- ☐ I have been in _____ (# number) of different foster homes.
- ☐ I had (have) a physical/mental abnormality that brought ridicule from peers.
- ☐ I experienced a severe trauma (e.g., house fire, accident, tragedy). Please explain.

- ☐ I was verbally abused as a child.
- ☐ I am adopted.
- ☐ I have an alcoholic or drug-dependent parent.
- ☐ My Mom / Dad was arrested and in jail during my childhood
- ☐ I have felt abandoned by family
- ☐ I have felt abandoned by friends
- ☐ I have had problems with the law (been arrested, served jail time)

❑   My family doesn't understand me very well.
❑   I love my family.
❑   I feel that I have let my family down—that I've disappointed them by what I've done..
❑   I was raised by (grew up with) my_____ (grandparents, aunt...)
❑   I've never felt "wanted" or accepted by my family.
❑   I felt loved growing up.
❑   I felt lonely growing up.

LIFE HISTORY (C): SELF

The following information helps us help you. Please clearly print your response to each question. If you are unable to complete some items, leave them blank. Please use additional paper as needed.

Name		Nickname	
Birthdate	/ /	Age	
Today's Date			

◼ About Me

How would you describe yourself? (write your own words then ✓ those below that apply)

_____

❑	Active	❑	Ambitious	❑	Self-confident	❑	Persistent
❑	Nervous	❑	Hardworking	❑	Impatient	❑	Shy
❑	Moody	❑	Leader	❑	Quiet	❑	Lonely
❑	Often blue	❑	Excitable	❑	Imaginative	❑	Calm
❑	Serious	❑	Easy-going	❑	Good-natured	❑	Submissive
❑	Self- conscious	❑	Passive	❑	Happy	❑	Likeable
❑	Extroverted	❑	Introverted	❑	Sensible	❑	Emotional
❑	Procastinator	❑	Organized	❑	Sensitive	❑	Tough

Please list your strengths—the things you are good at.

They may be an attitude or character trait, a skill or ability, an accomplishment, or something you've overcome:

_____

_____

What feelings are you experiencing now or in recent weeks? (*check any that apply to you*)

☐ Angry	☐ Guilty	☐ Unhappy	☐ Annoyed
☐ Happy	☐ Bored	☐ Sad	☐ Conflicted
☐ Restless	☐ Depressed	☐ Regretful	☐ Lonely
☐ Anxious	☐ Hopeless	☐ Contented	☐ Fearful
☐ Contented	☐ Fearful	☐ Hopeful	☐ Excited
☐ Panicky	☐ Helpless	☐ Optimistic	☐ Energetic
☐ Relaxed	☐ Tensed	☐ Envious	☐ Jealous
☐ Others:			

Behavior – *check any of the following behaviors that apply to you:*

☐ Suicidal attempts	☐ Can't keep a job	☐ Compulsions	☐ Insomnia
☐ Smoke	☐ Take too many risks	☐ Odd behavior	☐ Withdrawal
☐ Lack of motivation	☐ Drink too much	☐ Nervous tics	☐ Eating problems
☐ Work too hard	☐ Procrastination	☐ Sleep disturbance	☐ Crying
☐ Impulsive reactions	☐ Phobic avoidance	☐ Outbursts of temper	☐ Loss of control
☐ Aggressive behavior			

Which of the following are you currently experiencing or have experienced? (*Please check all that apply*)

☐ Overeating	☐ Rapid heart rate	☐ Compulsive behaviors	☐ Restless	☐ Taking drugs
☐ Depressed mood	☐ Impulsive behaviors	☐ Sweating	☐ Crying	☐ Trembling or shaking
☐ Odd behavior/ thoughts	☐ Fears/phobias	☐ Recent weight gain	☐ Difficulty concentrating	☐ Shortness of breath
☐ Anxiety	☐ Recent weight loss	☐ Low motivation	☐ Muscle tension	☐ Vomiting
☐ Jumpy	☐ Recent appetite changes	☐ Aggressive behavior	☐ Distrust	☐ Outbursts of temper
☐ Social withdrawal	☐ Feelings of worthlessness	☐ Nightmares	☐ Stomach problems	☐ Easily distracted
☐ Family problems	☐ Obsessions	☐ Dizzy or lightheaded	☐ Chest pain	☐ Fatigue/loss of energy

	Pain		Sleeping too much		Decreased need for sleep		Difficulty falling asleep		Difficulty staying asleep
❏	Pain	❏	Sleeping too much	❏	Decreased need for sleep	❏	Difficulty falling asleep	❏	Difficulty staying asleep
❏	Problems with school	❏	Housing problems	❏	Drinking alcohol	❏	Relationship problems	❏	Experienced a traumatic event
❏	Financial problems	❏	Can't turn my mind off	❏	Extremely angry				

Others:

Are there any specific behaviors, actions, habits that you would like to change?

■ Feelings Checklist

Below is a list of problems for you to rate indicating how often you have experienced them during the past week. Please circle the number that applies.

Sr. No.	Problems	Never	Rarely	Occasionally	Frequently	Constantly
1	Anger or Irritability	1	2	3	4	5
2	Anxiety, worry, or fear	1	2	3	4	5
3	Guilt or self-condemnation	1	2	3	4	5
4	Hopelessness or depression	1	2	3	4	5
5	Loneliness	1	2	3	4	5
6	Helplessness	1	2	3	4	5
7	Self-pity	1	2	3	4	5
8	Inferiority or worthlessness	1	2	3	4	5
9	Avoiding responsibility	1	2	3	4	5
10	Being undisciplined	1	2	3	4	5
11	Attacking others	1	2	3	4	5
12	Withdrawing from activity	1	2	3	4	5
13	Abusing drugs, alcohol, pills	1	2	3	4	5
14	Overeating/eating problems	1	2	3	4	5

15	Over-smoking	1	2	3	4	5
16	Sexual problems	1	2	3	4	5
17	Giving in too much	1	2	3	4	5
18	Religious concerns	1	2	3	4	5
19	Failure to achieve	1	2	3	4	5
20	Other	1	2	3	4	5

Are these responses descriptive of a "typical" week? ☐ Yes ☐ No ☐ Recent weeks only

☐ Yes ☐ No ☐ Recent weeks only

Comments:

Check the issues that pertain to you: rate degree of stress/urgency = 1 (low) to 5 (high).

☐ Depressionx	☐ Chronic illness	☐ Sexual Identity Issues	☐ Homosexuality
☐ Anger	☐ Relationship Problem	☐ Drug Addictions	☐ Insomnia
☐ Physical Abuse	☐ Eating Disorder	☐ Alchoholism	☐ Sexual Abuse
☐ Grief/Loss	☐ Low Self-Esteem	☐ Emotional Abuse	☐ Occult Oppression
☐ Career Decision	☐ Excessive Anxiety/ Fear	☐ Workaholism	☐ Financial Problems
☐ Loneliness	☐ Unforgiveness/ Bitterness		

☐ Other crises (describe briefly):

☐ I suffer with low self- esteem.

☐ I have clear memories of my childhood or

☐ Most of childhood memory comes from what I have been told (I can't remember it myself)

❑   I sometimes lose blocks of time I can't account for—time
passes and I don't know where I was or what happened.

❑   I sometimes have dreams about angry people surrounding me.

Please check any that relate to your experience and then explain below.

❑   Psychic abilities, clairvoyance, divination; feeling of having "special powers."

❑   Inward perception of a separate personality, name, or voice.

❑   Fearful, repetitive night visitations by an evil presence.

❑   Difficulty participating in prayer; agitation, nausea, anger, rebellion, etc.

❑   Uncontrolled thoughts/impressions; e.g., sexual perversion, cursing, violence.

❑   Uncontrollable compulsive behaviors: sexual behavior, anger, chemical indulgence.

❑   Preoccupation with thoughts of death, despair, and hopelessness.

❑   Uncontrollable, irrational, paralyzing fear.

❑   Unusual, non-typical emotional expressions, e.g., laughter, sadness, crying, anger.

❑   Extreme nervousness or negative reactions at the mention of the name of Jesus.

Please describe any additional factors:

LIFE HISTORY (D): HEALTH/MEDICAL

The following information helps us help you. Please clearly print your response to each question. If you are unable to complete some items, leave them blank. Please use additional paper as needed.

Name		Nickname	
Birthdate	/ /	Age	
Today's Date			

■ HEALTH and MEDICAL Information

Name of Doctor or Clinic while growing up
_____

City
_____

Date of last Dr./hospital visit (approximate)
_____

Please list any significant past or current health, medical, or psychiatric issues (including anything resulting in hospitalizations).

Dates	Problems & Treatment	Were you hospitalized (Y/N)

Have you ever experienced: (Please mark all that apply)

❑ Emotional abuse ❑ Physical abuse ❑ Sexual abuse ❑ Sexual assault

Have you, or anyone else, ever been concerned that you may have an eating disorder?

❑ Yes ❑ No

Do you get regular exercise? If so, what type and how often?
_____
_____

■ MEDICATIONS AND SUBSTANCES USED

If applicable, please list all medications you are now taking or have taken in the past six months, including birth control pills, vitamins, herbs, and supplements.

Medication	Dosage	Person prescribing	How long been taking?	Helpful (Y/N)

Amount of caffeinated beverages per day (#cups)

_____ Coffee   _____ Espresso   _____ Soda   _____ Tea   _____ Energy drink

If applicable, number of cigarettes
smoked per day

If applicable, how often do you use
marijuana per week? (No. of times/week)

Consider a typical week during the past month. Please fill in a number for each day of the week indicating the typical number of drinks you usually consume on that day: 1 Drink = 12 oz. beer / 4 oz. of wine / 1 oz. of hard alcohol.

of Drinks

Sunday	Monday	Tuesday	Wednesday	Thursday	Friday	Saturday

Think of an occasion where you drank the most in the past month.

How much did you drink? (# of drinks)

If applicable, other substances used

Do you use alcohol or drugs to (check all that apply)

❏ Manage stress	❏ To relax	❏ For sleep
❏ To change mood	❏ To deaden the emotional pain inside	❏ Other

How often do you gamble? (Circle one response)

❑ Never	❑ Once-A-Year	❑ 2-3 Times A Year
❑ Every Few Months	❑ Once A Month	❑ 2-3 Times/Month – Weekly
❑ A Couple Of Times/ Week	❑ Every Day	

PHYSICAL SENASTIONS (Check any of the following that often apply to you):

❑ Headaches	❑ Stomach trouble	❑ Skin Problems
❑ Dry mouth	❑ Palpitations	❑ Fatigue
❑ Burning or itchy skin	❑ Twitches	❑ Chest pains
❑ Tension	❑ Muscle Spasms	❑ Back pain
❑ Rapid heartbeat	❑ Sexual disturbance	❑ Fainting spells
❑ Tingling	❑ Watery eyes	❑ Visual Disturbance
❑ Numbness	❑ Flushes	❑ Hearing problems
❑ Tremors	❑ Unable to relax	❑ Don't like being touched

◼ MENSTRUAL HISTORY

❑	I was_____ years old when I had my first period.
❑	I wasn't really prepared for it.
❑	My period usually lasts _____ No. of days.
❑	My last period was: (date)
❑	My period is fairly regular.
❑	My period affects my moods. (I'm more emotional around that time of the month.)
❑	I have had one or more abortions. How many?_____
❑	I have had one or more miscarriages. How many?_____

■ BIOLOGICAL FACTORS

Do you have any current concerns about your physical health? ❑ Yes ❑ No

If yes then describe

Are you currently taking medications? ❑ Yes ❑ No

If yes, please list any medications you are currently taking, or have taken during the past six months. Include aspirin, birth control, prescription, or over the counter medicines.

CHECK any of the following that apply to you or members of your family

❑ Thyroid disease ❑ Kidney disease ❑ Neurological diseases ❑ Asthma

❑ Diabetes ❑ Cancer ❑ Epilepsy ❑ Glaucoma

❑ Prostate problems ❑ Gastrointestinal disease ❑ Other

Have you had accidents or injuries not previously describe? ❑ Yes ❑ No

Have you ever had any head injuries or loss of consciousness? ❑ Yes ❑ No

Have you had surgery? ❑ Yes ❑ No

If yes to any of these, please give details and dates:

19 THE BOOK ABOUT ME

Age	All	Setting	Individual or Group	Trauma Recovery	CARING-Collecting Information

Purpose	To provide the facilitator with a tool to use throughout the counseling process, which encompasses the various stages of the healing process.
Overview	This booklet (workbook) is given to the individual for the purpose of collecting helpful information and teaching about trauma, emotions, thoughts, and behavior, as well as opportunities to share about the abuse.

Approximate Time	Varies

Supplies Needed	Workbook and pen.

■ Activity Explained

- ⮑ The facilitator chooses which pages to include from the many activities provided in this book. Chosen activities are copied and compiled into a booklet for the person, including a title page for the person to write their name. Activity worksheets should reflect the various stages of trauma recovery and be kept in the intended order.
- ⮑ The facilitator and individual go through the book a few pages at a time.
- ⮑ The facilitator and individual celebrate the book's completion (which generally corresponds with the completion of trauma counseling).

■ Reflection

How do you like having a book about you? How do you feel after having shared about yourself, your experiences, and your goals?

■ Variations

Pages included vary according to age, culture, context, and for each individual or group.

■ Concerns

Individuals who are not able to read and write may need assistance filling out and compiling the book.

■ Story

This has been used with younger children, an adolescent support group, and adult women, all with positive results. The facilitator chooses which information and activities to include, personalizing it for the individual or group.

THE BOOK ABOUT ME

This booklet helps reinforce learning; explore identity; encourage self-efficacy; clarify beliefs and values; identify feelings, thoughts, and maladaptive responses; tell the trauma narrative; address trauma triggers, future goals, and more (depending on what pages the facilitator/program decides to include). Use of the booklet is incorporated into the ongoing counseling process rather than completed all at once.

The Facilitator chooses which pages to include from the many TRACTs (Trauma Recovery Activities) provided in this book (and from other sources). The activities are selected based on which are most appropriate for the age, setting, culture and context of the individual. Chosen activities are copied and compiled into a booklet for the person, including a title page for the person to write their name. The activities should reflect the various stages of trauma recovery and be kept in the component order. That is, activities on sharing one's trauma stories are located after the previous foundational steps have been completed.

■ Possible Content Pages (and possible # of pages)

- ➲ **Title Page with person's NAME:** Allow the person to write their name however they see fit. (1 page) Some have written their name quickly in pencil and others have created a colorful, elaborate name drawing.

- ➲ **Identifying Information:** name, age, date of birth, names and ages of parents and siblings, birthplace, etc. (1 – 2 pages) Refer to activities under Building Relationships.

- ➲ **Drawings (intermingled):** Family, Self and Safety, Happiness, Peace or Sadness (3+ pages) Include blank pages in the book for this purpose and ask for these various drawings every few pages at the beginning of the book's development.

- ➲ **Checking In/How I'm Doing:** Holistic self-evaluation which asks the person to rate and describe briefly how he/she is doing emotionally, socially, mentally, physically, and spiritually. (2 – 3 pages) Refer to the example under Collecting Info. It's best to put several weeks on one page.

- ➲ **Interesting information about the person:** Self-descriptors, strengths, personality traits, favorites, hobbies, experiences, etc. (1 – 3 pages) On these pages the person can be asked to list these items or is provided prompts or checklists. Refer to activities in Building Relationships.

- ➲ **Sentence completions and questions:** Clarifies values, interests…, hopes, etc. (2 – 5+ pages) Refer to activities in Building Relationships.

- ➲ **Life Before (the Trauma):** Drawing, collage, information completion, poem, perhaps a drawing of the person's home or village. (1 – 2+ pages) The person is asked to provide information about what life was like before the trauma experience.

- ➲ **What Happened (Trauma Narrative):** Drawing, collage, information completion, poem, written story…,etc. (1+ page) The telling of one's story or the trauma narrative must be done after a foundation of trust in built and there is an understanding about trauma and its effects, as well as accompanying thoughts. Refer to activities in Step 5 Sharing.

- ➲ **What Happened Afterwards (running away, police, detention, placement…,):** Drawing, collage, information completion, or poem. (1+ page) Ask the person to share a bit about what happened after the trauma event—who did what, how people reacted and what they wish had/hadn't happened. For some, this is a continuation of the trauma narrative.

- ⮕ **Life Now (how I feel and think, what I've learned, how I am different, what advice would I give to others):** Drawing, collage, information completion, or poem. (1+ page)
- ⮕ **Future Goals and Hopes:** Drawing, collage, information completion, or poem. (1+ page) Refer to activities in Living.

■ Sample Introduction

How to Use this Book

This book is about YOU—your past, present and future, what you like and don't like, what you've experienced, as well as your hopes and plans for your life. It also helps you learn more about yourself—how you think and feel, how you can heal from past hurts, and how you view yourself and your future.

Hopefully, you'll have some fun along the way as you explore more about YOU.

Each week, you'll be asked to go through a few pages. You can mark the top of the pages to indicate the ones that are private (you don't want others to see), and those that others are allowed to see. If you don't feel like doing a page, you can skip it for now and return to it later.

Also, you can be creative if you want to. You can use words, pictures, poems, make a collage, attach a photo, or write a song. And, you can use crayons, colored pencils, markers, or pens.

This is a book about YOU and for YOU. If you have any questions, just ask.

Contents Example

Approximate

No. of Pages	What
1	Title Page write your name
2-3+	Personal information: name, birthday, age, birthplace, family member names and ages...
4	Draw a picture of your family
5-6	Checking In (used for each session)
7	Include a measure of self-esteem
8-9	Interesting information about you: My Favorites, Get to Know You Questions
10	Draw a picture of yourself
11-13	Interesting information: Would you Rather Questions, My Uniqueness, What's Important to

No. of Pages	What
	Me
14-15	Include a measure of trauma and anxiety
16-21	Learning: choose activities from this step (5 – 7+)
22-23	Include a measure of depression
24	Draw a picture of "Safety" or "Happiness" or "Peace"
25-34	Feeling: Choose activities from this step (maybe 7 – 10+)
35-41	Thinking: Choose activities from this step (7 – 8+)
42-49	Sharing: Choose various activities from this step which are appropriate for the individual
50-60	Living Free, Safe and Well: Choose activities from this step specific to the person/program

HELPING
CAREGIVERS

CARING

20 STRENGTHS-BASED APPROACH

For Caregiver Training	Setting	Individual or Group	Trauma Recovery	CARING-Helping Caregivers

Purpose	To teach caregivers about the Strengths-Based Approach.
Overview	The Strengths-Based Approaches challenges caregivers to "find the good in the bad," to focus on the positive amidst the negative, and to concentrate on strengths rather than weaknesses.

Approximate Time	15-30 minutes

Supplies Needed	Workbook and pen.

■ Activity Explained

- ➲ The facilitator teaches caregivers about the Strengths-Based Approach (using the attached information). The facilitator provides a definition, explanations, and examples of how to incorporate the Strengths-Based Approach and how to ask questions that highlight strengths from the client's past successes.

- ➲ Helpers get in pairs and practice identifying strengths by asking questions that draw attention to a person's strengths and past success (included in the following information).

- ➲ Helpers come back together to share their experiences.

■ Reflection

Reflection focuses on how to use the Strengths-Based Approach both with an individual and within organizational practice. *How can you foster an environment where Strengths-Based practice is encouraged? How can each of us increase our ability to "find the good in the bad" and "the positive amidst the problems," focusing on "the potential and not just the problem"?*

■ Variations

Activity best done in a group setting with all caregivers.

■ Concerns

Helpers may initially need assistance in identifying strengths amidst challenging client behaviors.

STRENGTHS-BASED APPROACH

■ What it is?

- ➲ Focusing on strengths and not weaknesses. Looking for strengths amidst difficult behavior.
- ➲ Choosing to focus on the good and not the bad in behaviors and attitudes
- ➲ Strengths-based approach is designed to help caregivers focus on the trauma victim's strength and past successes rather than solely on current problems and failures.
- ➲ It comes from the approach that many people already possess or can develop strengths and abilities to address current problems.
- ➲ *Its focus is on strength-building rather than flaw-fixing. (unknown)*

Focus on:

- ❑ Strengths
- ❑ Abilities and Skills
- ❑ Past experiences of success
- ❑ Positive coping skills
- ❑ Survival skills
- ❑ Helpful characteristics

■ Asking Questions

When working with victims of trauma, here are some questions you can ask to help them identify their own strengths. We encourage them to draw upon past successes and situations in which they have overcome and/or survived.

- ➲ *How have you solved problems in the past? What helped?*
- ➲ *Have you had any problems or situations similar to what you are experiencing now? What happened and what did you do? What, if anything, did you learn from it?*
- ➲ *What do you consider to be some of your strengths and abilities? What are you good at?*
- ➲ Point out successes, strengths, and other times when the person has overcome challenges and adversity.

■ Questions to Consider as Care Providers

- ➲ In what ways does our organization foster resiliency? What can it do to improve?
- ➲ How can we foster an environment where Strengths-Based practice is encouraged?
- ➲ How can each of us increase our ability to "find the good in the bad" and "the positive amidst the problems"; focusing on "the potential and not just the problem"?

"Strengths-based practice dares us to find the good in the bad and see the positive and potential amidst the problems."

Dr. Becca Johnson

21 - STRENGTHS-BASED PRACTICE

For Caregiver Training	Setting	Group	Trauma Recovery	CARING-Helping Caregivers

Purpose	To teach caregivers about the Strengths-Based Approach, encouraging them to practice and use it when dealing with conflict resolution.
Overview	The Strengths-Based Approach challenges caregivers to "find the good in the bad," to focus on the positive amidst the negative, and to concentrate on strengths rather than weaknesses.

Approximate Time	20-30 minutes		Supplies Needed	Worksheet

■ Activity Explained

⊃ The facilitator teaches or reviews with caregivers about the Strengths-Based Approach (refer to previous activity).

⊃ The facilitator chooses a negative behavior and asks caregivers to identify possible strengths of that behavior.

⊃ The facilitator divides caregivers into small groups (2 – 4 people) and gives a list of negative behaviors, asking caregivers to list possible strengths and positive outcomes.

■ Reflection

Reflection focuses on why the strengths-based approach should be used. *Why is it important to focus on individual strengths? When should we use the strengths-based approach?*

■ Variations

Activity may be verbal or written and may be done individually, in large, or small groups.

■ Concerns

Helpers may initially need assistance identifying strengths.

"At a restoration home for victims of commercial sexual exploitation in Southeast Asia, caregivers didn't understand the concept of the strengths-based approach. After being asked for common behavioral problems experienced in the home, we developed a list of the possible strengths of each of these behavioral issues together as a large group. Then, they understood the what and how to of implementing the strengths-based approach and were able to continue identifying potential positives in small groups."

Dr. Becca Johnson

STRENGTHS-BASED PRACTICE

■ REVIEW: What it is?

- ➲ Strengths-based practice is an approach to helping people which focuses on the individual's strength and past successes rather than solely on current problems and failures.
- ➲ It believes that all people already have or can develop strengths and abilities to address problems.
- ➲ We focus on: strengths, abilities, and positive coping and survival skills

Strength-based practice dares us to find the good in the bad and see the positive amidst the problems

Dr. Becca Johnson

■ Identifying the Good in the Bad

For each negative behavior listed below, identify the possible strengths—those characteristics, attitudes, skills, abilities, perspectives, and potential positive outcomes.

Negative Behavior	Possible strengths, skills, abilities, positive outcomes
Lies	
Steals	
Manipulates	
Uses Drugs	
Hurts others (hits, kicks, pushes)	
Other	

Example: Some Possible Answers

Negative Behavior	Possible strengths, skills, abilities, positive outcomes
Lies	creative, good communicator, good memory, etc.
Steals	resourceful, focused, quick, attentive/alert, etc.
Manipulates	knows what he/she wants, persuasive, goal-oriented, etc.
Uses Drugs	problem-solver, solution-focused, aware of negative life aspects (aware of need to deaden the pain), etc.
Hurts others	physical skills, assertive, problem-solver, active, etc.

22 IDENTIFYING TRANSFERABLE SKILLS

For Caregiver Training		Setting	Group	Trauma Recovery	CARING-Helping Caregivers
Purpose		To teach caregivers about the skills and resilience that can come from traumatic experiences..			
Overview		Helpers work in a group to make a list of the possible skills, abilities, characteristics, and positive outcomes that might result from the traumatic experience.			

Approximate Time	15-25 minutes		Supplies Needed	Worksheet and pen

■ Activity Explained

- ⊃ The helpers select a traumatic experience (from a list or one common amongst those they serve).
- ⊃ The helpers brainstorm a list of possible, positive skills, abilities, characteristics, or outcomes that may result from the traumatic experience.
- ⊃ The helpers repeat the process for another traumatic experience.

■ Reflection

Are there ways that horrible experiences can bring positive results? How can good things come out of terrible experiences? For faith-based staff, what Scriptures address this issue of good coming out of bad situations?

■ Variations

Activity may be used individually or in groups. Activity may be verbal or written. This activity may also be used with trauma victims who can understand the concept.

■ Concerns

Helpers may need assistance in identifying positive transferable skills.

IDENTIFYING TRANSFERABLE SKILLS

Positive skills and abilities can develop during and after a traumatic event. Even amidst a horrifying experience, good things can happen. While this can be challenging, it is possible. Choose a trauma event (from those listed or one common to your culture and context) and make a list of the possible skills, abilities, characteristics, and positive outcomes that might be a result of the traumatic experience.

Example: Trauma = Exploitation / Prostitution

What skills, abilities and/or characteristics might a person gain from being exploited or prostituted?

Possible answers might include:

- Communication skills
- Money handling
- Promotion/Marketing abilities
- Loyalty
- Hard work
- Responsibility

- Customer Service (pleasing clients)
- Survival Skills
- Computer skills (for some)
- Alert and aware of surroundings
- Other _____

Choose a trauma event then make a list of potential positive skills, characteristics, abilities, and outcomes.

Trauma event examples: Sexual or Physical Abuse or Assault, Domestic Violence, Substance use/abuse, Death, Divorce, Forced Abortion, Natural Disaster, Terrorism, etc.

Trauma Event	Potential Positive Outcomes, Skills, Abilities, Characteristics developed, etc.

23 DISCIPLINE GUIDELINES

For Caregiver Training	Setting	Group	Trauma Recovery	CARING-Helping Caregivers

Purpose	To teach basic discipline guidelines to all caregivers.
Overview	Caregivers make a list of discipline techniques and brainstorm positive discipline guidelines.

Approximate Time	30-45 minutes

Supplies Needed	Worksheet and pen

■ Activity Explained

⊃ Caregivers should first be taught about trauma and trauma recovery in order to gain sensitivity to and understanding of victims' experiences, thoughts, feelings, and behaviors.

⊃ Caregivers are asked to develop a definition of discipline and to give examples of various techniques. Discuss the strengths and weaknesses, as well as pros and cons of the different methods.

⊃ The facilitator explains that effective discipline should be specific, consistent, and positive, and used to guide or shape behavior, not for punishment. (Other aspects of behavioral management are discussed in other activities, including giving attention and using behavioral charts and respite.)

⊃ The facilitator and caregivers generate new ideas for discipline and how these guidelines might be implemented. Remind caregivers to use a strengths-based approach.

⊃ Caregivers practice various scenarios to determine which technique to use for different situations.

■ Reflection

What techniques have you been using that meet these guidelines? How have they been working when caregiving? What techniques haven't been working? Do you have any concerns with how to use these guidelines? What's your biggest concern with disciplining the person you care for?

■ Variations

Activity may be verbal or written. Activity may be used individually or in groups.

If the program, culture, or laws include any information on discipline, please include these in the activity.

■ Concerns

Discipline techniques may need to be adjusted to be culturally appropriate.

BEHAVIORAL MANAGEMENT (DISCIPLINE IS THE SHAPING OF BEHAVIOR)

Focus on....

- ➲ Positive reinforcement (affirm desired behaviors)
- ➲ Strengths-based approach (focusing on abilities and strengths)
- ➲ Clear, consistent, and firm expectations
- ➲ Being patient and allowing time for the person to respond appropriately to a request
- ➲ Giving reminders of consequences if the person continues undesired behavior
- ➲ Explaining why rules and guidelines are needed for their safety and wellbeing
- ➲ Giving the person options (whenever possible; example: *You can clean up your room now or you can do it in an hour.*)

Avoid....

- ➲ Physical Punishment (ex: spanking)
- ➲ Yelling or raising your voice
- ➲ Focusing only on weaknesses and mistakes
- ➲ Acting out of impatience; reacting and "punishing"
- ➲ Saying "Because I said so" and relying on one's authority, power, and control

Approaches and Techniques to Use:

- ➲ Strengths-Based Approach
- ➲ Positive Reinforcement
- ➲ Focused Attention (Active Listening)
- ➲ Behavioral Management Charts
- ➲ Reward system: giving rewards or taking away privileges for specific desired behaviors
- ➲ Giving the person a respite (break, time out)

Scenarios *(discuss and/or role play the following, add other commonly experienced examples)*

If you ask the person to clean up a mess they made and they refuse, what would you do?

_____

_____

If you asked the person not to touch something and they grab it, what would you do?

_____

_____

If the person lied to you, what would you do?

_____

_____

If the person takes something without asking permission, what would you do?

_____

_____

If the person refuses to do something and becomes violent (yelling and hitting), what would you do?

_____

_____

Other common situations:

_____

_____

_____

24 FOCUSED ATTENTION

For Caregiver Training	Setting	Individual or Group	Trauma Recovery	CARING-Helping Caregivers

Purpose	To teach caregivers the behavioral management strategy of focused attention.
Overview	Caregivers practice utilizing a positive reinforcement approach by giving focused attention for expected behaviors and overlooking unwanted behaviors (whenever possible).

Approximate Time	10-15 minutes

Supplies Needed	None

■ Activity Explained

- ➲ The facilitator explains that focused attention is learning to overlook certain misbehaviors and focus primarily on desired behaviors. This is positive reinforcement.
- ➲ The caregiver should not give verbal or physical attention for unwanted behaviors such as outbursts, hostile looks, and disrespectful actions unless considered harmful to others.
- ➲ The caregiver should acknowledge and affirm desired behavior with verbal affirmations such as *Thank you for putting away your belongings. That was responsible.*
- ➲ Ask caregivers to practice with various common situations.
  What to ignore: rolling eyes, displays of disgust, some defiance...
  When to give attention: completing chores, putting bowl away, smiling at another person, etc.

■ Reflection

It may be challenging for the caregiver to shift their attention from the bad behaviors to the good, but they should practice consistently. Discuss any concerns by asking, "*Have you tried focused attention before? If you have tried this before, what worked well and what didn't? What behavior is the hardest for you to ignore? How can those around you support you with this strategy?*"

■ Variations

Activity may be taught individually or in groups.

■ Concerns

Always respond to behavior that is dangerous or abusive. The caregiver needs to reassure the person that the attention given is not an indicator of how much they are loved and valued.

25 GIVING ENCOURAGEMENT

For Caregiver Training	Setting	Individual or Group	Trauma Recovery	CARING-Helping Caregivers

Purpose	To teach helpers and caregivers how to best encourage those that they are helping and caring for.
Overview	Caregivers are given instructions on how to encourage those they serve by focusing on positive affirmations.

Approximate Time	20-30 minutes		Supplies Needed	Worksheet for person teaching unless all are given the information worksheet

■ Activity Explained

- ⊃ The facilitator explains that encouragement fosters hope and self-esteem and is often more effective than threat of punishment.

- ⊃ The facilitator asks for an example of a negative behavior and then re-words it for an example of a Strengths-based approach. Example: "You're always lying" can instead be "You are quite a creative person and a good communicator, but we want you to always tell the truth and not a lie."

- ⊃ The facilitator encourages helpers to practice a Strengths-based approach by providing words of encouragement and affirmation.

- ⊃ The facilitator encourages helpers in their efforts and then ask them to give each other encouragement.

■ Reflection

Helpers should reflect on how they feel when people encourage them and why it would be important to also encourage those they serve.

■ Variations

Though preferred completing with all caregivers, this activity can also be done individually.

■ Concerns

Helpers may need assistance in creating authentic affirmations and compliments or may feel uncomfortable giving them. Encourage them to practice this over and over until it becomes more natural.

GIVING ENCOURAGEMENT

We want to give those we care for hope and encouragement not discouragement and punishment. To do this, we give plenty of positive affirmations and we do it often.

◼ Strengths-Based Approach

As we've learned, the strengths-based approach challenges us to identify good qualities amidst the bad. We aren't to ignore harmful, negative behavior, but our job is to remain as encouraging and positive as possible.

We can identify the individual's strength then share desired behavior with statements such as: *You are quite a creative person and a good communicator, but we want you to always tell the truth and not lie.* or, *You have a good memory, but let's try to remember good things about people and not just the bad; let's not gossip about them.*

◼ Encouragement (Positive Reinforcement or Affirmations)

When giving affirmations or encouraging words:

- ⮑ Do it as soon as possible
- ⮑ Do not include "but" afterwards (it becomes a negative rather than positive comment)
  Thank you for cleaning your room but next time empty the rubbish bin too.
- ⮑ Be specific, commenting about a particular behavior, attitude, or characteristic observed.
- ⮑ Be enthusiastic, letting the person know that their action or attitude is genuinely appreciated.
- ⮑ Give it freely and frequently, not just once or twice.

Examples

- ⮑ *Thank you for remembering to clean up after yourself.*
- ⮑ *You did a good job paying attention in class today.*
- ⮑ *You really understand how to operate that machine.*
- ⮑ *Great job on _____.*
- ⮑ *You're good at _____.*
- ⮑ *I really appreciated when you _____.*
- ⮑ *You're a fast learner.*
- ⮑ *What you did was very thoughtful and kind.*
- ⮑ *When you helped _____, I could tell you are a caring person.*

Words of Affirmation (more examples)

- + Super, good, wonderful, great, awesome, fantastic, amazing, incredible
- + Good job, great work, that was kind/thoughtful, thanks for doing____, that was helpful
- + You're: improving, smart, resourceful, getting better, creative, strong, skilled at _____

26 RESPITE (TIME OUT, SELF-REGULATION TIME, TAKING A BREAK, REALIGNMENT TIME)

For Caregiver Training	Setting	Individual or Group	Trauma Recovery	CARING-Helping Caregivers

Purpose	To teach caregivers how to use respite or time outs as a behavior management strategy.
Overview	Caregivers are introduced to how to use respite or breaks to manage misbehavior. Using this strategy interrupts negative behavior and helps the person regain emotional and behavioral self-control.

Approximate Time	10-20 minutes	**Supplies Needed**	Worksheet

■ Activity Explained

➲ The facilitator explains that using respite or "taking a break" can help interrupt negative behavior and gives the person an opportunity to regain behavioral and emotional control (self-regulate).

➲ The facilitator teaches the process of respite (when it is needed and how to use it).

    a. Use a respite when the person has already been told to discontinue an unwanted behavior (after your first clear request to change) and yet continues the undesirable behavior. You might say something like, Let's take a break so that you can gain control of yourself and make better decisions about your behavior. Or, I think the best way to help you right now is to let you take a break from this situation. Or, You're going to have a respite now to help you decide what you want to do.

    b. Tell the person that they need to take a break and, if needed, walk the person calmly and without argument to the chosen location.

    c. For children, the chosen location should be "boring" or free of distraction and activities (ex: a chair in the corner of the room not surrounded by any toys)

    d. Tell the child to stay in that location for a specific amount of time. It is recommended to use a minute for each year of age (ex: a five-year-old would have a 5-minute break and a ten year old should be given 10 minutes).

    e. If the child doesn't stay in the chosen location or for the required amount of time, perhaps give the loss of a privilege (ex: a treat, a fun activity, playing outside).

    f. After the respite, be sure to either explain to the child or have them explain to you why they needed a break and the reasoning behind your original request.

▪ Reflection

Have you used this before? Do you think it will be helpful? What has been helpful in the past? How can we make sure this is not viewed as a punishment, but as an opportunity to self-regulate?

▪ Variations

Instead of calling this a time out, use a positive phrase like a self-regulation time, taking a break, or a time for realignment.

▪ Concerns

The purpose of having a respite should be explained to the child/youth so they view it as a time to take a break and regulate their emotions and behavior rather than a punishment (whenever possible). It is not a time to get out of work or helping, but to help regain one's emotional and behavioral control.

▪ Story

Having people (young or old) take a break is helpful for them to calm down, refocus, or to teach them that certain behaviors are undesirable and may have undesired consequences. When using this with my own children, the time and place for the break had to be clearly understood and I had to follow-up and be consistent. More than once I returned to find a sleeping child.

27 CHARTING PROGRESS

For Caregiver Training	Setting	Group	Trauma Recovery	CARING-Helping Caregivers

Purpose	To teach caregivers how to use behavioral charts to encourage desired behaviors.
Overview	The caregivers create a behavioral chart with rewards specific to the child/desired behaviors.

Approximate Time	15-20 minutes		Supplies Needed	Worksheet/blank paper and pen, stickers, or colored pens for marking the chart.

■ Activity Explained

➲ The caregivers select certain behaviors they want the child/youth to improve. It is best to focus on 3 to 5 behaviors/skills at a time, especially for younger children.

➲ The facilitator assists the caregivers in creating a chart with the desired behaviors listed on the left side and the days of the week across the top (see the following example). It is preferred that actual charts are created with the help of the child/youth.

➲ The caregiver decides when the acknowledgement (check mark/point/star) is awarded: immediately after observing the desired behavior or when the behavior is demonstrated for the majority of the day. They decide how many points the child needs to achieve before receiving a reward and what that reward should be. Rewards can include a special treat, a new toy or book, extra time on a favorite activity, or a special experience like going to the park/library. These, of course, are chosen considering the setting and resources.

➲ The facilitator asks caregivers to practice explaining the chart to each other as if they were explaining it to the child/youth. The facilitator reminds the caregivers to present it in a positive way and to develop mutually agreed upon rewards.

■ Reflection

How do you think this strategy will work in your setting/situation? If you have already used it, what worked well and what didn't?

■ Variations

This chart should be individualized, addressing the specific needs of the child/youth and caregiver.

■ Concerns

The behavioral expectations on the chart should be practical and attainable and should reflect the person's current behaviors and developmental age. All changes to the chart should be discussed with the child/youth in advance.

BEHAVIORAL CHART

Examples

Desired behaviors are listed on the left column of the chart with each day of the week listed across the top. Each box that has a star in it symbolizes that the child completed that task or practiced that behavior that day. Once a desired behavior becomes more consistent, the mastered behaviors are replaced with new behaviors.

■ For a Child *(example)*

My TO DO List	MON	TUE	WED	THUR	FRI	SAT	SUN
Clean my room, make my bed	★						
Get dressed	★	★	★	★			
Follow directions – obey first time	★			★			
Brush my teeth	★	★	★	★			
Help with meals: set table/clean up	★			★			
Other:							

GOAL: For every 15 stars the child earns, they can play at the park with a friend.

■ For a Youth/Adult *(example)*

My TO DO List	MON	TUE	WED	THUR	FRI	SAT	SUN
Clean my area, make my bed							
Follow directions – obey first time							
Help with meals: set table/clean up							
Attend school/work							
Complete household chores							
Other:							

GOAL: For every 15 stars the youth/adult earns, they can attend the weekly movie night.

28 EMOTIONALLY DIFFICULT TIMES

For Caregiver Training	Setting	Group	Trauma Recovery	CARING-Helping Caregivers

Purpose	To inform caregivers of times that may potentially be more emotionally difficult for those they serve.
Overview	Helpers are asked to identify potentially emotionally difficult times for those they serve in order to be more understanding and patient during those times, and to respond in ways that are helpful.

Approximate Time	20-30 minutes

Supplies Needed	Worksheet

■ Activity Explained

- ⮑ The facilitator asks helpers to think about when they personally experience emotionally difficult times.
- ⮑ The facilitator asks helpers to discuss why it is important for them to be aware of potentially emotionally difficult times for victims of trauma.
- ⮑ The helpers develop a list of when those they help may be more emotional.
- ⮑ When complete, place the worksheet in a place where it can easily be referred to and reviewed.

■ Reflection

Reflection should focus on how helpers should prepare or react when those they serve are going through an experience that is considered potentially more emotionally difficult. *How will you react when the participant is experiencing one of these times? How can you plan ahead to make things easier for the person if you know something will make them more emotional? How can this information help you to respond in ways that are more helpful?*

■ Variations

Activity may be done individually or in groups and may be verbal or written.

■ Concerns

Helpers may need assistance in listing all possible emotionally triggering times or in planning how to help those in their care during those identified emotionally difficult times.

■ Story

In Latin America the Day of the Dead (El Dia de los Muertos) is one that can trigger overwhelming emotions as people remember their dead relatives (ancestors). Both good *and* bad memories can trigger unwanted emotional responses.

EMOTIONALLY DIFFICULT TIMES

PREPARE Caregivers by discussing times that might be more emotionally difficult for the victims.

■ Reflect and Discuss

What are some of the times that are potentially more emotionally hard for those within your care?

_____

_____

_____

Examples of Emotionally Difficult Times:

- ➲ Counseling sessions (a time to focus on and talk about painful things)
- ➲ Bedtime (missing their family, sharing a bed, 'down time' to think)
- ➲ When new people arrive to the program
- ➲ On their birthday
- ➲ Special holidays and festivals: New Years, Religious
- ➲ When the person is going to have contact with family (phone call, letter, visit)

- ➲ When another person (friend) is going to have or has recently had contact with family (phone call, letter, visit)
- ➲ Anniversary of an event (happy or sad; example: a parent's death, of being sold/raped, sister's wedding)
- ➲ Legal proceedings (court date)
- ➲ During menstruation
- ➲ Others: _____

What can your organization do to better prepare both your staff and those you serve for times that are generally more emotional?

_____

_____

Why it is helpful to know WHEN it might be more emotionally difficult for victims of trauma?

_____

_____

Examples of why it is helpful to be mindful of emotionally difficult times:

- ➲ Helps the caregiver to be prepared for the possibility of misbehavior and/or various emotional outbursts.
- ➲ Helps to prepare the victims by talking about the difficult time as it approaches.
- ➲ Helps to prepare the caregivers and all staff who have contact with the victim.
- ➲ Can be the focus of counseling/group sessions.

✓ **Learning Trauma**
✓ **Sex Education**
✓ **Learning Relaxation Skills**

STEP 2

LEARNING

LEARNING

■ OVERVIEW

Providing information about abuse and trauma normalizes the experience and validate one's reactions, helping the victim realize that she is "not alone and not crazy." Providing information on other pertinent topics (such as sex, exploitation, assault, healthy relationships, and self-esteem) gives victims a needed, foundational understanding of healthy boundaries.

Information is provided in an educational, rather than personal way (not requiring personal disclosure, emotional vulnerability, and possible re-traumatization). The objective is to provide accurate information about abuse and trauma (and other pertinent topics) that will normalize and validate feelings and reactions and provide a helpful foundational understanding.

The relaxation techniques teach various ways to identify distress, to relax or calm oneself, and to deal with intrusive thoughts in ways that are personally useful, helpful, and self-sustaining.

We encourage the use of these skills when the person is overwhelmed by traumatic memories.

■ GOALS

- ➲ To educate victims about abuse and trauma (and other important related topics such as Sex Education, intimate partner violence, exploitation).
- ➲ To teach relaxation (anxiety reduction) skills and to identify helpful self-regulation tools.

■ PSYCHOEDUCATION

TEACH about trauma (and topics relevant to the person such as abuse, domestic violence, exploitation, human trafficking, rape, assault, coercion and control, lust and love, etc.)

Provide information on:

- ➲ Definitions and terms, types, and causes
- ➲ Who is victimized and who are the perpetrators?
- ➲ Statistics, prevalence, and known facts
- ➲ Common emotional, physical, mental, social, and behavioral responses (symptoms, reactions, possible behavioral outcomes, coping strategies., etc.)

PRESENT information on sex education (if needed):

- ➲ Body parts and functions
- ➲ Birth control, abortion
- ➲ Sexually transmitted diseases and AIDS
- ➲ Other helpful, related information

DISCUSS additional topics as needed:

- ➲ Self-esteem
- ➲ Healthy versus unhealthy relationships
- ➲ Love and lust
- ➲ Coercion and control
- ➲ Anger
- ➲ Other relevant topics

PRESENT Creatively:

- ➲ Be creative and age appropriate when presenting this information
- ➲ Utilize books on trauma/abuse/sex education, as well as information sheets, videos, activities, games, role plays, dramatic readings, art, sand play, toys, etc.
- ➲ Present information in a helpful, appropriate, and interesting manner

Note:

- ➲ The person may feel uncomfortable and/or be non-compliant when talking about *their* situation, life, and/or trauma. It is less potentially re-traumatizing and triggering to present the information in a more general or impersonal way. Instead of asking "Did *you* experience (know, do, feel) this?" ask "What might *a person* think or feel?" or "These are the common symptoms or experiences of *many who* have experienced trauma."

■ RELAXATION SKILLS

During my initial years of counseling (many years ago), I only taught relaxation skills to those individuals reporting high levels of stress. Those experiencing extreme emotional turmoil and tension were instructed in various helpful relaxation or calming activities. I've since realized the importance of teaching these skills to everyone. Whether the person is exhibiting high levels of stress and anxiety or not, these skills are beneficial. All of us need relaxation, body awareness, calming, and mindfulness skills. These skills are an integral component of all trauma therapy.

I encourage individuals to identify specific activities that personally help them to calm down, recuperate, and feel refreshed. We seek to discover those activities that are recuperative (bring us back to "normal"), those that are restorative (take us to a healthier place), and those that are refreshing (increase our energy).

Learning and practicing various relaxation techniques assists the individual in identifying those best suited for personal use when triggered or overwhelmed.

TEACH:

- ➲ Why relaxation skills are needed and helpful,
- ➲ About the body's reactions to trauma and stress, and how our bodies respond differently to stressful situations
- ➲ Encourage the use of these skills and techniques when feeling overwhelmed, anxious, scared, or angry.

PRACTICE various relaxation techniques:

- ➲ Focused breathing helps us calm down when feeling stressed or anxious and can help in re-focusing our negative thoughts.

- ➲ Progressive Muscle Relaxation incorporates a progressive tensing, then relaxing of the muscles while lying down or in comfortable position. The counselor provides an opportunity for the practice of this activity and may incorporate creative ways to present it, depending on the age of the person.

- ➲ Meditation (mindfulness) encourages the individual to focus on the present (being "mindful of the moment"). Some choose also to focus on a chosen phrase or word or to keep one's eyes on a specific focal point.

Other Relaxation Ideas: Encourage the person to identify (make a list) of those activities and exercises that he/she finds personally beneficial when wanting to relax or to calm themselves down.

IDENTIFY Personally Calming Activities by generating an extensive list of activities that help calm or refresh people. Then ask the person to identify those on the list that they find helpful.

- ➲ *Creative activities (dancing, art, drama and other forms of creative expression)*
- ➲ *Music (listening, playing, movement)*
- ➲ *Aesthetic focus, appreciation, and enhancement (visual, tactile, smells)*
- ➲ *Create and/or imagine a safe, peaceful person, place or thing*
- ➲ *Guided imagery (being verbally guided to a peaceful space; putting undesirable or overwhelming emotions in a locked container)*
- ➲ *Exercise and Activity: Physical activity and exercise are always recommended for those experiencing stress and depression because it activates positive chemicals in the brain. Such activities may include walking, running, swimming, bicycling, yoga, dance, sports, gardening...*

IMPLEMENT Thought-Stopping and Thought-Replacement strategies

Thought-Stopping techniques that help the person become aware of and then stop intrusive thoughts.

- ➲ Saying "No!" "Stop!" "Go away!" out loud
- ➲ Snapping a wristband (or rubber band) to snap when thinking "bad" thoughts as an attempt to draw attention to and stop one's focus of thought.

Thought-Replacement redirects one's unwanted, negative, and intrusive thoughts to a happy memory or to a safe person, place, or thing (real or imagined).

EQUIP with ideas for dealing with Nightmares and Flashbacks

Assist the client in identifying helpful ideas for dealing with nightmares, flashbacks, and sleep problems.

- ➲ Get up and do something (don't just lie there thinking about the nightmare)
- ➲ Turn the pillow over (like changing a channel on a television)
- ➲ Share it with someone
- ➲ Write it down
- ➲ Write/make YOUR own (positive or neutral) ending
- ➲ Play or do a distracting game or activity

Name		Program Location	

Tasks (some optional, depending on person/situation)	Date Completed	Notes
Psychoeducation		
Provide psychoeducation about trauma*		
Provide psychoeducation about intimate partner violence, abuse, sexual assault, exploitation, and human trafficking (if applicable)		
Provide developmentally appropriate sexual education (if needed)		
Provide psychoeducation on self-esteem, relationships, love and lust, coercion and control, anger, and other relevant topics		
Relaxation		
Provide information (psychoeducation) about the body's response to trauma and stress and how relaxation skills can help to lessen stress, anxiety, and fear reactions to abuse and trauma reminders		
Identify and discuss both negative and positive coping strategies (substance use, risk-taking...)		
Discuss client's personal triggers and coping mechanisms (*IF* applicable *AND* not uncomfortable or invasive)		
Teach Relaxation and Thought-Stopping strategies, as appropriate: ⮑ Deep Breathing ⮑ Progressive Muscle relaxation ⮑ Exercise and Physical Activity ⮑ Mindfulness, Guided Imagery, "Safe Place" ⮑ Thought stopping and replacement ideas ⮑ Personal anxiety-stress reduction activities (music, reading, bath, exercise, poetry...)		

Tasks (some optional, depending on person/situation)	Date Completed	Notes
Practice relaxation strategies		
Teach anger management/conflict resolution (if needed/ appropriate)		
Help client identify personally helpful calming activities		
Identify helpful ideas for dealing with nightmares, flashbacks and sleep problems.		
Other:		

* Terms and definitions, statistics, symptoms (emotional, behavioral, physiological, social, and mental), feelings, beliefs, reactions, coping mechanisms...

LEARNING: TRAUMA

29 TRAUMA LIST

Age	All	Setting	Group	Trauma Recovery	LEARNING-Trauma

Purpose	To educate the individual about types of traumatic experiences.
Overview	The facilitator and individual/group make a list of traumatic events and review the following worksheet to increase learning about the variety of experiences considered to be trauma.

Approximate Time	10-20 minutes		Supplies Needed	Worksheet

■ Activity Explained

○ The facilitator asks the participant(s) to share what they think trauma is and give as many examples as they can think of.

○ The facilitator shares an event or experience which might be traumatic to someone. The facilitator and participant(s) then discuss how an event may be traumatic for one person but not another.

○ The facilitator and participant(s) review the following worksheet listing various trauma events adding any from their list to it.

■ Reflection

Why may something be traumatizing to one person and not to another?

Did some of the items on the list surprise you? Why?

■ Variations

Activity may be used individually or in groups.

Activity may be verbal or written.

■ Concerns

Activity may be triggering or emotionally distressing for some.

TRAUMA EVENTS AND EXPERIENCES

This list is not comprehensive but includes events considered by most to be traumatic, or to cause trauma-related responses, reactions, and symptoms. Many other experiences can also be traumatic, some depend on the individual, such as a visit to the dentist, seeing a snake, being bitten by a dog, or being robbed. The list is endless and is affected by the individual and their culture, age, gender, race and more.

- Child Physical Abuse
- Child Neglect or Emotional Abuse
- Child Sexual Abuse
- Satanic Ritual Abuse
- Being Prostituted
- Domestic Violence
- Physical Assault
- Sexual Assault (Rape)
- Serious Accident
- Violent Death of A Close Loved One
- Witnessed Violent Death
- Accidental Death (Observed or Close Person)
- Exposed to War
- Exposed to Community Violence
- Exposed to School Violence
- Exposed to Gang Violence
- Exposed to acts of Terrorism

- Deprivation
- Unjust Imprisonment
- Serious Physical Injury or Illness
- Risky or Unplanned Medical Procedure
- Abortion
- Forced Separation and/or Relocation
- Drug Use
- Divorce of 'parents'
- Divorce (self)
- Adultery and/or Infidelity of Spouse
- Suicide
- Homicide/Murder
- Natural Disaster (earthquake, tornado...)
- Man-Made Disaster Affecting Many
- Torture (Self)
- Kidnapped (Self or Child)

Other Examples:

30 TYPES OF ABUSE

Age	All	Setting	Group	Trauma Recovery	LEARNING-Trauma

Purpose	To understand the different types of abuse and neglect.
Overview	The facilitator teaches about all the different types of abuse and neglect.

Approximate Time	20-30+ minutes

Supplies Needed	Worksheet and pen

■ Activity Explained

- ➲ The facilitator explains that people sometimes experience abuse but do not know it is abuse.
- ➲ The facilitator reads *and* explains the types of trauma listed, asking for any other examples.
- ➲ Individuals place checks by the statements that represent the thoughts or feelings they have about their abuse (optional).

■ Reflection

Were you surprised by any of the things on our lists? Has your perception changed about any of your own experiences?

■ Variations

Activity may be used individually or in groups. Activity may be verbal or written.

■ Concerns

Checking their own experiences should be optional as it can be triggering. Explanations must be adapted for children (or illustrated with dolls or stuff animals).

■ Story

While many people know right away that what happened to them was wrong, there are also many who have been surprised to know that what happened to them is considered abuse and illegal. Over the years, when I've listened to people share about their past and realized there was abuse, I've said, "What happened to you is considered abuse." The response is usually, "Really? Are you sure?" This list has helped many realize the truth about their past. This begins the possibility for them to heal and be free of the self-blame and shame that so frequently accompanies abuse and exploitation.

TYPES OF ABUSE

Below is a list of some of the many events that happen in sexual, physical, and emotional abuse and neglect. You can read the list to learn about types of abuse, or you could check those events that happened to you, marking as many as apply. If you know of other experiences that are not listed, add it to the list under *Other*.

■ Sexual Abuse:

- ❑ Fondling or touching
- ❑ Penile penetration (vagina), intercourse
- ❑ Sodomy (anal sex)
- ❑ Sexual violence (forced touching, sex act, etc.)
- ❑ Voyeurism (being watched during bathing, dressing, urination, etc.)
- ❑ Indecent exposure (other showing his or her private parts)
- ❑ Object or finger penetration (into vagina or anus)
- ❑ Oral sex (done on you or by you; cunnilingus or fellatio)
- ❑ Pornography (allowed, encouraged, or forced to watch)
- ❑ Pornography (photos or videos taken of you nude or scantily clad)
- ❑ Pornography (being filmed while doing sexual activities)
- ❑ Being given to others for sexual activities
- ❑ Being sold to others for sex (prostituted)
- ❑ Encouraged or forced to provide sexual activities in exchange for basic needs (food, clothing, shelter, money; survival sex)
- ❑ Masturbation (watching or doing on self or others)
- ❑ Sexual activities with animals (bestiality)
- ❑ Parading or dancing around (nude or few clothes)
- ❑ Ritual abuse involving sexual activities
- ❑ Forced to take drugs then participate in sex activities
- ❑ Forced to participate in multiple-member sex orgies
- ❑ Any sexual activity done by a family member

Other: _____

Other: _____

■ Physical Abuse:

- ❏ Kicked
- ❏ Beat, hit, shoved, pushed, slapped, thrown
- ❏ Cut, bitten, punctured, stabbed
- ❏ Trapped, smothered
- ❏ Burned

- ❏ Whipped, slashed
- ❏ Closeted (for several hours, several days, or long amounts of time)
- ❏ Exposure to elements (sun, wind, cold, or storms) without proper clothing or gear

■ Resulting in:

- ❏ Stitches
- ❏ Fractures
- ❏ Dislocations
- ❏ Bruises, black eye, welts
- ❏ Bleeding
- ❏ Lacerations and cuts

- ❏ Need for medication
- ❏ Need for bandaging
- ❏ Difficulty with daily physical activities: walking, sitting, running, standing
- ❏ Emergency room visit
- ❏ Doctor's visit

Other: _____

Other: _____

■ Neglect:

- ❏ Lack of food
- ❏ Lack of clothing
- ❏ Lack of shelter (safe place to stay and sleep)

- ❏ Lack of nurturance (love, affection, bonding)
- ❏ Lack of medical care
- ❏ Lack of proper supervision

Other: _____

Other: _____

■ Emotional Abuse:

- ❏ Degradation, belittling, ridicule, insults
- ❏ Continual, intentional withholding of emotional support (ignoring or silent treatment as punishment)
- ❏ Verbal threats
- ❏ Witnessing family violence

- ❏ Put in the middle of parental disputes and/or forced to take sides
- ❏ Used by an adult to vent inappropriate content and/or emotions
- ❏ Depended upon as an adult's emotional support

Other: _____

Other: _____

31 COMMON FEELINGS (1)

Age	All	Setting	Group	Trauma Recovery	LEARNING- Trauma

Purpose	To identify feelings that victims of trauma often feel.
Overview	The Facilitator will teach the participant(s) about the various common feelings experienced by trauma victims.

Approximate Time	10-15 minutes	**Supplies Needed**	Worksheet

■ Activity Explained

- ➲ The facilitator explains that experiencing a trauma can be emotionally overwhelming.
- ➲ The facilitator presents a list of feelings commonly experienced by victims of trauma, explaining any as needed.
- ➲ The facilitator presents a list of statements that reflect common thoughts and feelings experienced by victims of trauma.

■ Reflection

What did you learn about victims' common thoughts and feelings? Any surprises?

■ Variations

Activity may be verbal or written. Activity may be used individually or in groups. If used in groups, individuals can take turns reading the lists if desired. Adapt when using with children, incorporating simpler words and explanations.

■ Concerns

Activity may be triggering for some individuals. We do not ask direct personal questions but present the information in a general rather than personal way. We say *These are common feelings and statements made by people who have experienced trauma (abuse)*, rather than asking, *Did you experience any of these?* Do not invite personal reflection unless the person chooses to do so, wants to share, and/or it seems an appropriate time for brief sharing.

COMMON FEELINGS WORKSHEET

When a person experiences a trauma, it may be emotionally overwhelming. The victim is often not sure what to feel, how to feel, or how much to feel. They experience a variety of feelings simultaneously or say they feel emotional numbness.

Here is a list of feelings that are commonly experienced by trauma victims:

❑ Fearful	❑ Sad
❑ To blame	❑ Anxious, worried
❑ Shame	❑ Confused (ambivalent)
❑ Deceived	❑ Numb
❑ Guilty	❑ Betrayed
❑ Angry	❑ Helpless
❑ Special	❑ Embarrassed
❑ Loved	❑ Hopeless or depressed
❑ Excited	❑ Stuck
❑ Aroused	❑ Powerless
❑ Dirty	❑ Sneaky
❑ Stupid	❑ Other: _____

■ Overwhelming Feelings

Common victim thoughts and feeling are reflected in these statements:

❑ I felt dirty.	❑ I was scared, afraid of what could happen.
❑ I felt stupid.	❑ I was afraid I'd get in trouble.
❑ I didn't want to do anything that I used to enjoy.	❑ I felt lonely.
❑ I felt exhausted and lethargic.	❑ I felt like nobody cared about me.
❑ I worried a lot.	❑ I felt like I'd never be normal.
❑ I cried a lot.	❑ I felt like I was to blame for everything.
❑ I wanted to scream a lot.	❑ I didn't know who to trust or what to do.
❑ I found it hard to think or focus.	❑ I felt ashamed about what happened.
❑ I hated myself.	❑ I was frustrated, discouraged, depressed.
❑ I hated my caregiver (non-offending).	❑ I felt confused or like it wasn't real.
❑ I hated the person who hurt me.	❑ I yearned for the attention and interaction
❑ I felt I was a bad person.	

32 BELIEFS ABOUT ABUSE

Age	Youth and Adults	Setting	Group	Trauma Recovery	LEARNING-Trauma

Purpose	To teach participant(s) about common victims' beliefs about abuse.
Overview	Presenting and explaining a list of common victims' beliefs helps normalize the participant(s) responses to their own experiences.

Approximate Time	15-30 minutes

Supplies Needed	Worksheet and pen

■ Activity Explained

↪ The facilitator presents the checklist which explores abuse victims' beliefs, explaining as needed.

■ Reflection

What did you learn about victims' common beliefs? Anything unexpected, new, or surprising?

■ Variations

Activity may be verbal or written. Activity may be used individually or in groups.

■ Concerns

Activity may be triggering for some individuals. We do not ask direct personal questions but present the information in a general rather than personal way. We say, "*These are common beliefs made by people who have experienced trauma (abuse)*" rather than asking, "*Did you experience any of these?*" If the person has a strong emotional reaction to the prompts, do not continue with the activity. Do not invite personal reflection unless the person chooses to do so, wants to share, and/or it seems an appropriate time for brief sharing.

BELIEFS AND RESPONSES

Those who have experienced a trauma, such as abuse or exploitation, develop many unhealthy beliefs.

Here's some examples of what many people who have been abused believed:

- ❑ I believed that abuse was rare.
- ❑ I believed that, since abuse was rare, then there must be something wrong with me because it was happening to me.
- ❑ I didn't know that what was happening was abuse.
- ❑ I believed that I wasn't supposed to tell.
- ❑ I believed that I would be blamed.
- ❑ I believed that if I told, no one would do anything about it.
- ❑ Other:_____

■ Responses to Abuse

When abuse happens, people often tell themselves:

- ❑ I just thought it was strict discipline, not abuse.
- ❑ I didn't know it was wrong.
- ❑ I thought it was wrong but wasn't sure.
- ❑ I knew it was wrong.
- ❑ I didn't think it was that bad.
- ❑ I enjoyed the attention.
- ❑ I enjoyed the way my body felt.
- ❑ I hated myself so much that I felt I deserved the harsh punishment (abuse).
- ❑ I thought it was normal or what families do.
- ❑ I wanted it to stop but didn't know how.
- ❑ I didn't know what to do or who to talk to.
- ❑ I didn't want to tell anyone.
- ❑ I thought I was supposed to do it or put up with it.
- ❑ I thought it didn't matter.
- ❑ I didn't think I had any choice.
- ❑ Other _____
- ❑ Other _____

33 WHAT WE WERE TOLD

Age	All	Setting	Group	Trauma Recovery	LEARNING-Trauma

Purpose	To understand that offenders use verbal and non-verbal tactics in order to perpetuate abuse.
Overview	Individuals will learn about tactics offenders commonly use, as well as statements they often say, in order to control or force their victims. This can help validate and/or normalize the participant(s) own experiences or responses to their experience.

Approximate Time	15-25 minutes		Supplies Needed	Worksheet

Activity Explained

⊃ The facilitator explains that often those who abuse or exploit others use various statements to coerce, force, shame, blame, demand, and degrade their victims into doing what they want them to.

⊃ The facilitator presents the list of commonly used offender tactics, explaining as needed.

⊃ The facilitator explains that offenders may or may not say things aloud to coerce their victims.

⊃ The facilitator presents the list of spoken or implied statements, explaining as needed.

Reflection

What did you learn about offenders' tactics? Anything unexpected, new, or surprising?

Variations

Activity may be verbal or written. Activity may be used individually or in groups. Adapt when using with children, incorporating simpler words and explanations.

Concerns

The facilitator may need to explain what *implied* means.

Some statements or coercion tactics may be triggering to individuals. Do not invite personal reflection unless the person chooses to do so, wants to share, and or it seems an appropriate time for brief sharing.

WHAT WE WERE TOLD

Those who abuse or exploit others use various statements to coerce, force, shame, blame, demand, and degrade their victims into compliance. Sometimes these are said aloud, sometimes they are not. They want you to believe what they are saying or not saying (but clearly infer). They have a strategy and use tactics to get you to keep quiet.

■ Commonly Used Offender Tactics:

❑ Blame and shame the victim

❑ Imply mutual consent and/or enjoyment

❑ Imply victim blame and responsibility

❑ Make verbal, physical, and/or emotional threats

❑ Imply or say that nothing is wrong with the sexual acts

❑ Imply or say that no one cares

❑ Imply or say that no one will believe the victim

❑ Imply or say that the victim is worthless and deserves such treatment

❑ Make promises of future benefits—bribery or incentives (of gifts, events, care, etc.)

❑ Make promises of future behavior (not to harm sibling or others if victim complies)

❑ Use force, fraud, or coercion

❑ Threaten harm and/or the loss of basic needs

❑ Deceive and tell lies

Whether said aloud or not, the communication was generally loud and clear, and clearly understood. The following statements represent those that victims may have heard or received, whether spoken or *implied*.

■ Spoken or implied messages by abusers may include:

❑ It is because you're so pretty that I do these things.

❑ I will hurt you if you tell anyone.

❑ Let this be our little secret.

❑ I will hurt (or kill) your pet if you tell anyone.

❑ This is fun, isn't it?

❑ You must apologize for making me feel this way (i.e., angry, sexually stimulated).

❑ I will hurt your (mom, dad, family) if you tell or if you don't obey.

❑ I will abuse your sister or brother if you don't do what I say.

❑ I do this because I love you (to show my love).

❑ This is happening because you are a bad little girl (or boy).

❑ This is your punishment.

❑ Sex is a beautiful thing.

❑ I am supposed to teach you these things (i.e., sexual acts).

❑ You are worthless (a whore, slut, filthy, stupid, dirty).

❑ You deserve this (being used, abused, hit, beat, yelled at).

❑ I will teach you to enjoy this.

❑ The way you dressed made me do this.

❑ You're a dirty (naughty) girl or boy.

❑ I am your father (and you are supposed to obey me).

❑ There's nothing wrong with what we do.

❑ I'm glad you like it too.

❑ It's your fault.

❑ If you do this, I won't... (hurt you, hurt someone you love, etc.)

❑ If you do this, you will be... (popular, liked, accepted, desirable, sexy; or receive the toy, clothes, electronics that you want).

❑ Don't tell anyone, or it will be on social media (Facebook, Twitter, Instagram, etc.).

❑ If you do this, I'll help you... (go to college, get a job, become famous, etc.).

❑ You won't get any food (clothes, bed, love) unless you do what I say.

❑ You are promiscuous.

❑ God made sex so He wants us to do this.

❑ Your parents know about this and say it is okay.

❑ Other:

34 WHY VICTIMS DON'T TELL

Age	All	Setting	Group	Trauma Recovery	LEARNING-Trauma

Purpose	To identify and understand the reasons victims don't tell about or keep silent about their abuse.
Overview	The facilitator teaches the participant(s) about why victims do not report abuse. Although presented in a general, rather than personal way, this can provide healing validation for those learning about the topic.

Approximate Time	10-20 minutes

Supplies Needed	Worksheet and pen

■ Activity Explained

⊃ The facilitator shares or reads through why victims often do not share or are afraid to share their abuse and the main reasons people don't tell, explaining as needed.

■ Reflection

What did you learn about victim silence? Anything new or surprising? Does anything not make sense?

■ Variations

Activity may be verbal or written. Activity may be used individually or in groups. Adapt when using with children, incorporating simpler words and explanations.

■ Concerns

Some information may be triggering to individuals. Do not invite personal reflection unless the person chooses to do so, wants to share, and/or it seems an appropriate time for brief sharing.

WHY VICTIMS DON'T TELL

Did you know the following regarding cases of sexual abuse?

- ➲ Fewer than one in four sexual abuse survivors disclose immediately after the abuse occurs.
- ➲ A majority of victims keep it to themselves, never disclosing what happened. When or if they do tell, it is generally many years later (typically eight to fifteen years). Most who experience child sexual assault do not disclose until adulthood, and many never tell at all.

(Jonzon and Lindblad, 2004; Smith et al., 2000)

- ➲ Some victims tell and then recant (take back) the disclosure of abuse, due to the repercussions or consequences experienced.

■ Main Reasons

In a study on why people don't tell, reasons were grouped:

Threats made by the perpetrator

- ➲ Threats of violence, getting in trouble, having no friends or money, or parents' anger.

Fears

- ➲ Fear of the perpetrator, negative repercussions and emotions by caregivers, what would or could happen to the victim, possible consequences of telling, being judged, or being forced to leave home.

Lack of opportunity

- ➲ Not knowing who or how to tell or having the opportunity to tell.

Lack of understanding

- ➲ Not understanding what is or isn't abuse, what would happen if they told, and not wanting others to know.

Relationship with the perpetrator

- ➲ The victim expressing positive emotions toward perpetrator, relative, or friend, or wanting to maintain the relationship even amid the abuse.

(Schaeffer, Leventhal, and Asnes, 2011)

Victims Of The Trauma Of Abuse And Exploitation Usually Don't Tell Because They Believed:

- ❑ I was too young and didn't have the words or understanding to tell anyone.
- ❑ I didn't know it was wrong, so I didn't tell anyone.
- ❑ I was afraid for my safety.
- ❑ I was afraid for my family's safety.
- ❑ I was afraid of what my family would think.
- ❑ I was afraid of what others would think.
- ❑ I was afraid others would blame me.
- ❑ I was afraid of what might happen.
- ❑ I was afraid of what would happen to the abuser.
- ❑ I was afraid the abuser would stop loving me.
- ❑ I was afraid people would think I'm a bad person.
- ❑ I was afraid no one would believe me.
- ❑ I was afraid for my younger siblings.
- ❑ I was afraid I'd get in trouble.
- ❑ I was afraid my parent would get mad.
- ❑ Other: _____
- ❑ Other: _____

- ❑ I felt helpless and hopeless.
- ❑ I feared being abandoned and rejected.
- ❑ I was ashamed.
- ❑ I didn't know I could or should tell.
- ❑ I thought it was my fault.
- ❑ I enjoyed the attention and didn't want it to stop.
- ❑ I enjoyed the physical touch (stimulation) and didn't want the abuse to stop.
- ❑ I thought I'd get in trouble.
- ❑ I pretended that it didn't happen.
- ❑ I was afraid our family would fall apart if I told.
- ❑ I didn't know who to tell.
- ❑ I didn't know who I could trust.
- ❑ I didn't want to stop getting what I received (candy, toys, money, clothes, etc.).
- ❑ I was dependent on abuser (financially, emotionally).

We must listen, understand, and believe what is and is not being said. Disbelieving and blaming the victim can compound the damage done by the trauma. We must continue to discover ways of making the unspeakable safely speakable and thus promote healing.

35 POSSIBLE INDICATORS OF ABUSE

Age	All	Setting	Group	Trauma Recovery	LEARNING-Trauma

Purpose	To identify the various attitudes, behaviors, and events that may indicate abuse is happening.
Overview	An extensive list is provided with possible indicators of abuse to be reviewed with the participant(s). This can help in understanding abuse, its effect, and normalizing one's own experience.

Approximate Time	20-30 minutes

Supplies Needed	Worksheet

■ Activity Explained

⟳ The facilitator teaches the individual about possible indicators of sexual, emotional, and physical abuse, as well as neglect, explaining as needed.

■ Reflection

Do you think it is easy or hard to miss most of these indicators? Why? Which of these indicators seem obvious; which do not?

■ Variations

Activity may be used individually or in groups. If used in groups, have individuals take turns reading through the lists aloud (if they are able). Adapt when using with children, incorporating simpler words and explanations.

■ Concerns

Some individuals might find this activity overwhelming and question why significant others didn't understand that abuse was happening. Do not invite personal reflection unless the person chooses to do so, wants to share, and/or it seems an appropriate time for brief sharing.

POSSIBLE BEHAVIORAL AND PHYSICAL INDICATORS OF ABUSE

The following checklist includes *possible* indicators of abuse. Caution must be given when using this list. Children and adolescents experience many of these without being abused. It is meant to provide insight and assistance in the identification of child abuse when numerous indicators are observed together. Only a few items (*), in and of themselves, are stronger possible indicators of child abuse.

This can be used to educate others on possible indicators of abuse or be used for programs working with minors. A checklist could be used for each child or youth, with staff who observe their ongoing behaviour completing the checklist.

Name		Nickname	
Birthdate	/ /	Age	
Sex			

■ Sexual Abuse - *Behavioral Indicators*

- Reluctance to change clothes in front of others
- Withdrawn
- Sexualized behavior: toward adults or other children which is unusual sexual behavior and/or knowledge beyond that which is common for the particular developmental age
- Poor peer relationships
- Either avoids or seeks out adults
- Pseudo-mature
- Manipulative
- Self-conscious
- Problems with authority and rules

- Eating disorders
- Self-mutilating
- Obsessively clean
- Drug and/or alcohol abuse
- Delinquent behavior/running away
- Extreme compliance or defiance
- Fearful, anxious
- Suicidal gestures and/or attempts
- Promiscuous/prostitution
- Engages in fantasy or infantile behavior
- Unwilling to participate in sports activities
- School difficulties

■ Sexual Abuse - *Physical Indicators*

- Pain and/or itching in the genital area
- Bruises or bleeding in the genital area
- Venereal disease
- Private parts are swollen
- Difficulty walking or sitting

- Torn, bloody, and/or stained underclothing
- Experiences pain when urinating
- Pregnant
- Vaginal/penile discharge
- Bedwetting

Emotional Abuse - *Behavioral Indicators*

- Over-anxious to please
- Seeks out adult contact
- Views abuse as warranted
- Changes in normal behavior
- Excessive anxiety
- Depression
- Unwillingness to discuss problems
- Aggressive or bizarre behavior
- Withdrawn
- Emotional apathy
- Passivity
- Unprovoked yelling or screaming
- Inconsistent behavior at home and school
- Feels responsible for the abuser
- Running away
- Suicide attempts
- Low self-esteem
- Gradual impairment of health and/or personality
- Difficulty sustaining relationships
- Unrealistic goal setting
- Impatient
- Inability to communicate or express feelings, need or desires
- Sabotages success
- Lack of self-confidence
- Self-deprecation and negative self-images

Emotional Abuse - *Physical Indicators*

- Sleep disorders (nightmares, restlessness)
- Bedwetting
- Developmental lags (stunting of child's physical, emotional and mental growth)
- Hyperactivity
- Eating disorders

Physical Abuse - *Behavioral Indicators*

- Wary of adults
- Either extremely aggressive or withdrawn
- Often clingy and indiscriminate with attachments
- Uncomfortable when other children cry
- Generally controls own crying
- Exhibits a drastic behavior change when not with parents/caregiver
- Manipulative
- Poor self-concept
- Delinquent behavior and/or running away
- Drug and/or alcohol use
- Self-mutilation
- Frightened of parents or going home
- Overprotective of or responsible for parents
- Suicide attempts and/or gestures
- School behavior problems

Physical Abuse - *Physical Indicators*

- Unexplained* bruises or welts (often clustered or in a pattern)
- Unexplained* and/or unusual burns (cigarettes, donut-shaped, immersion lines, object patterned)
- Unexplained* bite marks
- Unexplained* fractures or dislocations
- Unexplained* abrasions or lacerations
- Bedwetting (*or explanation is inconsistent or improbable

■ Neglect - *Behavioral Indicators*

- ⊃ Often truant or tardy to school or arrives early and stays late
- ⊃ Begs or steals food
- ⊃ Suicidal gestures and/or attempts
- ⊃ Uses/abuses alcohol and/or drugs
- ⊃ Extremely clingy or detached

- ⊃ Engages in delinquent behavior, prostitution, stealing
- ⊃ Appears exhausted
- ⊃ States frequent or continual absence of parent/guardian

■ Neglect - *Physical Indicators*

- ⊃ Frequently dirty, unwashed, hungry or inappropriately dressed
- ⊃ Unsupervised and therefore engages in dangerous activities
- ⊃ Tired, listless
- ⊃ Has unattended physical problems
- ⊃ May appear overworked and/or exploited

36 WHERE ABUSE HAPPENS

Age	All	Setting	Group	Trauma Recovery	LEARNING-Trauma

Purpose	To understand where abuse takes place.
Overview	The facilitator teaches about the different places where abuse can happen in order to provide opportunities for validation and normalization of one's experience.

Approximate Time	10-15 minutes	**Supplies Needed**	Worksheet and pen

■ Activity Explained

- ⊃ The facilitator explains that abuse can happen anywhere and asks participants to list or guess some locations.
- ⊃ The facilitator presents the following list of locations where abuse most often happens, explaining as needed.

■ Reflection

What did you learn about where abuse happens? Anything surprising or confusing?

■ Variations

Activity may be used individually or in groups. If used in groups, individuals can take turns reading the list, if appropriate. Adapt when using with children, incorporating simpler words and explanations.

■ Concerns

Activity may be triggering to some individuals. Do not invite personal reflection unless the person chooses to do so, wants to share, and/or it seems an appropriate time for brief sharing.

WHERE ABUSE HAPPENS

Here's a list of some of the places where people have been abused: Add to the list if you want.

- ❏ In their home
- ❏ At a friend's house
- ❏ At a relative's house
- ❏ In a barn, storage shed
- ❏ At a gym, sports field
- ❏ At a neighbor's house
- ❏ At a carnival, party
- ❏ In the living room
- ❏ In the family room
- ❏ In the bedroom
- ❏ In the bathroom
- ❏ In the attic
- ❏ In the basement
- ❏ At a store, business, work
- ❏ In a car, bus, vehicle
- ❏ On a boat, train, plane
- ❏ At school

- ❏ At a park or in the woods
- ❏ In a pool or hot tub
- ❏ In a tent
- ❏ In the office, study
- ❏ In another country
- ❏ In the kitchen, pantry
- ❏ At a park, playground
- ❏ Mosque, church, synagogue (religious building)
- ❏ Underground (in a shelter, culvert, cave)
- ❏ In a public building (library, office, etc.)
- ❏ At doctor's or dentist's office
- ❏ In a dressing room, public bathroom
- ❏ In a tree house, kids' fort, playhouse
- ❏ Other: _____
- ❏ Other: _____
- ❏ Other: _____

Unfortunately, abuse can happen anywhere.

The vast majority of abuse—whether physical, sexual, emotional, or neglect—happens in one's own home; the place that is supposed to be safe, warm, and loving.

37 FLIGHT, FLIGHT, OR FREEZE

Age	All	Setting	Group	Trauma Recovery	LEARNING-Trauma

Purpose	To learn about our body's responses to a traumatic situation.
Overview	The facilitator teaches about fight, flight, or freeze and how we often feel ashamed when we 'freeze' because we don't understand that it is our body's automatic, involuntary reaction.

Approximate Time	10-20 minutes

Supplies Needed	Nothing or Worksheet

■ Activity Explained

⮑ The facilitator explains that in intense and traumatic situations, our bodies respond in one of three ways: fight, flight, or freeze.

⮑ The facilitator explains that often when facing a threat, our body freezes. This is called **involuntary compliance** and is a normal response to a traumatic situation.

⮑ The facilitator shares more about the freeze response and emphasizes how those who have reacted with the freeze response need to understand that freezing is a normal response and to release self-condemnation.

■ Reflection

Would knowing about the freeze response change someone's perception of their story? Once people realize that freezing is a good and natural response, do you think they will feel better if they too froze? Explain.

■ Variations

Activity may be used individually or in groups. Adapt when using with children, incorporating simpler words and explanations.

■ Concerns

Activity may be triggering to some individuals. Do not invite personal reflection unless the person chooses to do so, wants to share, and/or it seems an appropriate time for brief sharing.

HOW OUR BODIES REACT

Our bodies sometimes react without our permission. Something happens and the next thing we know, our bodies have taken control, and we don't have a say in the matter. This is what happens during a trauma.

■ Fight, Flee, Freeze

When we are threatened, our response is to fight, flee, or freeze. This is part of our automatic defense system. When we are unable to engage the fight or flight responses, we instinctively utilize the freezing response. It is not a conscious, voluntary choice, but an involuntary physiological response. That is, we don't choose it, it happens whether we want it or not.

Freezing indicates **involuntary compliance**. Even if you seemed to *allow* the abuse to happen, this reaction is often the result of your internal, generally subconscious, assessment that it would be dangerous to resist. This seeming compliance can be due to the desire to avoid punishment, to fit in, or to not cause problems. Going along with the abuse may also be due to thinking that what was happening was normal or okay.

■ Don't be so hard on yourself.

With freezing, however, the body assesses the danger and makes the decision for us. It is normal and common for abuse victims to freeze (not fight or flee) during the trauma (abuse).

In *Waking the Tiger—Healing Trauma (1997)*, author Levine summarizes it well:

> "When neither fight or flight will ensure safety, there is another line of defense: immobility (freezing) which is just as universal and basic to survival. This defense strategy is rarely given equal billing in texts... yet freezing... is an equally viable survival strategy in threatening situations. In many situations, it is the best choice... It is not a sign of inadequacy or weakness."

Whether we froze or didn't run or fight, too many victims carry extra shame and blame for not responding more forcefully to the abuser.

Over the years, many have shared of feeling deep shame and guilt for not fighting back or fleeing the abusive situation. Both of these options seem to bring less shame than freezing.

"If only I'd yelled or screamed or kicked or..." or "I should have run away and gotten out of there." Again, it feels like a retrospective, critical, improbable assessment. *We are so hard on ourselves for doing something over which we had no control.*

38 LOSSES

Age	All	Setting	Group	Trauma Recovery	LEARNING-Trauma

Purpose	To bring awareness to the losses encountered by many who have experienced abuse, trauma and/or interpersonal violence.
Overview	The facilitator teaches about loss and takes individuals through a list of potential losses. As with most of the LEARNING activities, the purpose is to enhance the persons awareness and bring a sense of personal validation and normalization; the "I'm not alone and I'm not crazy" perspective.

Approximate Time	10-20 minutes

Supplies Needed	Worksheet

■ Activity Explained

- ➲ The facilitator teaches the participant(s) about loss—what it means and what it looks like.
- ➲ The facilitator presents the following list of "losses."

■ Reflection

Are there any other losses we could add?

■ Variations

Activity may be used individually or in groups. If in groups, individuals can help read through the list of losses. Adapt for children, incorporating simpler words, phrases and explanations.

■ Concerns

Activity can be overwhelming and induce sadness. Do not invite personal reflection unless the person chooses to do so, wants to share, and/or it seems an appropriate time for brief sharing.

■ Story

When I presented this list of Losses to a group of women survivors of prostitution, they stopped me when I shared that one of the losses was education. They explained that not only did they lose opportunities to go to school, but also to graduate, to be a part of a sports team or club, to go to a school dance, to be a part of the cheering crowd during sporting events, to have close school friends, and more. I was thankful that they helped me better understand the many losses experienced by victims of abuse, exploitation, and other traumas.

LOSSES – TRAUMA VICTIMS

Survivors of exploitation experience a wide variety and number of losses. Losses are those opportunities or things they did not have but should have, but they can also be those experiences or things they had but shouldn't have had.

Some losses are tangible (they can be touched and felt, such as possessions) but most are intangible (i.e. hopes, dreams, feeling safe).

What are some of the losses experienced by those who have been abuse or traumatized? What events and relationships do victims not have the opportunity to experience? What characteristics, emotions, and beliefs do they not have the opportunity to develop? Make a list.

■ Losses can include:

- ❑ A sense of what "normal" is
- ❑ Belonging
- ❑ Boundaries
- ❑ Communication skills
- ❑ Confidence
- ❑ Contentment
- ❑ Control
- ❑ Dignity
- ❑ Dreams
- ❑ Education
- ❑ Enjoyment
- ❑ Faith
- ❑ Family
- ❑ Friends
- ❑ Future
- ❑ Healthy relationships
- ❑ Hope

- ❑ Identity
- ❑ Innocence
- ❑ Material possessions
- ❑ Meaning and purpose
- ❑ Morality
- ❑ Motivation
- ❑ Nurturing
- ❑ Respect
- ❑ Safety
- ❑ Security
- ❑ Sense of self
- ❑ Stability
- ❑ Support
- ❑ Treasures
- ❑ Trust
- ❑ Virginity

39 QUESTIONS WONDERED

Age	All	Setting	Group	Trauma Recovery	LEARNING-Trauma

Purpose	To identify with the internal questions often asked by trauma/abuse victims.
Overview	Numerous questions are listed which reflect common victim thoughts. The facilitator reviews and explains them.

Approximate Time	15 minutes

Supplies Needed	Worksheet and pen

■ Activity Explained

⊃ The facilitator teaches the individual that victims of trauma and abuse often ask themselves several questions.

⊃ The facilitator presents the list of questions, explaining as needed.

■ Reflection

Why do you think people ask these questions? What did you learn about questions victims ask?

■ Variations

Activity may be used individually or in groups. If in groups, individuals can take turns helping read through the list of questions. Adapt for use with children, incorporating simpler words and phrases.

■ Concerns

Activity can be overwhelming and induce sadness. Do not invite personal reflection unless the person chooses to do so, wants to share, and/or it seems an appropriate time for brief sharing.

QUESTIONS VICTIMS ASK

Along with the many negative beliefs (lies) victims think about themselves, they also ask many questions. Victims do not generally voice these questions aloud, but, none-the-less, they wonder about them continually.

- Why did this happen to me?
- Will it happen again?
- Why me?
- Why did I have to keep silent?
- What can I do to protect myself?
- What would have happened if it went on?
- Why do I feel so responsible for everything that's happened?

- Who knows about this?
- Who needs to know and who doesn't need to know?
- What will counseling/treatment be like?
- Why did the offender (abuser/trafficker) interfere with my life?
- Will the pain ever go away?
- Other: _____

◼ Faith—Spiritual Questions

- Where was God?
- Why didn't He answer my prayers?
- How can God allow this? Why didn't He stop what happened?
- Does God really care about me?
- Is God a loving Father?
- Am I forgiven? Do I have to forgive the abuser?

- Am I loved and accepted by God? Am I lovable?
- What part does God have, if any, in my healing process?
- Does prayer really work? Does God answer prayer?
- How come this hurts so much and for so long?
- Is God a loving, powerful, compassionate God?
- Is it okay to be angry? Is it okay to be mad at God?

To live is to suffer, to survive is to find some meaning in the suffering.

Friedrich Nietzsche

Although the world is full of suffering it is also full of the overcoming of it.

Helen Keller

40 TRAUMA'S VICIOUS CYCLE

Age	All	Setting	Group	Trauma Recovery	LEARNING-Trauma

Purpose	To bring awareness of re-victimization and how one becomes more susceptible to being re-traumatized.
Overview	The facilitator teaches about the cycle or trauma and how someone is more likely to be re-traumatized if they have already experienced trauma once.

Approximate Time	10-15 minutes

Supplies Needed	Worksheet

■ Activity Explained

- ⊃ The facilitator explains that often when someone has been traumatized, they are much more likely to be traumatized again.
- ⊃ The facilitator provides and overview of *"Trauma's Vicious Cycle."*
- ⊃ The facilitator explains more in-depth each step of the cycle.

■ Reflection

Why do you think someone is more susceptible to trauma if they have already experienced it?

■ Variations

Activity may be used individually or in groups. Adapt for use with children, incorporating simpler words and explanations.

■ Concerns

Activity may be triggering to some individuals. Do not invite personal reflection unless the person chooses to do so, wants to share, and/or it seems an appropriate time for brief sharing.

TRAUMA'S VICIOUS CYCLE

Unfortunately, it is all too common for victims of abuse and exploitation to be re-victimized. Research confirms it: once you've experienced a trauma, you are much more likely to experience more in the future. Why? Let's look at **Trauma's Vicious Cycle**.

A vicious circle is a term used when a situation repeats itself over and over again. It is as if you're on a merry-go-round where you can't get off.

When a person experiences an interpersonal trauma, re-victimization is even more likely to be repeated as it generally puts into motion a series of events:

After an interpersonal trauma, victims usually develop negative self-beliefs and feelings. In order to cope with the overwhelming negative thoughts and feelings, the individual implements various coping strategies to feel better and to deaden the pain of self-blame and/or shame. These coping mechanisms are generally unhealthy and harmful. The person then becomes more vulnerable to being re-victimized.

Trauma experience: abuse, violence, rape, assault, death, accident...

Negative thoughts and feelings: It's my fault. I should have tried harder. I'm so stupid. I can't do anything right or make good decisions. I'm worthless. Self-focused anger, shame, guilt, fear, loneliness, low self-esteem set in...

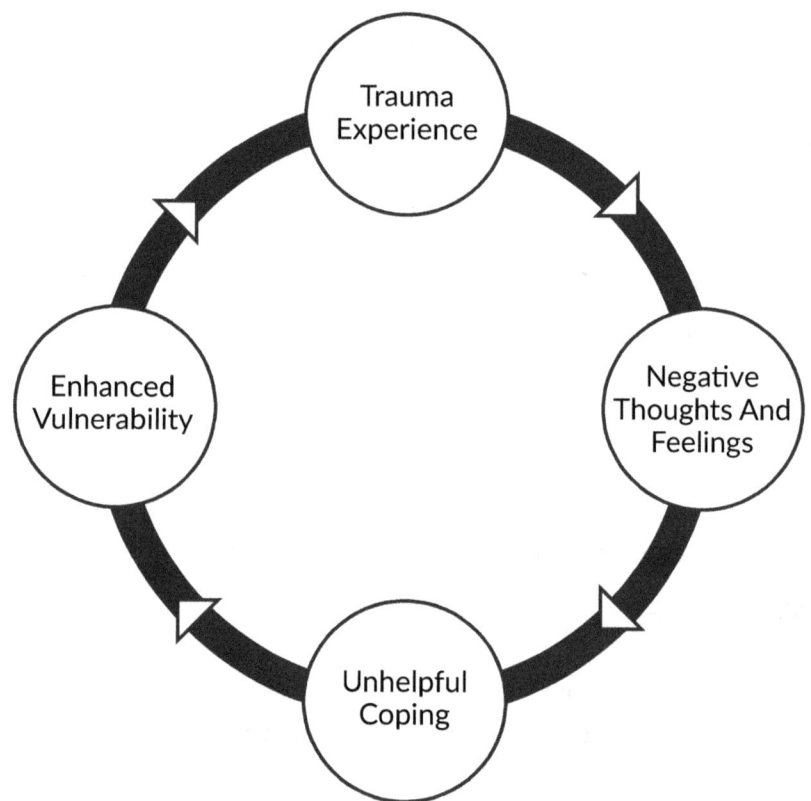

Unhelpful coping: substance abuse, self-harm, lying, stealing, poor decision-making, workaholism...

Enhanced vulnerability: due to the negative thoughts and feelings and the ineffective and unhelpful coping skills, the person is now more likely to be re-victimized...

Trauma experiences: person is re-victimized, experiencing yet another traumatic situation. The vicious cycle continues.

41 HEALTHY RELATIONSHIPS

Age	All	Setting	Group	Trauma Recovery	LEARNING-Trauma

Purpose	To learn characteristics of both healthy and unhealthy relationships.
Overview	The facilitator and participant(s) generate a list of characteristics of both healthy and unhealthy (good and bad) relationships.

Approximate Time	10-20 minutes

Supplies Needed	Worksheet and pen

■ Activity Explained

➲ The facilitator and participant(s) generate a list of the characteristics of both good and bad relationships.

➲ Review and discuss the list.

■ Reflection

How can someone tell if a relationship is unhealthy at the beginning? What things should someone be aware of or cautious about? What should someone do when they realize a good relationship has turned bad? Why do some people compromise and put up with unhealthy relationships?

■ Variations

Activity may be verbal or written. Activity may be used individually or in groups. Adapt when using with children, incorporating simpler words and explanations such as *What are good people like? Bad People?*

■ Concerns

Participants may need assistance in the beginning.

■ Story

One group of women survivors of sexual exploitation in North America shared how helpful it was to make the two lists. They said that it quickly brought into focus how unhealthy and bad their relationships were with their boyfriends (pimps) and how they didn't want that in the future.

COMPONENTS OF HEALTHY AND UNHEALTHY RELATIONSHIPS *(BC JOHNSON, 2009)*

Make a list of characteristics (attitudes and behaviors) of both healthy and unhealthy relationships. The examples provided should be presented after your own list has been written.

Healthy Relationships	Unhealthy Relationships
Selfless	Selfish
Helpful	Demanding
Kind	Often mean
Positive. Optimistic attitude	Negative, pessimistic attitude
Mutual decision-making	Makes most/all decisions
Considers other's thoughts and feelings	Motivated primarily by self-concerns
Able to empathize	Unable or unwilling to understand others' feelings
Loving	Verbalizes love statements but actions don't seem loving or contradict statements of affection
Unconditional love	Conditional love
Clear communication	Confusing, often misunderstood communication
Encouragement	Critical and judgmental attitude
Shared positive values	Militaristic or unclear values
Play and pray together	Primarily individualistic pursuits
Limits and boundaries understood	Enmeshed or distant boundaries
Consistency in actions and attitudes	Inconsistency and unpredictability
Ability to identify and express emotions	Emotions devalued or overvalued
Sense of equality	Sense of inequality
Shared or clear roles	Unclear roles or strict adherence to predefined roles

42 CONSENT OR COMPLY?

Age	Youth and Adults	Setting	Group	Trauma Recovery	LEARNING-Trauma

Purpose	To identify the difference between consent and compliance.
Overview	The facilitator will teach about the difference between consent and compliance.

Approximate Time	10-15 minutes

Supplies Needed	Worksheet

■ Activity Explained

- ➲ The facilitator teaches about the difference between compliance and consent (using the following worksheet). If available, watch the short video about consent and tea (https://www.youtube.com/watch?v=pZwvrxVavnQ).
- ➲ The individual or each small group creates a definition of "consent" and for "comply."
- ➲ The facilitator or participants read the "Consent or Comply" statements.

■ Reflection

Did any of the statements resonate with you? Do you have a better understanding of what it means to comply versus what it means to consent?

■ Variations

Activity may be used individually or in groups. While this could be used with children, it would require significant adaptations. Children also need to understand the difference between consenting and complying, so creativity in presenting is needed.

■ Concerns

Activity may be triggering to individuals.

■ Story

After watching the Tea and Consent video, some survivors of prostitution commented that they were often forced to drink tea, (have sex) when they didn't want to.

COMPLY OR CONSENT?

Abusers want you to think that you deserved, agreed with, or consented to the abuse. Some believe this themselves. They want to convince you that you are more responsible or to blame for what happened than you actually are. The message is that you consented and were compliant—which is absolutely absurd. Even if you enjoyed the attention or the bodily sensations of sexual abuse, or wanted the anger release or punishment to deaden the pain of physical abuse, or welcomed the self-affirming negative rants of verbal abuse—you did not initially agree to abuse.

If you were physically and verbally abused, you probably thought it was due to some disobedience or fault of your own. You might not have even known that the behavior was abusive. Therefore, you bit the bullet, got tougher, tried harder, avoided more, and kept quiet.

Did you comply? **Yes.**   Did you consent? **No.**

When we disobey as children, we may need discipline and guidance, but we never deserve physical abuse. No disobedience gives a parent or someone in authority permission to abuse us. Punishment is punitive and should be replaced by positive parenting and corrective discipline. Child rearing should never be abusive.

You may have thought that you agreed to or consented to the abuse because you didn't say anything or tell anyone, but you didn't.

As already stated, many who are sexually abused are confused and unaware that what happened was wrong and illegal. When a thirteen-year-old girl is forced to do sexual things with a much-older boy, that is abuse. When a teacher has sex with a minor under his or her authority, even if the victim is a teenager, that is abuse. When there is an age difference and/or a position of authority over the minor, it is considered sexual abuse. Few, if any, exceptions apply. Even if you allowed the abuse, it is still abuse, whether you did comply or thought you consented.

One victim shared that her older sister's boyfriend would force her to do sexual things with him. She stated, "Even though I didn't want it or like it, I didn't know it was against the law. I thought I had consented because I didn't tell anyone."

Was she coerced? **Yes.**   Did she comply? **Yes.**   Did she consent? **No.**

■ Comply or Consent

- ❑ I complied with the abuse because I thought I didn't have a choice.
- ❑ I complied with the abuse because I didn't know it was wrong or abuse.
- ❑ I complied with the abuse and felt I deserved it.
- ❑ I complied with what was happening to me but didn't like it and thought I didn't deserve it.
- ❑ I was coerced or forced to do things I didn't want to do. I didn't think I had a choice.
- ❑ I thought that I consented because I said nothing and told no one.
- ❑ I now know that I didn't really consent.

LEARNING:
SEX EDUCATION

43 SEX EDUCATION

Age	All	Setting	Group	Trauma Recovery	LEARNING-Sex Education

Purpose	To educate individuals on proper terms for body parts and reflect on the use of slang terms.
Overview	The facilitator discusses any terms the participant(s) know for body parts, the meanings associated with those slang words, and then teaches the proper body part names.

Approximate Time	20-30 minutes

Supplies Needed	Worksheet and pen

◼ Activity Explained

- ⮑ The facilitator starts the discussion by asking the participant(s) what terms they know for various body parts, particularly genitalia (vagina and penis). The facilitator writes down the list of terms.

- ⮑ After creating a list, the facilitator discusses the meaning behind these slang/inappropriate terms (i.e. as insults, adjectives) by asking, "*When people use this word, what are they using it for?*" Then discuss how the meaning behind these slang terms can influence how someone might feel about their own body. "*How do you feel when you hear this word?*"

- ⮑ The facilitator discusses the proper terms for genitalia, using a diagram if needed. The facilitator reads the definitions of different body parts (see example on next page), using culturally appropriate and relevant language.

◼ Reflection

Did you find the information helpful today? Was any of this information new to you? Do you think any of this information will change the way you view your own body?

◼ Variations

Activity may be used individually or in groups. When teaching children, simplify the information to make it understandable and developmentally appropriate. The terminology used can be replaced with what is culturally relevant and appropriate. Definitions can be added to or removed if needed. Other related topics that could be covered during this activity are puberty, pregnancy, sexually transmitted infections, or HIV/AIDS.

◼ Concerns

Applicable cultural language is key. The lesson must be taught in a culturally sensitive manner. Activity should only be used if developmentally appropriate or to correct false information about the individual's body.

SEX EDUCATION

■ Names of Body Parts

Teach the names for various body parts so that the person has the vocabulary or words needed if/when they want to tell someone something is happening. This should be taught in a way that makes saying the words not embarrassing nor shaming. *"Your body is very special. It belongs to you. You have all kinds of different parts of your body—some parts of your body don't need clothes all the time, but other parts need clothes most of the time, even when you go swimming. These are your private parts. What do you call your private parts?"*

Use a diagram and/or drawing to facilitate the learning of body parts related to sex education.

■ Female Genitalia (private parts)

Ovaries: contain eggs, the female reproductive organ, and produce the hormones estrogen and progesterone.

Fallopian tubes: how eggs travel from the ovaries to the uterus.

Uterus: where a fertilized egg develops to form a baby.

Cervix: the narrow pathway from the uterus to the vagina, dilates during birth.

Vagina: the opening and muscular tube that leads to the uterus through the cervix.

Urethra: the opening that urine leaves the body through.

Anus: the opening where waste leaves the body.

■ Male Genitalia (private parts)

Testes/Testicles: produce sperm, the male reproductive organ.

Penis: the passageway that sperm and urine travel through.

Scrotum: the skin that contains the testicles.

Foreskin: skin that covers the urethral opening and might be removed surgically.

Urethral opening: the opening through which semen and urine leave the body.

Anus: the opening where waste leaves the body.

Prostate: a gland that secretes semen to protect the sperm.

44 SEXUAL ACTIVITIES

Age	All	Setting	Group	Trauma Recovery	LEARNING-Sex Education

Purpose	To educate individuals about different sexual activities and consent.
Overview	The facilitator and the participant(s) discuss different sexual activities and define consent.

Approximate Time	20-30 minutes		**Supplies Needed**	List of activities, dolls if needed.

■ Activity Explained

⮕ The facilitator states, *"This can be a sensitive or uncomfortable topic to discuss, but we are just learning about different activities and discussing what you already know without talking about personal experiences. If it becomes too uncomfortable, we can come back to it at another time."*

⮕ The individual describes what they know about sex. If needed, the facilitator can prompt them by asking, *"What are the different ways you can have sex? What is sex?"*

⮕ If the individual does not know anything, the facilitator can tell them a brief overview of the sexual activities listed below. If helpful, the facilitator can use dolls to briefly show positioning. The facilitator discusses that when participating in these activities it is important that both people have consented. The facilitator asks the individual if they know what consent is. If they do not know, the facilitator should say, *"Consent is when permission is given and the activity is discussed together beforehand. Consent is about both people having equal power in the sexual activity and both having the power to ask to stop if desired. Both people should feel respected and safe and trust each other. If consent is not given, but the act is done or forced, this is considered abuse and is wrong; and in many places, it is a crime."*

⮕ The facilitator closes the activity by reassuring the individual/group that this activity is just to educate and not about sharing personal experiences. If the activity triggers any individuals, those experiences can be discussed during a one-on-one session with a trusted facilitator.

■ Reflection

Did you learn any new information today? Do you feel comfortable talking about sexual activities? Do you understand and can you explain the concept of consent?

■ Variations

Activity may be used individually or in groups. A demonstration with dolls, showing various positions and sexual acts, can be done with children if developmentally appropriate.

■ Concerns

Do not use this activity if it would be too traumatic for those struggling with past sexual abuse. Cultural sensitivity and appropriate language use for the cultural context are necessary. Make changes to the worksheet to ensure activity is developmentally and culturally appropriate.

SEXUAL ACTIVITIES

■ **Anal Sex**

When a man inserts his penis into another person's anus. This may also be performed by a female wearing a man-made penis belt (sex apparatus).

■ **Bestiality**

When a sexual act is performed between a human and an animal. This is illegal in many places in the world.

■ **Masturbation**

When a male's penis or female's vagina is stimulated by using one's own hand or someone else's hand.

■ **Oral Sex**

The stimulation of a male or female's genitals using another's mouth.

Types of oral sex include: Cunnilingus (Oral Vaginal Contact) which is oral stimulation of a woman's vagina and/or vulva, especially her clitoris, by her partner's lips and tongue. Fellatio (Oral Penile Contact) which is stimulation of a man's penis by his partner's mouth-usually by licking or sucking.

■ **Orgy**

A sexual encounter involving many people.

■ **Sexual Abuse**

When someone coerces, forces, or manipulates a minor and sexually uses the person for their own pleasure. The person is usually older (an adult) and in a position of authority over the minor but can also be another minor.

■ **Sexual Intercourse**

Is performed between a male and female when the male places his penis inside of the female's vagina until he releases semen inside of her, which can result in pregnancy if not using contraception.

■ **Other Sexual Activities** *(list and explain)*

45 - LOVE AND AFFECTION VS. LUST AND ABUSE

Age	Youth and Adults	Setting	Group	Trauma Recovery	LEARNING-Sex Education

Purpose	To learn the difference between love and lust; affection and abuse.
Overview	Information will be presented on what love/affection looks like and what lust/abuse looks like in relationships.

Approximate Time	10-20 minutes

Supplies Needed	Worksheet and pen

◼ Activity Explained

- ➲ The participant(s) creates a list of people that they love and a list of people that love them. The facilitator asks, *"How do you know you love someone? How do you know someone loves you?"*

- ➲ The facilitator explains that love is an attachment to a person that is unconditional and wants what is best for that person. Love is unconditional, which means it is not based on certain behaviors or things you do. If some says, "I will love you if you do this for me," that is not love; it is based on the condition that you do something for them. True love for a friend, family member, or partner is unconditional and always wants the best for them.

- ➲ The facilitator discusses what physical touch is between loving people, and what types of physical touch are appropriate and healthy. Touch in abusive relationships is generally manipulative and focuses on the abuser's needs as most important.

- ➲ The facilitator explains that lust is superficial and based on appearance, characteristics, or behaviors. Lust offers a false or temporary sense of attraction. It can lead to abuse and to exploitation—when someone is treated unfairly and tricked into certain behaviors.

◼ Reflection

Who do you unconditionally love from your list? Have you seen examples of unconditional love in your life? Who unconditionally loves you from your list? Have you ever experienced lust? Attraction? Abuse? Which relationships have been the healthiest in your life?

◼ Variations

Activity may be verbal or written. Activity may be used individually or in groups.

◼ Concerns

Sensitivity needs to be taken with individuals who may feel that they are unloved.

LEARNING: RELAXATION SKILLS

LEARNING

46 CALM OR TENSE

Age	All	Setting	Group	Trauma Recovery	LEARNING- Relaxation

Purpose	To learn to identify emotions from calm to tense.
Overview	The individual completes a worksheet by looking at pictures and rating each on a scale of 1 to 5, 1 representing very calm and 5 representing very tense.

Approximate Time	5-10 minutes	Supplies Needed	Worksheet and pen

■ Activity Explained

- ⮕ The facilitator explains and asks the participant(s) to look at various images and rate how calm or tense the person is in each image.
- ⮕ Discuss the difference between tense and calm, what they look like, how one might feel and think, and how one might behave (what they might do) when feeling that emotion.

■ Reflection

Were any of the images difficult to rate? How did you decide to rate each image? What does tense look and feel like? Calm?

■ Variations

Activity may be used individually or in groups.

The facilitator may make facial expressions for the individual to rate instead of using the worksheet.

■ Concerns

Developmentally appropriate language will be needed.

If the facilitator makes facial expressions, remind the person that the emotions presented are not aimed towards the individual in any way.

CALM OR TENSE

Look at each image and then circle the number that represents how calm or tense the person seems to you, where 1 = calm, 2 = relaxed, 3 = in the middle, 4 = uptight, 5 = very tense.

Calm   Tense

1   2   3   4   5

Calm   Tense

1   2   3   4   5

Calm   Tense

1   2   3   4   5

Calm   Tense

1   2   3   4   5

47 FOCUSED BREATHING

Age	All	Setting	Group	Trauma Recovery	LEARNING- Relaxation

Purpose	To encourage awareness of breathing and to increase stress tolerance.
Overview	A breathing exercise is introduced to bring awareness to the benefits of focused and intentional breathing.

Approximate Time	5-15 minutes	**Supplies Needed**	Soft instrumental music may be used to enhance the relaxation experience.

■ Activity Explained

➲ The facilitator explains that although breathing is done unconsciously (without awareness), when we bring attention to our breathing, it provides our bodies with more oxygen and helps us relax by regulating our emotions.

➲ The individual follows the facilitator's demonstration of sitting up tall in a chair with their feet on the ground or, if possible, lying down. One hand should be placed on the stomach and one hand on the chest.

➲ The facilitator and the participant(s) breathe in together and call awareness to how their stomach expands with each inhale and how the stomach shrinks with each exhale. Practice until the individual notices how their stomach moves with each breath, then focus on slowing down the breath and taking in deeper breaths by breathing in and out for longer time periods. The facilitator can count as the participants breathe in and out slowly increasing the number counted to, so the breaths are deeper and longer.

■ Reflection

How did you feel after taking a few deep breaths? How might you use this when you feel anxious? If variations were introduced, "Which variation did you find most useful?"

■ Variations

If lying down, a light object (ex: a small book) may be placed on the stomach so the individual is able to see their stomach rise and fall with each breath.

If helpful, the illustration of breathing in as if smelling a flower or your favorite food may be used. Instruct the participants to exhale as if they are blowing out a birthday candle or cooling off a hot dish. These examples can be changed to best fit the age and cultural relevance of the individual.

■ Concerns

Use developmentally appropriate language based on the person's age.

■ Story

When I was interacting with a very anxious young adult, I encouraged her to practice focused breaths, reminding her the importance of taking deep breaths in and out. We breathed in together, while I counted to 10, and then we breathed out slowly together to help regulate her breath, helping to calm her anxiety. It is useful for all ages and is used by paramedics to calm shock victims and by pregnant women during the birthing process. This practice can be especially useful for helping younger children regulate their emotions.

48 GROUNDING YOUR SENSES

Age	All	Setting	Group	Trauma Recovery	LEARNING-Relaxation

Purpose	To create mindfulness to help "ground" the individual in the present moment.
Overview	The person focuses on one of their senses in order to become more aware (mindful) of their surroundings and their own body.

Approximate Time	5-10 minutes		Supplies Needed	Soft instrumental background music (if available)

■ Activity Explained

- ➲ The individual sits or lays in a comfortable position and closes their eyes to increase their other senses.
- ➲ The facilitator instructs the individual to focus on one of their senses at a time (sound, touch, or smell work best) and asks them to pay attention to what they are hearing, smelling, or feeling around them and in their body. The individual continues this for 1 to 5 minutes depending on their comfort level.
- ➲ The facilitator and individual discuss what they noticed and how they felt.

■ Reflection

What did you smell, hear, or feel? What smell, sound, or feeling was the strongest/weakest? What did you notice about your body? Which parts of your body feel relaxed? Which parts of your body feel tense? Did you notice your breath at all? How did you feel after opening your eyes again?

■ Variations

If helpful, the facilitator can demonstrate first by describing what he/she is smelling, hearing, or feeling as their eyes are closed. When focusing on touch, the facilitator can offer different textiles or objects to hold. When focusing on smell, the activity may be conducted outside, with an open window, or with incense or other pleasant smells introduced.

■ Concerns

Some smells, sounds, and things could be triggering of traumatic experiences, so the facilitator should start by asking the individual if there are certain things to avoid before starting this activity.

If the facilitator makes facial expressions, remind the person that the emotions presented are not aimed towards the individual in any way.

49 PROGRESSIVE MUSCLE RELAXATION

Age	All	Setting	Group	Trauma Recovery	LEARNING-Relaxation

Purpose	To decrease muscle tension by alternately tensing and relaxing various muscle groups.
Overview	The individual practices tensing certain muscle groups for a period of time before relaxing them in order to help build awareness and to teach the ability to release tension.

Approximate Time	5-10 minutes

Supplies Needed	Mats (if available)

Activity Explained

- The facilitator explains that often when we experience anxiety, our bodies become tight and our muscles become tense, causing pain and soreness. *We are going to practice a technique that will help you and your muscles relax.*
- The individual finds a comfortable position (lying down or sitting in a chair)
- The facilitator explains the technique and demonstrates if needed. All are instructed to tense different muscle groups one at a time (hand, forearm, thigh, calf, leg, foot, neck, stomach, back, face).
- The facilitator tells which muscles to tense, hold (to the count of 10), then relax.

Reflection

How do you feel after tensing and relaxing your muscles? Are there any muscles that still feel tight? If they still feel tight, repeat the activity for that muscle group.

Variations

Activity may be used individually or in groups.

If the person needs help tensing and relaxing muscles, the example of stiff uncooked rice versus soft cooked rice, being hard like a rock and then free like water or being as stiff as a plastic doll and then as relaxed and soft as a stuffed animal, may be used. Language and examples need to be culturally relevant and age appropriate for the specific individual.

Concerns

Developmentally appropriate language must be used based on the age of the individual.

50 A PEACEFUL PLACE

Age	All	Setting	Group	Trauma Recovery	LEARNING-Relaxation

Purpose	To encourage the person to focus on a positive, safe, and calming place when anxious.
Overview	The individual is led on a journey to visualize a calm, peaceful place while the facilitator describes the sights, sounds, smells, tastes, and feelings of that place, based on the person's preferences.

Approximate Time	10-15 minutes		**Supplies Needed**	Soft instrumental background music (if available)

■ Activity Explained

⮂ The facilitator asks the person (or group) if they prefer being by water, in the mountains, or in an open, grassy area. The individual should elaborate what that location would look like to them (Example: If by the water, is it a lake or the ocean? In a grassy area, is it a park or a desert oasis?)

⮂ The individual sits or lays in a comfortable position and closes their eyes while the facilitator uses a calming voice to describe the chosen location.

⮂ The facilitator starts describing the location with as much detail as possible based on what one might see, smell, hear, taste, and feel during perfect conditions at that location. (See example dialogue on the next page). The facilitator should speak in a slow and soft voice, letting words flow with the tempo of the story.

⮂ After describing the location fully, the individual opens their eyes and shares what the experience was like for them, what they enjoyed, and what they would have changed.

⮂ Repeat the activity again later, making the desired changes to the description of the location.

■ Reflection

How was that exercise for you? What did you like? Dislike? What would you change? Where else would be a peaceful place for you?

■ Variations

Activity may be used individually or in groups. Locations may include by a lake, a river, or the ocean, a dessert oasis, mountain meadow or another preferred, positive, peaceful place.

If the person needs help tensing and relaxing muscles, the example of stiff uncooked rice versus soft cooked rice, being hard like a rock and then free like water or being as stiff as a plastic doll and then as relaxed and soft as a stuffed animal, may be used. Language and examples need to be culturally relevant and age appropriate for the specific individual.

■ Concerns

Avoid locations that may be triggering to the individual.

A PEACEFUL PLACE

■ Example Dialogue:

(Speak slowly and softly and use soothing background music if available.)

■ Beach

Imagine you are at a beach. The sun is warm, but not too hot. There are shady areas under trees where you can lie in the cool breeze. The waves are rolling up to the beach (facilitator slowly inhales) and back down to the ocean (facilitator slowly exhales). Back and forth, they gently come in (breathe in) and go out (breathe out).

There are a few people further down the beach, but this area is just for you. The sand feels warm beneath you as you wiggle your toes and feel the sand move beneath you. A few birds fly overhead while other birds, bobbing up and down beyond the waves. They sing melodiously, in time with the rhythm of the waves. You lick your lips and taste the cool, salty air as you take a deep breath in (facilitator slowly inhales) and slowly breath out (facilitator slowly exhales). You are relaxed and start to feel sleepy.

Your worries fade away and you are enjoying just resting in this peaceful place.

■ Desert Oasis

Imagine you are in a dry, hot desert. Your throat feels tight and sore as you long for a drop of cool water. Your feet and whole-body ache from walking and from the scorching heat. Then as you reach the top of a sand dune your eyes see something green in the distance. You race down the hill moving until you reach the oasis. Your feet step on the cool green grass and the air feels dramatically cooler as you are embraced by the shade from the trees. A spring nearby is bursting with fresh drinking water. As you drink, your throat feels the sweet relief and healing touch of the liquid refreshment.

You dive into a fresh pool and feel awakened and refreshed, like your body is brand new. You take a deep breath (facilitator slowly inhales) before diving back in. You hold your breath under water before breathing out as you swim towards the bottom (facilitator slowly exhales). You come back to the surface and feel the sun on your face as you take another deep breath (facilitator slowly inhales). You climb out of the pool and lay on the grass. You feel the tingling sensation of the water evaporating on your skin. You feel cool now. You feel invigorated, refreshed, and relaxed.

Your cares and worries fade away, and you feel safe and at peace.

51 - MY SAFE PLACE

Age	All	Setting	Individual	Trauma Recovery	LEARNING-Relaxation

Purpose	To help the individual focus on personal memories about a place that is positive and safe.
Overview	The individual is asked to describe a positive place and/or person from their past. They are encouraged to use as much detail as possible and to use this memory when anxious. The facilitator helps them by asking many questions about the sights, sounds, smells, tastes, and feelings of that place, based on the person's description.

Approximate Time	10-20 minutes	**Supplies Needed**	Soft, instrumental background music (if available)

■ Activity Explained

- ⮑ The facilitator asks the individual to identify a place where they felt safe, secure, and happy. The individual should be encouraged to think about it and then describe it to the facilitator in as much detail as possible (for example the sights, smells, tastes, sounds, events, and people).

- ⮑ The facilitator asks the individual to sit or lie in a comfortable position with their eyes closed. Discuss the location they chose, what memories they have in that place, and how they felt there. Clarifying questions should be asked to gain a better understanding of the location they chose (What time of year did you most enjoy going to this place? Who was there? What positive memories happened in this place? What activities did you do? What did look it look like? Were there any pleasant nearby smells? Was there a favorite food associated with this place?)

■ Reflection

How did you feel when you reflected upon your safe place? Did you feel more relaxed and calmer? Is there anything that you would want to add or change?

■ Variations

If the individual prefers to draw a picture rather than describe their safe place, then materials may be provided to do so.

If the individual cannot identify a personal safe place, the facilitator should refer to A Peaceful Place (the previous activity).

After questioning, the facilitator may choose to retell the story of the person's safe place and creatively embellish (add details) to make the story more interesting, fun, and safe.

■ Concerns

Developmentally appropriate language must be used based on the age of the individual.

MY SAFE PLACE

■ Example Dialogue

(Speak slowly and softly)

The person said they remember helping their grandmother cook dinner.

Your safe place is a memory of being at your grandmother's house and cooking with her. So, close your eyes and let's picture being back at your grandmother's house. You knock on the door and she welcomes you with a warm smile and big hug. As she hugs you, you can hear the steady sound of her heartbeat. As she gently squeezes you, you melt into her arms and feel at peace. You can smell her floral perfume and can almost taste the food cooking in the kitchen behind her. You walk in the door. Everything in her home has a place and it looks just like you remember it from your last visit.

The further you walk into her house, the more you smell dinner cooking on the stove—a warm soup with fragrant smells of garlic and onions. You lift the lid off the pot of soup and take a deep breath (facilitator slowly inhales) as the warm steam hits your skin and the delicious smells bring a smile to your face. You breathe out (facilitator slowly exhales) and feel at home in your grandmother's house.

You ask to help and begin peeling the potatoes. As you finish each one, your grandmother takes it and dices it into little pieces before adding it to the aromatic soup. You hear the chickens squawking outside and wonder if the neighbor's dog is chasing them. After the potatoes, you peel a bunch of carrots while your grandmother watches you with a look of pride and love.

You feel loved, proud, competent, and safe.

52 CALMING ACTIVITIES

Age	All	Setting	Group	Trauma Recovery	LEARNING-Relaxation

Purpose	To generate a list of calming activities that can be used as a resource when worried, anxious, or fearful.
Overview	The participant(s) create a long list of calming activities, then select those activities most helpful to him/her.

Approximate Time	10-15 minutes

Supplies Needed	Large paper, black/whiteboard, or paper and pen

■ Activity Explained

- ⮑ The participant(s) develop a list of any activities that people might do to help calm themselves down (Example: reading, sleeping, journaling, singing, listening to music, going on a walk, exercising, etc.). Someone writes the activities while the facilitator encourages others to add to the list.

- ⮑ Each person is then told to choose 5 to 7 of these activities that are personally effective in calming him/her down when feeling fearful, worried, or anxious.

- ⮑ The participant(s) keeps the full list as a resource for when they are feeling anxious but should memorize those personally chosen to use whenever they need to calm down.

■ Reflection

Which ideas are you most excited to try? Have you ever used any of these in the past? Which activity have you found most helpful in calming yourself?

■ Variations

Activity may be used independently or in groups.

If done with an individual, the list of activities can be created independently and then brought to the session in order for the individual to consult others for ideas.

■ Concerns

Activities suggested and listed need to be possible and relevant in the context of the individual's culture.

■ Story

One survivor shared, "Creating a list of helpful activities is a great resource for me to turn to when I started feeling anxious."

53 FINGER REMINDERS

Age	All	Setting	Group	Trauma Recovery	LEARNING-Relaxation

Purpose	To refocus one's mind using each finger to recall specific memories
Overview	With clasped hands, the individual raises corresponding fingers on both hands and recalls a specific memory associated with that finger to refocus and relax.

Approximate Time	5 minutes

Supplies Needed	None

■ Activity Explained

⮑ The individual sits in a comfortable position with eyes closed and takes a few deep breaths. The facilitator instructs them to clasp their hands together with fingers interlaced.

⮑ The facilitator continues to instruct the individual:

    a. "First, put your thumbs up together and think of a time when you felt strength."

    b. "Then, put your index or pointer fingers up and think of a time where you helped someone."

    c. "Next, put your middle fingers up together and think of a time where you were able to forgive someone and overcome the hurt they caused you."

    d. "Then, put up your fourth fingers, the one next to your little finger (often called your ring finger) and think of someone that you love or someone that loves you.

    e. "Last, put up your little fingers and think of a happy memory."

⮑ Afterwards, ask the person to practice it again then ask how that activity made them feel.

■ Reflection

Which memory was your favorite to recall? How could you use this when you are feeling stressed or anxious? Is there anything you would like to change?

■ Variations

Activity may be used individually or in groups, with people of all ages.

If needed, the facilitator may demonstrate this activity first or change any of the finger memories to best fit the person's needs.

■ Concerns

The individual should be instructed to think only of pleasant memories.

54 RELAXED, NOT AFRAID

Age	All	Setting	Group	Trauma Recovery	LEARNING- Relaxation

Purpose	To bring awareness to the connection between the mind and physical body.
Overview	The individual is asked to focus on something they are afraid of while, at the same time, changing their physical response.

Approximate Time	15 - 20 minutes

Supplies Needed	None

■ Activity Explained

➭ The facilitator asks the individual to think of something they are afraid of (i.e. snakes, the dark, spiders)—not a traumatic memory or event.

➭ The individual closes their eyes and imagines that they are facing whatever they are afraid of (i.e. *"Close your eyes and imagine there is a snake coming towards you."*) The facilitator should remind them that this is just an imagination activity and they are in no real danger.

➭ The individual is asked to describe out loud how they are feeling in their physical body. *"Does their body feel tense, tight, heavy, frozen? Where do they feel it?"*

➭ Then, the facilitator instructs the individual to relax their body, take a deep breath, and pay attention to how their body feels now. If desired, other activities could be used such as the Peaceful Place, My Safe Place, or breathing and progressive muscle relaxation.

➭ After getting in a relaxed state, the facilitator then instructs the individual to imagine what they are afraid of again and asks them if their body feels any differently than the first time. *"Are you more relaxed? Are you still scared?"*

■ Reflection

How did the first experience of imagining your fear compare to the second?

How could you use this activity with other memories that cause physical responses?

■ Variations

Activity may be used individually or in groups.

■ Concerns

The object imagined should not be triggering in any way to the individual.

> *"What a difference it made to engage in relaxation techniques before I told my trauma story."*

55 FREE WRITING

Age	Children – Youth – Adults - All	Setting	Individual - Group - Both	Trauma Recovery	LEARNING- Relaxation

Purpose	To teach the relaxation strategy of freewriting for processing thoughts and emotions.
Overview	The individual writes about something for an extended period of time to release thoughts and emotions on paper.

Approximate Time	5-15 minutes

Supplies Needed	Paper and pen

■ Activity Explained

- ⮑ The facilitator explains to the individual that Free Writing or journaling can help many people relax and release various thoughts and emotions.

- ⮑ The individual decides what they want to write about, or the facilitator may use a simple object for the individual to write about. (Example: a toy, a spoon, flowers, a lamp, a bowl, a picture.)

- ⮑ The facilitator asks the person to write continuously about something of their choosing (or the object that was brought in). The individual will be asked to keep writing for the whole time without correcting grammar or spelling, writing down anything that comes to mind.

- ⮑ The individual should write for a certain amount of time, starting with 5 minutes, and slowly increase the time if they continue using this strategy on their own. The time can also be decreased if it is too difficult.

■ Reflection

How was that experience for you? Did it feel like it was too much time or not enough? Did you find it hard to focus on that specific topic or object? Did your mind wander? Was it hard or easy for you to ignore writing mistakes you made? Do you think you might use this activity?

■ Variations

The individual can bring in their own object to write about.

■ Concerns

If the individual is struggling with writing about the object, the facilitator can provide them with the prompts and time to think before starting to write: *How does this object/thing make you feel? How would you describe it? Does it bring up any memories? How would you describe it to a blind person? What color is it? Size? Shape? What is its purpose?*

56 MINDFULNESS

Age	Youth & Adults	Setting	Group	Trauma Recovery	LEARNING- Relaxation

Purpose	To create mindfulness, awareness of emotion, and how these are connected to your body.
Overview	The individual focuses on an emotion they are feeling and how it affects their body.

Approximate Time	5-15 minutes		Supplies Needed	None

■ Activity Explained

- ➲ The individual sits up tall in a chair with their feet on the ground and hands in their lap or lies down on their back with their legs straight and arms by their sides. The facilitator instructs the individual to fix their gaze on one object or to close their eyes.

- ➲ The facilitator instructs the individual to pay attention to how their body is feeling. The person is asked to practice doing a body scan by bringing awareness to each part of the body, working slowly up from their toes to their head. They are asked if different parts of their body are tense, relaxed, heavy, or light, and to pay attention to their breathing—if it's deep and slow or quick and shallow.

- ➲ The facilitator asks the individual to label what emotion they are feeling. Are they happy, sad, frustrated, afraid, nervous, content, angry, anxious? They are then asked to describe how their body is responding (feeling) while feeling that emotion.

- ➲ The individual opens their eyes slowly and then the individual and facilitator reflect on the experience together.

■ Reflection

How did that activity make you feel? What did you notice about your body? Were there areas where you felt tension or heaviness? Did bringing awareness to those areas make you more relaxed or tense? What emotional label do you think best fits what you're feeling?

■ Variations

If helpful, the facilitator can talk the individual through the activity by telling them to "Bring awareness to your toes, to your feet, to your ankles, your lower legs, etc."

This activity can be separated to just focusing on the physical feelings of their body and labeling their emotions. Activity may be used individually or in groups. Adaptations are needed for use with children.

■ Concerns

This activity may need to be adjusted for those with physical disabilities or limitations.

■ Story

"Through doing this activity, I learned that I carry a lot of my anxiety in my chest with a tight and heavy feeling. This made me more aware of when I was feeling anxious since I was able to recognize the physical signs."

57 YOGA

Age	All	Setting	Group	Trauma Recovery	LEARNING-Relaxation

Purpose	To improve muscular strength and flexibility, reduce tension of muscles, and to improve mindfulness through meditation and breathing.
Overview	Yoga includes a series of physical positions connected to breathing and body awareness.

		Supplies Needed	
Approximate Time	10 - 15 minutes		A trained instructor, books/online resources (websites, videos, applications), and yoga supplies if needed (mat, blocks, bands, etc.)

Activity Explained

- Find a yoga instructor, yoga studio, website, video, book, or app that teaches the practice of yoga.
- Practice and continue if desired.

Reflection

If the individual enjoys doing yoga, they should be encouraged to continue if able. Discuss the benefits of Yoga in relaxing and also in improving one's mental and physical awareness.

Variations

There are many variations of yoga based on the focus, difficulty, pace, and duration of the class. It is recommended to start with shorter classes, focusing on gentle stretching at a slow pace, and then, if desired, progress to longer or faster-paced classes.

If a staff member or volunteer is trained, ask if they can teach a class at your location.

Concerns

Only recommended for those who are physically able to do yoga and for calming practices.

Poses used should be based on abilities and adapted when using with children.

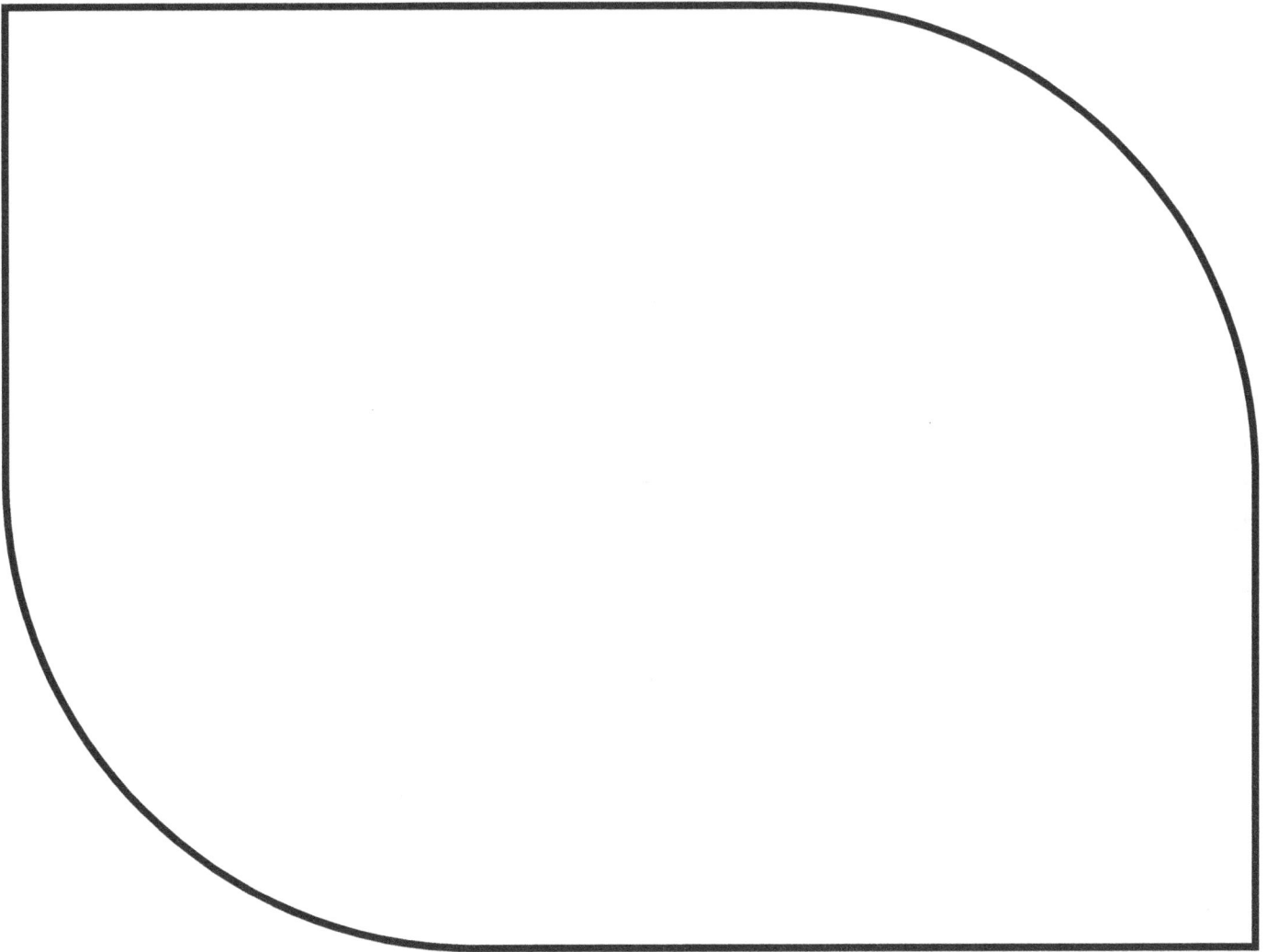

STEP 3

FEELING

FEELING

■ OVERALL GOAL

- ⮑ To empower the individual to identify and demonstrate a variety of emotions, when they are experienced, and at what intensity.
- ⮑ To bring awareness of personal emotional triggers and helpful strategies for self-regulation.

■ OVERVIEW

Because traumatized individuals experience various and overwhelming feelings, they often have difficulty identifying, understanding, regulating, controlling, and expressing emotions. This step helps the victim progress toward affective regulation as they learn to identify and express emotions in healthy ways, and also to identify people, places, and things that trigger upsetting emotions.

During this step, we help the individual:

IDENTIFY

A variety of emotions to expand their "feelings" vocabulary. Using photos or picture cards, feelings posters, and/or newspapers, we ask What might this person be feeling? Why?

EXPRESS

A variety of emotions, using activities which incorporate awareness of facial expressions and body language. Activities can include playing charades (acting without words) with various emotions and/or asking What are the ____ (eyes, mouth, arms, body) doing when someone feels _____ (emotion)? In this part of the exercise, clients are allowed to express themselves however they want in order to demonstrate an emotion, even if the behavior or words are offensive or inappropriate.

APPROPRIATELY EXPRESS

A variety of emotions, with focus on when, where, why, what, how much, and how best to communicate them. This is where the facilitator guides the client in expressing themselves effectively and appropriately according to the given situation/example, but with more control over their emotions.

Helpful questions could include:

- *What emotion might a person feel WHEN _____ (event) happens?*
- *WHEN might a person feel _____ (an emotion)?*
- *When should/shouldn't we express our emotions?*
- *To what degree (intensity) should we express our feelings?*
- *How intense/strong of an emotion would a person feel if _____happens?*
- *How _____(emotion) would a person feel if _____ (event) happens?*
- *On a scale of 1 to 10 (1 being no emotion and 10 being intense emotion) how much _____(emotion) would a person feel if_____(event) happened?*

RECOGNIZE

Triggers of upsetting emotions.

Identify what people, places, things, or events trigger unpleasant memories and emotions, and develop a plan in managing, facing, or avoiding them. Here's some suggestions:

- Recognize distress signals
- Implement relaxation (stress reduction) activities and techniques
- Implement thought-stopping and thought-replacement strategies as needed

FEELING

■ Goals
- ⮑ To empower victims to identify and appropriately express a variety of emotions
- ⮑ To foster self-regulation skills and their use
- ⮑ To increase awareness of emotional triggers

Name		Program Location	

Tasks (some optional, depending on person/situation)	Date Completed	Notes
Identify a variety of emotions and other feelings words (sad, gloomy, blue, down, depressed)		
Practice identifying and labeling emotions using photos, games, posters, drawings.		
Practice recognizing and expressing various emotions, when they are generally experienced, and to what degree of intensity.		
Present psychoeducation (information) regarding emotional expression including: What, How, When, Why, and How much (intensity).		
Discuss the role of body language and facial expressions in emotional communication		
Provide opportunities for role plays, charades, story-reading, and other activities that encourage the identification and/or appropriate expression of various emotions		
Practice applying relaxation and stress reduction techniques to emotional distress signals and triggers (if not done previously)		

Note:

The person may feel uncomfortable and/or be non-compliant when talking about their emotions. It may be more effective (less vulnerable and/or potentially re-traumatizing) to discuss feelings in a more general or impersonal way, such as What might someone feel who has experienced _____?

In this step it is important that the facilitator identifies spoken and unspoken family and cultural "rules" or values regarding what to share and what is and isn't appropriate emotional expression.

58 FEELINGS LIST

Age	All	Setting	Group	Trauma Recovery	Feeling

Purpose	To identify a variety of emotions and increase "feelings" vocabulary.
Overview	The individual lists as many emotions or "feeling" words as possible.

Approximate Time	5-10 minutes

Supplies Needed	Paper and pen

■ Activity Explained

- ➲ The facilitator challenges the individual to name as many "feeling" words as possible in a certain amount of time (i.e. 3 minutes).

- ➲ The individual writes the list of emotions or the facilitator offers to write the feelings words as the individual says them aloud.

- ➲ The facilitator and individual review the list afterwards, adding any new words that come to mind. If preferred, the lengthy list given in the next activity could be referred to after this list has been completed.

■ Reflection

The individual should be encouraged to continue to add to their list as they go about their day or week.

■ Variations

Activity may be verbal or written.

Activity may be narrowed to focus on certain categories of feelings, "List as many words as possible that represent the feeling of being mad." (Examples: irate, angry, upset, frustrated, enraged, hot, ticked off). Categories might be: happy, mad, sad, scared, jealous...

Consider repeating the activity again periodically as a way to measure the individual's increasing vocabulary of emotion words.

■ Concerns

The facilitator should be cautious of discouragement or self-condemnation (I.e. "I'm so stupid. I couldn't think of very many.") if the individual struggles with this task.

59 FEELINGS CHARADES

Age	All	Setting	Group	Trauma Recovery	Feeling

Purpose	To act out and identify a variety of emotions.
Overview	Using facial expressions and body language, various emotions are acted out for the other(s) to identify. Whether in a group or with the facilitator, numerous feelings are individually acted out for the other(s) to guess.

Approximate Time	10 - 20 minutes		**Supplies Needed**	Paper, pen, and open container

■ Activity Explained

- ➲ The facilitator will take a list of feelings (from the previous activity or the following page) then copy/print it in a readable size, cut the list into separate pieces of paper, and place them in an open container such as a bowl, hat, or basket.

- ➲ The facilitator instructs the individual in the activity. Let's play charades about emotions. We'll take turns picking a feeling out of the bowl, then act it out for the other(s) to guess. *Remember that in Charades, we don't talk or make noises. Any questions?*

- ➲ The individual goes first unless he/she asks the facilitator to do so. A piece of paper is randomly picked and acted out, without talking, for the other person(s) to guess.

- ➲ Occasionally, or after each of the charades, the facilitator might choose to ask the person/group *How did you know to guess that emotion? What were the clues (body language, facial expressions)?*

■ Reflection

Were some of those emotions hard to act out? Which ones? Have you ever felt that emotion? When have you felt that emotion? What was going on? When might someone experience that emotion? What event might have happened?

■ Variations

Activity may be used individually or in groups. Both young and old can enjoy this activity which helps the individual both identify and express a variety of emotions, thus increasing his/her affect awareness

■ Concerns

An age and language-appropriate feelings vocabulary is necessary. Keep the simple words for children or those of a different native language.

The facilitator should avoid embarrassing those unable to understand the word or how to act it out. Allow flexibility to let others help, to ask the helper for the meaning of the word, or to pass on a word and choose another.

FEELING LISTS

■ For Young Children:

- Happy
- Sad
- Mad
- Scared
- Worried
- Ashamed
- Surprised
- Glad
- Unhappy
- Angry
- Afraid
- Anxious
- Shy
- Frightened
- Content
- Sorry
- Upset
- Silly
- Concerned
- Bored
- Grouchy
- Thankful
- Gloomy
- Furious
- Fearful
- Panicked
- Curious
- Jealous

■ Additional Words For Older Children and Youth:

- Sweet
- Down
- Ticked off
- Disturbed
- Guilty
- Sassy
- Timid
- Wicked
- Blue
- Doomed
- Horrified
- Confused
- Lonely
- Impatient
- Hot
- Awful
- Frustrated
- Terrified
- Moody
- Helpless
- Unloved
- Cool
- Crushed
- Infuriated
- Tense
- Weird
- Heartbroken
- Satisfied

For Adults

- Affectionate
- Alive
- Amazed
- Angry
- Annoyed
- Anxious
- Ashamed
- Bad
- Bitter
- Bored
- Calm
- Comfortable
- Compassionate
- Confident
- Confused
- Conscientious
- Content
- Courageous
- Curious
- Depressed
- Despairing
- Determined
- Disappointed
- Discouraged
- Disgusted
- Eager
- Elated
- Embarrassed
- Empty
- Encouraged
- Energetic
- Enraged
- Envious
- Excited
- Foolish
- Frustrated
- Frightened
- Furious
- Grateful
- Grieving
- Guilty
- Happy
- Heartbroken
- Hopeful
- Hostile
- Hurt
- Impulsive
- Inadequate
- Inferior
- Insecure
- Inspired
- Irritated
- Jealous
- Joyful
- Lonely
- Lost
- Loving /Loved
- Lucky
- Mad
- Miserable
- Motivated
- Nervous
- Offended
- Optimistic
- Overwhelmed
- Passionate
- Pathetic
- Peaceful
- Pessimistic
- Pleased
- Proud
- Rejected
- Reliable
- Relieved
- Resentful
- Responsible
- Sad
- Satisfied
- Scared
- Self-conscious
- Shocked
- Silly
- Skeptical
- Sorrowful
- Stupid
- Surprised
- Suspicious
- Sympathetic
- Tense
- Terrified
- Thankful
- Tired / Fatigued
- Trapped
- Uncomfortable
- Worried
- Worthless

60 GUESSING FEELINGS

Age	All	Setting	Group	Trauma Recovery	Feeling

Purpose	Guessing Feelings
Overview	Using a variety of pictures or drawings of people's faces, the individual is asked to guess what the person might be feeling.

Approximate Time	20 - 30 minutes

Supplies Needed	Large blank paper, glue, scissors, pencils, and old magazines or picture books

Activity Explained

- ➲ The facilitator and/or person cut out different faces from old magazines, newspapers, or other sources to make a collage of the various faces.
- ➲ The facilitator asks the person what the individuals in the photos/drawing might be feeling. (We will use this collage again in the next section, Thinking, to ask what the people might be thinking.)

Reflection

What emotion might that person be feeling? Why do you think the person might be feeling that emotion? Have you ever experienced this emotion?

Variations

Activity may be used individually or in groups. If done in a group, each individual can create his/her own page full of faces or the group can collaboratively make one big collage.

The same exercise with faces/drawings is used for guessing thoughts. If done together, the difference between thoughts and feelings, a goal in recovery, is exemplified.

Concerns

If used in groups, participation should be monitored so that one person is not directing and telling others what to do and how to answer.

61 RECOGNIZING FEELINGS IN FACES

Age	All	Setting	Group	Trauma Recovery	Feeling

Purpose	For identifying feelings from various facial expressions.
Overview	Given drawings of various faces, the individual identifies the emotion and/or identifies with the face.

Approximate Time	5 - 15 minutes

Supplies Needed	Worksheet (with or without emotion word labels) and pen or pencil

■ Activity Explained

Without Labels

- ⮑ The facilitator instructs: "Write what emotion you think is being displayed by each of the drawings."
- ⮑ The facilitator and participant(s) discuss what was written.

    How challenging was labeling the faces for you? Were some expressions easier to name than others?

    Did some drawings seem to represent more than one emotion? Which ones?

- ⮑ If desired, participant(s) can add to the drawings (for example, hair, moustache, beard...)

With Labels

- ⮑ The facilitator asks: *"Which of these emotions have you experienced? Is that similar to what you look like when you experience those feelings?" "What are the differences between the drawings? Eyebrows, mouth, eyes?"*
- ⮑ The facilitator asks: *Which emotion(s) are you feeling right now? Which did you feel yesterday?*
- ⮑ If desired, participant(s) can add to the drawings (for example, hair, moustache, beard...)

■ Reflection

What have you learned about reading facial expressions? About figuring out what feelings people are showing?

■ Variations

The worksheet may be used with or without labels.

Activity may be used individually or in groups and may be done verbally with only the facilitator having a copy of the illustrations.

■ Concerns

Individuals may need assistance identifying/writing the emotions displayed.

HOW ARE YOU FEELING

Happy

Joyful

Content

Silly

Sad

Angry

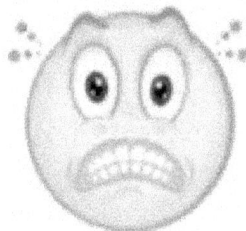

Scared

Worried

Confused

Surprised

Hurt

Embarrassed

This "Feelings Chart" was developed by Priceless Parenting, available free of charge at https://www.pricelessparenting.com/chart-for-kids.

HOW ARE YOU FEELING?

Here's what you can do:

⮑ Guess what emotion the Smiley faces are showing and write it below each face. Or

⮑ Match a feeling (list below) with the various Smiley faces. Or

⮑ Share which of the emotions you have felt or which ones you've felt this week or today.

List of Possible Feelings:

⮑ Happy	⮑ Mischievous	⮑ Uncertain
⮑ Angry	⮑ Playful	⮑ Friendly
⮑ Sad	⮑ Obedient	⮑ Shy
⮑ Upset	⮑ Ashamed	⮑ Embarrassed
⮑ Scared	⮑ Surprised	⮑
⮑ Bored	⮑ Lonely	
⮑ Funny	⮑ Insecure	
⮑ Loving	⮑ Cheerful	
⮑ Confused	⮑ Humorous	

62 FEELINGS ON FACES

Age	All	Setting	Group	Trauma Recovery	Feeling

Purpose	To identify a variety of emotional expressions; to increase one's emotional vocabulary.
Overview	The individual looks at a variety of facial expressions and guesses the probable emotion displayed. This activity provides a baseline of the individual's emotional vocabulary and helps in understanding the extent of the person's emotional dysregulation (impairment, disconnectedness).

Approximate Time	5-15 minutes

Supplies Needed	Feelings Poster, magazine, or variety of facial photos.

Activity Explained

➲ The facilitator instructs the individual that they will be looking at a variety of pictures and will be asked to guess what the person might be feeling.

➲ The facilitator shows the pictures and asks what emotion the pictured person might be showing.

Reflection

Why do you think he/she is feeling that way? What facial expressions or body language (indicators) led to your decision? Why might he/she be feeling that way? What might have happened? Anything else to add?

Variations

Activity may be used individually or in groups.

Smiley faces, caricatures, or actual photos can be found via an internet search or purchased through education or therapy supply sites. A small feelings poster can be printed from the internet. Cover any emotions words labels so that the person must guess the emotion.

Concerns

The facilitator should be careful not to frustrate, discourage, or shame the person if the guesses are often dissimilar to the suggested or expected responses.

If the individual guesses an emotion differently than suggested or as most would guess, the facilitator should ask, *Could the person in the picture be feeling anything else?* or, *Some people have guessed that this person is feeling a different emotion.*

What do you think it could be? The facilitator could also ask: Why do you think the person is feeling what you guessed?

Story

For this I use a set of cards (like baseball cards) with that show different children expressing a variety of emotions. Both young and old enjoy guessing what emotion the children are showing.

63 WHAT I WOULD FEEL 'IF'

Age	All	Setting	Group	Trauma Recovery	Feeling

Purpose	To identify one's feelings in response to various scenarios.
Overview	The individual is instructed to share what a person (or they) might feel in different situations.

		Supplies Needed	A copy of the following list and pen/pencil for the person to write responses. If done verbally, then only the leader needs a copy to read aloud.
Approximate Time	10-20 minutes		

■ Activity Explained

➲ Facilitator instructs: *In this activity we want to think about what and how we feel. You will be asked to write and/or share what you might FEEL, what might be going through your heart, given different situations.*

➲ Inform the person that he/she may choose to not answer any of the items.

➲ Responses are written for all scenarios (if not done in written form, responses are shared aloud one by one).

■ Reflection

Now, let's share what you wrote and talk about it. In what circumstances might your answers change? What affects your emotions? Was it hard to write what you might FEEL instead of what you might THINK?

■ Variations

Activity may be used individually or in groups.

Activity may be verbal or written.

The same exercise is used for identifying thoughts. If done together, the difference between thoughts and feelings is discussed.

■ Concerns

The individual may need assistance in writing their responses.

■ Story

The information gained from this activity has been an invaluable tool, that has taught me much about the client, their feelings, and their thought processes.

WHAT I WOULD FEEL 'IF'...

If I was given a surprise birthday party	
If I flunked a math test	
If a good friend died	
If someone tried to kidnap me	
If I got the highest score on a test at school	
If a dog jumped out of the bushes and growled	
If I was accused of doing something I didn't do	
If my friend saw my parent drunk	
If I wet my pants	
If I was leaving on a trip	
If my parents were fighting	
If my mom was crying	

If someone touched my private parts	
If no one was around and there was nothing to do	
If my friend didn't show up on time	
If my friend was missing	
If my parents treated my brother/sister better than me	
If my cell phone was taken away	
If I told a lie and got caught	
If I let someone down and didn't do what I said I would	
If I was in a car accident	
If I was invited to go to a special event	
If the teacher announced the test was cancelled	
If I tried and tried, but couldn't do something	
If I fell and hurt myself	

64 WHAT I'VE FELT

				Trauma Recovery	Feeling
Age	All	**Setting**	Group		

Purpose	To identify emotions experienced by the person, increasing awareness of self and emotions.
Overview	The individual indicates which emotions (refer to Feelings List), which ones he/she has personally felt or experienced (refer to Feelings List).

Approximate Time	5-15 minutes

Supplies Needed	Feelings List and pen

■ Activity Explained

➲ The facilitator reads a list of emotions and the individual lets the facilitator know (yes or no) whether or not they have personally experienced that emotion. If preferred, the individual can be given the feelings list and asked to mark (check, circle) which ones they have experienced.

➲ Explain or describe any unfamiliar words to the individual.

➲ The individual simply identifies which emotions he/she has experienced and does not need to discuss when and where the emotion was felt unless they choose to do so. If preferred, the individual can be given the feelings list and asked to mark which ones they have experienced.

■ Reflection

How do you feel about identifying emotions you have experienced? Were you surprised by how many emotions you have experienced?

■ Variations

Activity may be done verbally or written. Activity may be used individually or in groups.

The list can be read aloud, or the individual can mark the personally experienced emotions on the list.

■ Concerns

The words used need to be age-appropriate and in one's native tongue.

If the individual becomes withdrawn, the facilitator should either ask what's going on inside their head and heart or discontinue and return to this activity later. As always, prior to the Sharing step, we do not encourage nor invite the sharing of one's trauma stories. While we do not want to stop someone who begins to share, we do not ask questions to further the discussion, but gently move on to other topics. We wait to ask about the person's trauma narrative until all of the previous steps are completed.

65 UNDERSTANDING MY FEELINGS

Age	All	Setting	Group	Trauma Recovery	Feeling

Purpose	To understand how feelings are experienced throughout the body.
Overview	The individual will complete a worksheet to describe how they experience certain emotions in their face, body, heart, and thoughts.

Approximate Time	10-20 minutes

Supplies Needed	Worksheet and pen

■ Activity Explained

⊃ The individual fills out the following worksheet to explain what happens to their face, body, heart, and thoughts when certain emotions are felt. The facilitator may need to provide an example or demonstration to help the person better understand the activity.

⊃ The facilitator and individual discuss their responses.

■ Reflection

Why do you think you respond to this emotion in this way with your face, body, heart, or thoughts? Have you ever noticed before how your body responds to this specific emotion? What emotion was the hardest to think of your response to? What emotion was the easiest to think of your responses to?"

■ Variations

Activity may be used individually or in groups.

This worksheet can be completed independently and brought to the session.

If the individual is having a hard time expressing how they experience certain emotions, encourage them to close their eyes and imagine something that makes them feel that emotion so they can be aware of how they respond to it.

■ Concerns

Support for identifying emotions may be needed.

The individual may need assistance in filling out the worksheet.

UNDERSTANDING MY FEELINGS

When I'm feeling

Here's what happens:

My face	
My body	
My heart	
My thoughts	

When I'm feeling

Here's what happens:

My face	
My body	
My heart	
My thoughts	

When I'm feeling

Here's what happens:

My face	
My body	
My heart	
My thoughts	

66 INSIDE-OUTSIDE FEELINGS

Age	All	Setting	Group	Trauma Recovery	Feeling

Purpose	To bring awareness to how we often show different feelings on the outside than what we are experiencing on the inside.
Overview	The facilitator and individual discuss how internal emotions are often hidden inside and not shown on the outside.

Approximate Time	15-30 minutes	**Supplies Needed**	paper plate or blank sheet of paper (preferably stiff, cardstock) and colored pens/art supplies

■ Activity Explained

- ➲ The facilitator explains that often when we experience an emotion, we keep it inside and show a different feeling on the outside. When people are in a more comfortable setting, with people they know well, they are more willing to show their inside feelings on the outside. *We may feel discouraged but smile on the outside and tell others we're fine. Or, we may feel excited but show a calm outside.*

- ➲ Using a paper plate (or piece of paper), the individual draws a face on each side. One side represents how they feel on the inside and the other is the face that they want on the outside for others to see. For the outside face, ask the person to choose who it is for: a stranger, acquaintances, classmates, close friend, family member, etc.

- ➲ *Optional*: Give an inside emotion then ask the individual what *a person* might show on the outside. Then reverse this by giving an outside emotion and ask what a person might feel on the inside.

■ Reflection

What did you learn from this activity? Do you think your inside and outside emotions match or are they completely different? Does your outside face change according to who you are with? Are there certain inside emotions that are harder for you to show on the outside?

■ Variations

Activity may be repeated with different situations and people for the individual to identify possible inner and outer feelings.

Activity may be verbal or written.

■ Concerns

The individual may need assistance identifying emotions.

67 CHANGING FEELINGS

Age	All	Setting	Group	Trauma Recovery	Feeling

Purpose	To identify feelings and ways to alter them.
Overview	The individual is asked to brainstorm ideas (several preferred) of ways to change an emotion.

Approximate Time	10-15 minutes		Supplies Needed	None needed, though the facilitator may want to show pictures of the various emotions and/or use pen and paper or whiteboard to record/show the suggestions.

■ Activity Explained

- The facilitator explains the purpose and overview of the activity (in an age appropriate manner).
- The facilitator instructs, *We're going to talk about what we could do to help change unwanted feelings. For example, what ideas do you have for changing a feeling like anger? What are some things you could do to help you, or a friend, not feel angry? Let's try to identify at least three suggestions.*
- The facilitator and individual complete the first example together. If the individual is uncomfortable or it is too difficult to ask "you," then use "a friend".

   "If you (or a friend) were feeling nervous, what might help you (him/her) calm down?"

   "If you (or a friend) were feeling mad, what might help you (him/her) feel less angry?"

   "If you (or a friend) were feeling scared, what could help you (him/her) feel less frightened?"

   "If you (or a friend) were feeling sad (distraught), what might help you (him/her) feel better?"

   "If you (or a friend) were feeling overwhelmed, what could help?"

   "If you (or a friend) were feeling hopeless, what might help you (him/her) feel more hopeful?"

■ Reflection

Do you think people can change their emotional responses? What did you learn (if anything) from doing this activity? How do you think people can get better at identifying their options? How are you doing with changing your own emotions? How can you improve? What did you like or not like about this exercise?

■ Variations

Activity can be verbal or written.

Writing the suggestions down can increase responses as it visually illustrates the multitude of ways one can alter their emotional state. The facilitator, however, can choose whether or not to write down the responses or, depending on the age/ability of the individual, ask them to write them down.

■ Concerns

If using "you" (referring to themselves), is uncomfortable, use "a friend."

68 BEFORE, DURING, AND AFTER

Age	All	Setting	Group	Trauma Recovery	Feeling

Purpose	To identify how emotions can change given a variety of situations.
Overview	The individual identifies what a person (or they) might feel before, during, and after a specific situation.

Approximate Time	10-20 minutes		Supplies Needed	Worksheet and pen

■ Activity Explained

⮑ The facilitator discusses how our feelings can easily change according to what is happening in our lives. The facilitator gives examples:

Before my friend yelled at me I felt good. During the argument I felt angry. Afterwards, I was frustrated.

Before I talked to my Mom, I was lonely. During the phone call to my Mom, I was happy. Now, I feel content.

⮑ The individual is given a scenario on the worksheet and determines how one would feel before, during, and after the given situation.

■ Reflection

How was this activity for you? Would you like to answer any of the situations for yourself? How you would feel before, during, and after a personal situation?

■ Variations

Can be completed in writing or verbally through a conversation. Activity may be used individually or in groups.

■ Concerns

The individual may need assistance writing their answers.

Situations may need to be changed to be age/culturally appropriate.

■ Story

Some people forget how they felt before a situation, focusing just on what they currently feel. This activity has been helpful to remind people of positive emotions experienced prior to negative ones. Many have found this encouraging, especially later when we do talk about their trauma stories, as they have remembered that they didn't always feel sad and ashamed, but once felt happy and proud.

BEFORE, DURING, AND AFTER

How might a person feel before, during, and after...

Having a fight with a close friend.	
Before	
During	
After	

Going to the store to buy a treat and finding out the store has none left.	
Before	
During	
After	

Finding out that one's grandfather has died.	
Before	
During	
After	

Being told by a stranger that he/she is stupid.	
Before	
During	
After	

Learning they successfully passed a hard test.	
Before	
During	
After	

_____ (make up a situation)	
Before	
During	
After	

_____ (make up a situation)	
Before	
During	
After	

69 WHAT I'M FEELING

Age	All	Setting	Group	Trauma Recovery	Feeling

Purpose	To identify various emotions and how those emotions are often represented physically.
Overview	The individual is given a list of physical reactions and writes down what the emotions behind the reaction could be.

Approximate Time	10 minutes

Supplies Needed	Worksheet and pen

■ Activity Explained

- ➲ The facilitator explains that the individual will be identifying different emotions.
- ➲ The individual reads the sentences and identifies what emotion may be represented.

■ Reflection

Was it easy or hard to identify which emotions were being represented? Do you ever have these same reactions to these emotions?

■ Variations

Activity may be verbal or written.

Activity may be used individually or in groups.

■ Concerns

The individual may need assistance in identifying the emotions.

EXPRESSING FEELINGS

Complete the following sentences by guessing what emotion(s) might be happening:

If I had butterflies in my stomach, I am probably feeling:

If I was looking around and my heart was pounding, I'm probably feeling:

If I was crying, I could be feeling:

If my muscles were all tense and I was pacing the floor, I'm probably feeling:

If my eyes are looking down and I move slower, I could be feeling:

If my eyes are squinted and my eyebrows are facing inward, I'm probably feeling:

Other Examples/Ideas

If _____ (is happening), I am probably feeling:

If _____ (is happening), I am probably feeling:

If _____ (is happening), I am probably feeling:

70 WHAT MAKES ME FEEL...

All	Group	FEELING
Age	**Setting**	**Trauma Recovery**

Purpose	To identify what causes us to feel certain emotions.
Overview	The individual completes a worksheet and identifies what causes them to feel specific emotions.

Approximate Time	10-15 minutes

Supplies Needed	Worksheet and pen

■ Activity Explained

- ➲ The facilitator explains that different events and experiences make us feel different emotions.
- ➲ The individual follows the worksheet and writes down what makes them feel various emotions, such as happy, proud, excited, angry, etc.

■ Reflection

Are some of these emotions easier to feel than others?

Were there any emotions that were hard to choose what makes you feel that way?

■ Variations

Activity may be verbal or written. Activity may be used individually or in groups.

■ Concerns

The individual may need assistance filling out worksheet.

WHAT KIND OF THINGS MAKES ME FEEL

ANGRY	
ASHAMED	
BORED	
CURIOUS	
EMBARRASSED	
EXCITED	
GROUCHY	
HAPPY	
JEALOUS	
LONELY	
PANICKED	
PROUD	
SAD	
SCARED	
SHY	
SILLY	
SORRY	
SPECIAL	
SURPRISED	
WORRIED	

71 DRAWING FEELINGS FACES

Age	All	Setting	Group	Trauma Recovery	Feeling

Purpose	To increase emotional awareness and identification.
Overview	The individual is asked to draw a basic face with pencil and eraser on a paper plate or blank paper, then asked to make changes on the face with various emotions.

Approximate Time	10-15 minutes

Supplies Needed	Pencil, eraser, paper (or paper plate), and mirror (if available)

■ Activity Explained

- ⊃ The individual is given supplies and asked to draw a basic face.
- ⊃ The individual is asked to describe the emotion the face is expressing.
- ⊃ The facilitator instructs the individual to now change the drawing so that the face reflects another emotion (happy, mad/angry, sad, fearful, embarrassed, bored and/or whatever emotions the facilitator chooses).

■ Reflection

What changed? How do we show emotions on our faces? How do we know if someone is happy or scared, angry or sad? What role does body language play in how we determine how someone is feeling?

■ Variations

Activity may be used individually or in groups.

Computer images: If the helper has access to a computer and/or internet program that incorporates changing faces, this can also be used effectively for this exercise.

Pre-made facial parts: Pre-made mouths, noses, eyebrows, and eyes could be used and interchanged on a pre-made blank face. The person can choose which combination to use for each emotion indicated. (Refer to the examples on the following page.)

■ Concerns

The individual's frustration level should be monitored to determine when to discontinue or when to give another blank paper. Those prone to perfectionism might be uncomfortable with the erasing aspects.

DRAWING FEELINGS FACES

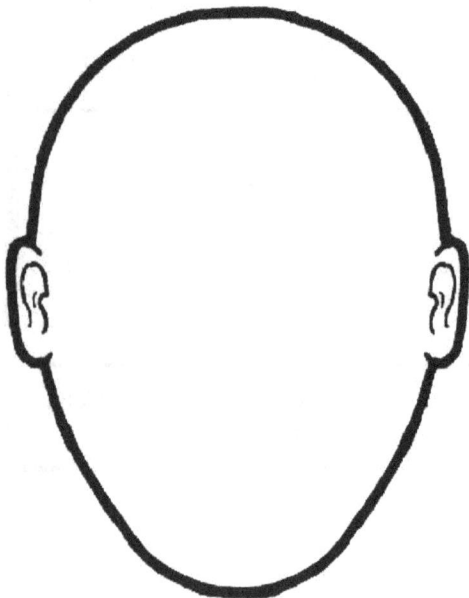

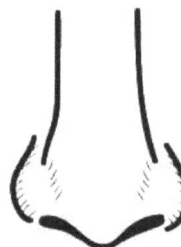

72 WHEN I FEEL...

Age	All	Setting	Group	Trauma Recovery	Feeling

Purpose	To bring awareness to what behaviors result from feeling certain emotions.
Overview	The connection between emotions and behaviors is explored through completing a worksheet asking what emotion the individual or group feel(s) when behaving in a certain way.

Approximate Time	15-30 minutes

Supplies Needed	Worksheet and pen

■ Activity Explained

- ⊃ The individual completes the following worksheet about what emotion they are feeling when they are behaving a certain way. Either the person or the facilitator can write down the answers. The person is reminded that he/she can skip any undesirable, unknown or complicated item (pass and not answer).
- ⊃ Facilitator asks questions to elicit a discussion about the relationship between emotions and behaviors.

■ Reflection

How was this activity for you? Do you think emotions come from behaviors or behaviors from emotions? Have you ever noticed before that certain behaviors come from certain emotions? Are there some behaviors that you wish you could change? Emotions?

■ Variations

The worksheet can be completed independently or during a session.

The worksheet can be written out or discussed verbally.

■ Concerns

The worksheet may need to be adjusted to be culturally relevant and age appropriate.

WHAT I DO WHEN I FEEL...

I find a place to be alone when I feel	
I don't do my work when I feel	
I act silly when I feel	
I hit others when I feel	
I share my things with friends when I feel	
I say mean things to others when I feel	
I brag about things I can do when I feel	
I disrupt others when I feel	
I give presents to people when I feel	
I take extra food when I feel	
I say things that aren't true when I feel	
I go for a walk when I feel	
I crawl in bed and get under the blankets when I feel	
I like to listen to music and sing out loud when I feel	
I argue with others when I feel	
I skip school/work when I feel	
I gossip about people when I feel	
I run away when I feel	
I draw lots of doodles (scribbles) when I feel	

73 WHEN I'M ANXIOUS

Age	All	Setting	Group	Trauma Recovery	Feeling

Purpose	To bring awareness regarding how a person (or the individual) experiences anxiety.[4]
Overview	The facilitator defines anxiety for the client so that there's a clear understanding. The individual then completes a worksheet about symptoms and experiences of anxiety.

Approximate Time	10-20 minutes

Supplies Needed	Worksheet and pen

■ Activity Explained[5]

➲ The individual fills out the worksheet describing the symptoms and experiences of anxiety.

■ Reflection

What do you think about anxiety? Do you think of it as a good or bad emotion? Did you learn anything new about how people experience anxiety by answering these questions? Have you ever felt any anxiety symptoms?

■ Variations

This worksheet can be filled out from the perspective of another person or can be made personal with how the individual deals with anxiety.

Activity may be verbal or written.

■ Concerns

The worksheet may need to be adjusted to be culturally relevant and age appropriate.

4   Konkel, L. (2018, January). What Are Common Symptoms of Anxiety Disorders?. Retrieved from https://www.everydayhealth.com/anxiety/guide/symptoms.
5   Adapted from What does your body do when you feel anxious? The C.A.T. Project, Harborview Center for Sexual Assault and Traumatic Stress.

WHAT HAPPENS WHEN I'M ANXIOUS?

Physical symptoms may include:

- ➲ Rapid or pounding heartbeat
- ➲ Shortness of breath
- ➲ Excessive sweating
- ➲ Tremors or twitches
- ➲ Headache

- ➲ Fatigue or weakness
- ➲ Insomnia
- ➲ Nausea or upset stomach
- ➲ Frequent urination or diarrhea

Psychological Symptoms may include:

- ➲ Feelings of apprehension or dread
- ➲ Feeling restless or irritable
- ➲ Feeling tense or jumpy

- ➲ Anticipating the worst
- ➲ Constantly watching for signs of danger

Questions

What might make a person feel anxious?

_____

_____

What might a person THINK about when they are anxious?

_____

_____

What might a person FEEL when they are anxious?

_____

_____

What do some people DO (how do they BEHAVE) when they have these anxious thoughts and feelings?

_____

_____

What are some things that people could/should do differently? What different THOUGHTS could they have? What could they do to calm down and not be so anxious?

_____

_____

74 WHEN I'M ANGRY

Age	All	Setting	Individual	Trauma Recovery	Feeling

Purpose	To bring awareness to how a person (or the individual) experiences anger.
Overview	The individual will complete a worksheet about symptoms and experiences of anger.

Approximate Time	10-20 minutes

Supplies Needed	Worksheet and pen

■ Activity Explained[6]

⊃ The individual fills out the worksheet describing symptoms and experiences of anger.

■ Reflection

What do you think about anger? Do you think of it as a good or bad emotion? Did you learn anything new about how people experience anger by answering these questions? Have you experienced any of these anger symptoms?

■ Variations

Activity may be verbal or written.

This worksheet can be filled from the perspective of another person or can be made personal by asking how the individual experiences anger.

■ Concerns

The worksheet may need to be adjusted to be culturally relevant and age appropriate.

6   Adapted from What does Your Body do when you feel Anxious? The C.A.T. Project, Harborview Center for Sexual Assault and Traumatic Stress.

WHAT HAPPENS WHEN I'M ANGRY?

Physical symptoms of anger may include:

- Heart Pounding
- Heart Racing
- Deep breaths

- Clenched fists
- Tense body
- Other: _____

Psychological symptoms of anger may include:

- Internal and/or external frustration and irritability
- Impulsive behaviors
- Irrational thoughts
- Inability to see others' perspectives

- Self-justification, rationalization, minimization of self-blame
- Thoughts of revenge (may or may not include planning)
- Other: _____

Questions

What is something that might make a person feel angry?
What might a person THINK about when they are mad?
What might a person FEEL when they are mad?
What do some people DO (how do they BEHAVE) when they have these angry thoughts and feelings?
What are some things that people could/should do differently? What different THOUGHTS could they have? What could they do to calm down and not be so angry?

75 WHEN I'M SCARED

Age	All	Setting	Group	Trauma Recovery	Feeling

Purpose	To bring awareness to how a person (or the individual) experiences being scared.
Overview	The individual will complete a worksheet about their symptoms and experiences of being scared.

Approximate Time	10-20 minutes	**Supplies Needed**	Worksheet and pen

■ Activity Explained[7]

⮂ The individual fills out the worksheet describing the symptoms and how they deal with being scared.

■ Reflection

How do you feel about this activity? Did you learn anything new about how you experience being scared by answering these questions? Have you felt any of these symptoms of when someone feels scared?

■ Variations

Activity may be verbal or written.

This worksheet can be filled from the perspective of another person or can be made personal by asking how the individual deals with being scared.

■ Concerns

The worksheet may need to be adjusted to be culturally relevant and age appropriate.

---

[7]   Adapted from What does Your Body do when you feel Anxious? The C.A.T. Project, Harborview Center for Sexual Assault and Traumatic Stress.

WHAT HAPPENS WHEN I'M SCARED?

Physical symptoms of fear may include:

- ⮑ Physical exhaustion
- ⮑ Skin rashes
- ⮑ Heartburn
- ⮑ Cold or tingly hands and feet

- ⮑ Sleep disturbance
- ⮑ Other: _____
- ⮑ Other: _____

Psychological symptoms of fear may include:

- ⮑ Irrational and or obsessive thoughts and beliefs
- ⮑ Pessimism (negative outcomes perspective)
- ⮑ Avoidance
- ⮑ Hyper-sensitivity to external stimuli

- ⮑ Difficulties with trust and safety
- ⮑ Other: _____
- ⮑ Other: _____

Questions

What is something that might make a person feel scared?
What might a person THINK about when they are scared?
What might a person FEEL when they are scared?
What do some people DO (how do they BEHAVE) when they have fearful thoughts and feelings?
What are some things that people could/should do differently? What different THOUGHTS could they have? What could they do to calm down and not be so afraid?

76 EMOTIONAL INTENSITY #1

Age	All	Setting	Group	Trauma Recovery	Feeling

Purpose	To identify possible emotions and their intensity, increasing self-awareness.
Overview	Given various scenarios, the individual rates the intensity of probable emotions on a scale of 1 to 10.

Approximate Time	10 minutes

Supplies Needed	Worksheet and pen

■ Activity Explained

- ➲ The facilitator explains that we feel emotions at various intensities and gives examples.
- ➲ The facilitator instructs the individual to read each scenario on the worksheet and rate the intensity of the emotion that would be felt in each scenario on a scale from 1 to 10. (1 = low intensity, 10 = high intensity, strongly-felt emotion).
- ➲ The worksheet focuses on what *a person* might feel and the intensity of the emotions. If appropriate, the scenarios could be answered personally, *what I would feel and how strongly?*
- ➲ Discuss answers and situations in an effort to increase understanding of the levels of intensity of various emotions.

■ Reflection

Who or what determines the intensity of how an emotion is experienced? How are emotions experienced differently? How did you decide the intensity for each situation? Would your answer change if you did this again, say, in a month? Can someone feel different intensity levels of the same emotion? Explain.

■ Variations

Activity may be used individually or in groups. Activity may be verbal or written.

■ Concerns

The worksheet may need to be adjusted to be culturally relevant and age appropriate.

EMOTIONAL INTENSITY

After each brief story, write what emotion a person might feel. Then mark how strong you think that emotion would be on a scale of 1 to 10.(1 = not a very strong emotional response to 10 = very intense.)

The person receives an award in school for good behavior.										
Feeling(s)										
Intensity (check)	1	2	3	4	5	6	7	8	9	10

The person's pet dies.										
Feeling(s)										
Intensity (check)	1	2	3	4	5	6	7	8	9	10

The person was lied to.										
Feeling(s)										
Intensity (check)	1	2	3	4	5	6	7	8	9	10

The person was physically and/or sexually abused.										
Feeling(s)										
Intensity (check)	1	2	3	4	5	6	7	8	9	10

The person is chosen to be on a special sports team.										
Feeling(s)										
Intensity (check)	1	2	3	4	5	6	7	8	9	10

The person witnesses someone being hit and hurt.										
Feeling(s)										
Intensity (check)	1	2	3	4	5	6	7	8	9	10

Someone yells "I hate you!" at the person.										
Feeling(s)										
Intensity (check)	1	2	3	4	5	6	7	8	9	10

The person is told that they are really smart and pretty (or handsome).										
Feeling(s)										
Intensity (check)	1	2	3	4	5	6	7	8	9	10

77 EMOTIONAL INTENSITY #2

Age	All	Setting	Group	Trauma Recovery	Feeling

Purpose	To identify different levels of intensity of emotions and words used to describe them.
Overview	The individual rates the intensity of probable emotions on a scale of low to high. Focus is placed on learning how to communicate and differentiate between different emotions.

Approximate Time	10-20 minutes	Supplies Needed	The following list of emotions (categorized according to intensity level) and/or your own list of emotions (refer to earlier FEELING activities if it's helpful), a large piece of paper taped to the wall (or a white board/chalk board), and markers.

■ Activity Explained

➲ The facilitator draws the "Intensity Scale" at the top of the paper/wall/board. Then the facilitator writes four words on the wall (Anger, Happiness, Fear, Sadness), leaving a lot of space beneath the words to add more words later during the activity. These are the four main categories.

➲ The facilitator focuses on one category at a time and asks the individual to identify a variety of words to represent each of the four main words: anger, happiness, fear, and sadness. Note: Additional words and categories could be used, such as jealousy (envy, covetous, desirous), tired (fatigue, exhausted, drained, sleepy), etc.

➲ Once all of the words in a specific category have been listed, the individual indicates where the emotions would fit on the scale. OR, the individual places the words in order of intensity, from less intense to more. (For example, sleepy ▶ tired ▶ fatigued ▶ drained ▶ exhausted.)

■ Reflection

How did you decide the order? Did you think that some of the words reflected the same intensity level? How do we determine which words to use to express the intensity of our emotions? If we only had one word for "mad," for example, how would we communicate the difference between when we are very, very mad and when we are just a little mad?

Variations

Activity may be verbal or written. Activity may be used individually or in groups.

If it is a verbal activity, the facilitator reads the list of emotions on the following page (choosing emotions from various intensity levels), asking the person to state what he/she thinks to be the intensity level of that emotion. *"I will read an emotion and you'll tell me where you think it fits on the intensity scale. If I said "sad," would you consider it a mild, moderate, strong, or intense feeling? What about "depressed"? What about "dislike", "hate"?*

Concerns

The facilitator needs to emphasize that there are no right or wrong answers. Adapt for children by incorporating basic and simple emotional words and cartoons to illustrate intensity levels.

FEELINGS WORD LIST[8]

Intensity Scale (decide which scale to use: drawings or cartoons and/or numbers or words)

Examples

1	2	3	4
25	50	75	100

Mild	Moderate	Strong	Intense

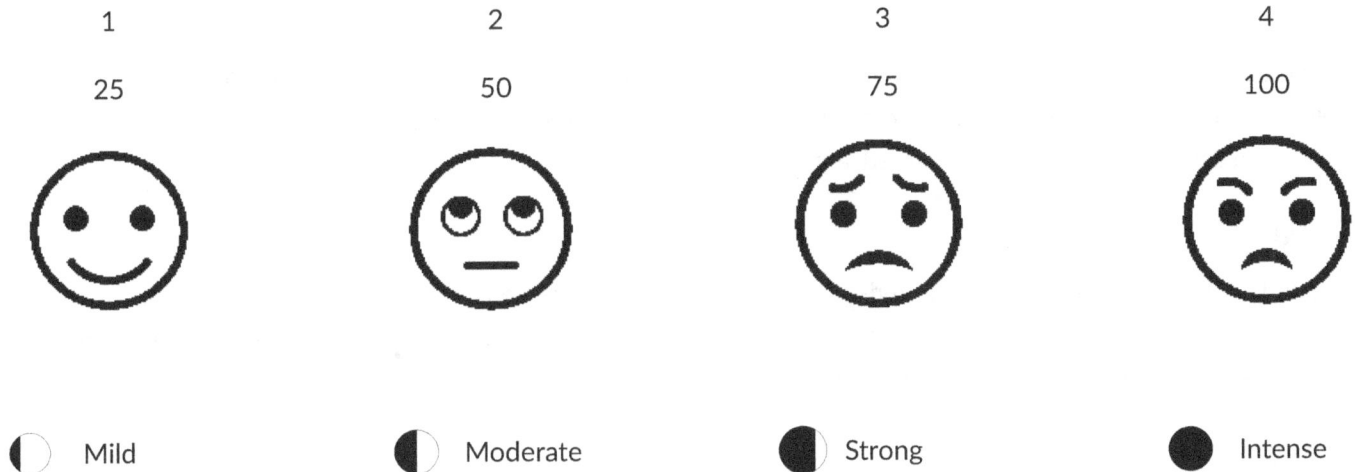

■ Positive Feelings

Mild

friendly, regarded, benevolent, wide awake, at-ease, relaxed, comfortable, content, keen, amazed, alert, sure, attractive, approved, untroubled, graceful, turned on, warm, amused, daring, comfortable, smart, interested.

Moderate

liked, cared for, esteemed, affectionate, fond, excited, patient, strong, gay, inspired, anticipating, amused, yearning, popular, peaceful, appealing, determined, pleased, excited, jolly, relieved, glad, adventurous, peaceful, intelligent.

Strong

enchanted, ardor, infatuated, tender, vibrant, independent, capable, happy , proud, gratified, worthy, sympathetic, important, concerned, appreciated, consoled, delighted, eager, optimistic, joyful, courage, hopeful, valiant, brave, brilliant.

Intense

loved, adored, idolized, alive, wanted, lustful, worthy, pity, respected, empathy, awed, enthusiastic, zealous, courageous.

---

8   Nadig, Dr. L. (2010, July). Feelings Word List. Retrieved from www.drnadig.com/feelings_list.htm (permission granted)

■ Negative Feelings

Mild

unpopular, listless, moody, lethargic, gloomy, dismal, discontented, tired, indifferent, unsure, impatient, dependent, unimportant, regretful, bashful, puzzled, self-conscious, edgy, upset, reluctant, timid, mixed-up, sullen, provoked.

Moderate

suspicious, envious, enmity, aversion, dejected, unhappy, bored, forlorn, disappointed, wearied, inadequate, ineffectual, helpless, resigned, apathetic, shy, uncomfortable, baffled, confused, nervous, tempted, tense, worried, perplexed, troubled, disdainful, contemptuous, alarmed, annoyed, provoked.

Strong

disgusted, resentful, bitter, detested, fed-up, frustrated, sad, depressed, sick, dissatisfied, fatigued, worn-out, useless, weak, hopeless, forlorn, rejected, guilty, embarrassed, inhibited, bewildered, frightened, anxious, dismayed, apprehensive, disturbed, antagonistic, vengeful, indignant, mad, torn.

Intense

hate, unloved, abhor, despised, angry, hurt, miserable, pain, lonely, cynical, worthless, impotent, futile, accursed, abandoned, estranged, degraded, humiliated, shocked, panicky, trapped, horrified, afraid, scared, terrified, threatened, infuriated, furious, exhausted.

78 COMMON FEELINGS (2)

Age	All	Setting	Group	Trauma Recovery	Feeling

Purpose	To present feelings common to trauma victims in order to normalize and validate the emotional response to their experience.
Overview	The facilitator reviews some of the common emotions experienced by the traumatized, providing explanations and examples. This increases one's understanding as well as their sense of not being alone or "crazy" (normalization and validation). (Refer also to activity #31 and #79, *Common Feelings 1 and 3*.)

Approximate Time	15 minutes

Supplies Needed	Worksheet and pen

Activity Explained

- The facilitator explains that there are many emotions that people feel when they experience traumatic events.
- The facilitator presents the following information on various common feelings that trauma victims feel and gives examples for each.
- Discuss in a general rather than personal way.

Reflection

Can you think of other common emotions that victims of abuse and trauma might feel?

Variations

Activity may be used individually or in groups. Individuals may take turns reading each common feeling (from the worksheet) aloud to the group (if used in a group).

Concerns

Some feelings may be triggering to individuals, so proceed with caution. Please remember that the focus is on reviewing common emotions from an informational perspective. We do not ask the person to share personally about their own trauma experiences until we come to *Sharing* section.

"Many have shared that they had not been able to identify what they felt until we reviewed these common feelings together. They said it was especially helpful when it was time to tell their trauma narrative. 'You've help me finally understand what I was feeling. You've given me words that describe what I have felt.'"

Dr. Becca Johnson

COMMON FEELINGS

There are many emotions people feel after experiencing traumatic events (abuse, violence, accident, exploitation, death...). Unwanted, engulfing, and constant emotions flood the hearts of those who have experienced trauma. Each of these emotions can be crushing, but when you experience a combination of these feelings simultaneously, it can be overpowering and devastating. That's why so many become angry or depressed, shut down their feelings, or develop unhealthy coping strategies. Below is a list of emotions victims of trauma often experience after the event takes place.

■ Guilt

The victim may have taken responsibility for what happened, blaming themselves. Whether directly told that they were to blame or feeling self-imposed guilt, the victim incorrectly believes they are at fault for the abuse. Thus, guilt floods the heart.

> *"I always believed it was my fault."*

> *"I think my guilt has been the root belief that led to many of my problems."*

■ Fear

The person may experience fear of bodily harm, fear of the loss of the affection, fear of the possibility of a broken home, fear of the future, fear for their life, fear of loneliness, fear of the abuse being disclosed, or fear of the abuse not being disclosed. While safety and fear of physical harm are common, the majority of fears generally focus on emotional and relational concerns.

> *"I was more afraid of what others thought of me than of what happened."*

> *"Fear of being hurt, fear of others finding out, fear of rejection. I had a lot of fears."*

■ Anger

While anger at the person(s) who caused a trauma are understandable, much of the victim's anger, however, is often misfocused onto themselves. Anger at the perpetrator, anger at those who didn't protect him/her, anger at God (or fate, or karma) might be present, but self-anger is most common.

> *"I remember hating myself and wishing that I'd die. I was so mad at myself."*

> *"The anger was eating me up inside because I kept it there and didn't let it out."*

▮ Shame

Shame has been defined as humiliating disgrace. It implies that the person is not only to blame for doing something wrong, but that what happened was disgusting and offensive. Unfortunately, many traumatized people, especially of interpersonal abuse and violence, not only feel guilty, they also feel that they are worthless, shameful, and despicable.

"I felt completely worthless, a nobody."

"Guilt and shame have been my companions for many, many years."

▮ Powerless/Helpless

Unpredictable, unwanted, unexpected trauma events often cause victims to realize their inability to control life's circumstances. They begin to feel powerless and out of control, which can lead to helplessness.

"The harder I tried, the worse it got."

"Nothing can help. It's hopeless."

▮ Confused/Overwhelmed

Feeling confused and overwhelmed is also very common among trauma victims. Uncertainty, doubts, questions, suspicions, and mistrust are accompanied by caution, fear, hypervigilance, and a feeling of impending gloom.

"There was always so much going on in my head. It felt chaotic."

"It was like I was living in a fog, unable to see clearly what was going on and always feeling stressed out."

▮ Depression and Loneliness

Profound sadness, fatigue, loss of energy, lack of enjoyment, apathy, difficulty concentrating, eating and sleep problems, hopelessness, low self-esteem (feelings of worthlessness), and suicidal thoughts are all common symptoms of depression. It has been referred to as anger turned inward, and it plagues most abuse victims.

"I cried a lot when I was alone. I felt that no one cared or understood me or what was going on."

"Being in bed alone at night was the hardest for me. The sadness and loneliness overwhelmed me."

"I think my depression was rooted in my low self-esteem. I felt like a nobody."

▮ Betrayal

Many victims of interpersonal trauma experience profound betrayal by their perpetrator, especially if they had a close relationship. Some refer to this as betrayal trauma because it deeply alters your worldview, beliefs about trust, relationships, love, kindness, safety, and more. The person feels betrayed, not only by the offender, but also by your own natural human longings for closeness, nurturance, and affection.

"I loved him and I trusted him—and he betrayed me. That hurts so deeply."

"I still want to think that all the abuse was a big mistake; that he really is good."

79 COMMON FEELINGS (3)

Age	All	Setting	Group	Trauma Recovery	Feeling

Purpose	To present feelings common to trauma victims in order to normalize and validate the emotional response to their experience.
Overview	The individual describes or defines, in their own words, some of the common emotions experienced by the traumatized, providing examples if possible.

Approximate Time	15 minutes

Supplies Needed	Blank paper and pen

■ Activity Explained

⮑   The facilitator explains that there are many emotions that people feel when they experience traumatic events.

⮑   The facilitator lists the common feelings people often feel after a traumatic experience.

⮑   The facilitator asks individuals to explain, define, or describe each of these common feelings in their own words.

■ Reflection

Can you think of other common emotions that victims of abuse and trauma might feel?

■ Variations

Activity may be verbal or written. Activity may be used individually or in groups.

■ Concerns

Individuals may need help identifying or writing down feelings. Some feelings may be triggering to individuals, so proceed with caution. Please remember that the focus is on reviewing common emotions from an informational perspective. We do not ask the person to share personally about their own trauma experiences until we come to the Sharing section.

COMMON FEELINGS

There are many emotions people feel after experiencing traumatic events (abuse, violence, accident, exploitation, death...). Each of these emotions can be crushing, but when you experience a combination of these feelings simultaneously, it can be overpowering and devastating. That's why so many become angry or depressed, shut down their feelings, or develop unhealthy coping strategies. Below is a list of emotions victims of trauma often experience after the event takes place. How would you describe, define, or explain each of these common victim emotions?

Guilt

_____

Fear

_____

Anger

_____

Shame

_____

Powerless/Helpless

_____

Confused/Overwhelmed

_____

Depression and Loneliness

_____

Betrayal

_____

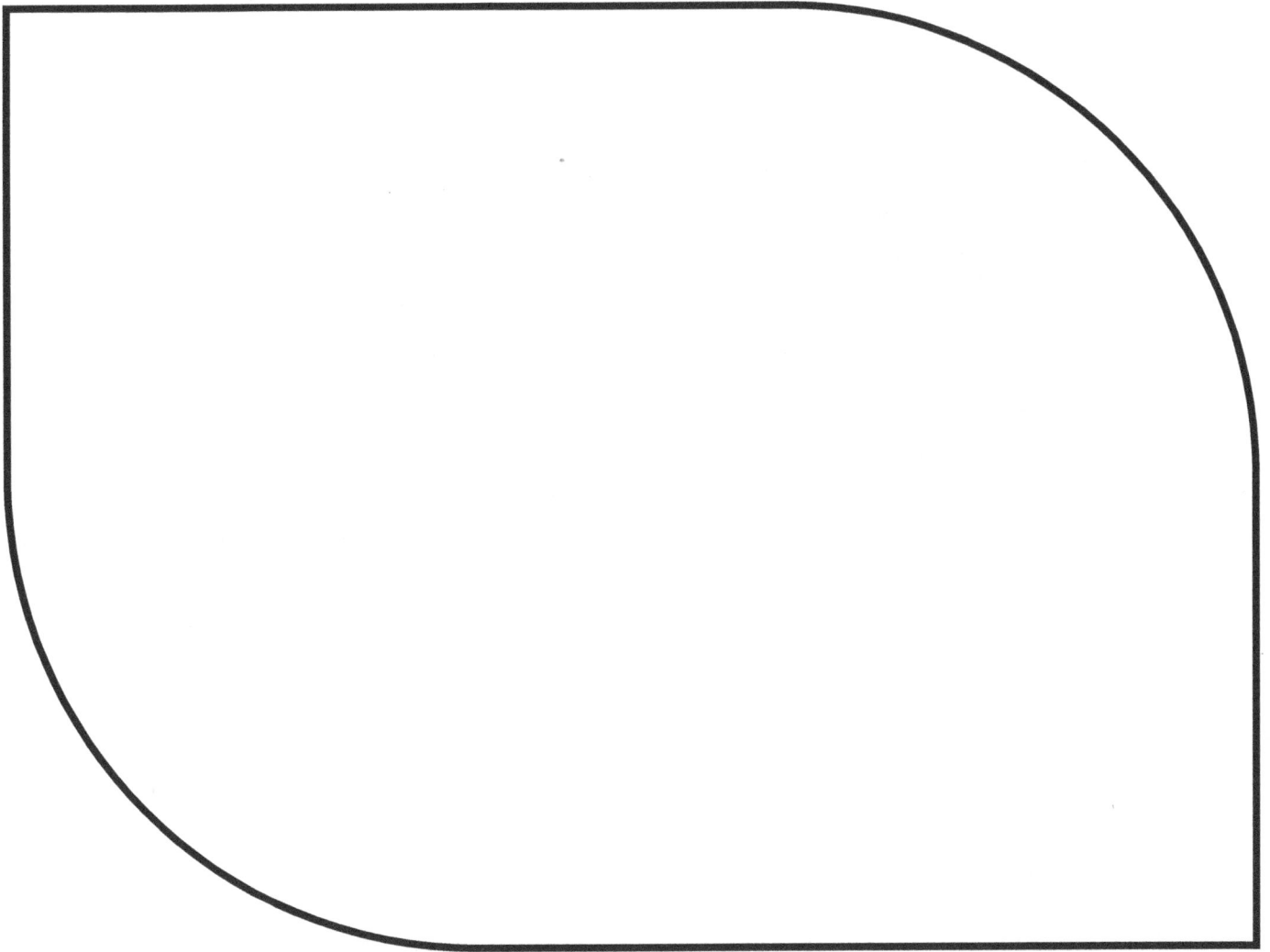

STEP 4

THINKING

THINKING

■ OVERALL GOAL

- ➲ To identify the difference between thoughts and feelings
- ➲ To acknowledge the existence of inner thoughts
- ➲ To understand the relationship between thoughts, feelings, and behavior
- ➲ To expose wrong (inaccurate, unhealthy) thoughts and how to correct/replace them

■ OVERVIEW

Understanding the difference and relationship between thoughts, feelings and behaviors greatly helps individuals in the process of overcoming trauma's negative effects. Recognizing one's negative, often repeated, inner thoughts and combating the inaccurate and harmful thinking, provides needed insight and help in overcoming these intrusive thoughts.

During this step, we want the person to:

DISTINGUISH between feelings and thoughts, identifying and clarifying the difference between them.

Examples of activities:

What would you THINK if _____ (event) happened?

What might a person FEEL if _____ (event) happened?)

UNDERSTAND the relationship between Thoughts – Feelings – Behavior (the Cognitive Triangle).

What we think affects how we feel and influences how we behave.

Example: If I think, *It's my fault*, I would probably feel guilty and angry at myself. Then, I might start taking drugs (behavior) to deaden the pain of the guilt.

RECOGNIZE the existence of our inner thoughts (our internal self-messages or inner dialog).

Examples of activities:

Make drawings with thought bubbles (like those used with cartoon characters) and write in what the person might be thinking given various scenarios.

IDENTIFY wrong, inaccurate, harmful thinking. Make a list of common inner self-messages (refer to the activity named *The Lies*). Then ask questions about their accuracy and helpfulness.

Examples of Harmful Thinking (cognitive distortions) include:

- ➲ *I will always be this way.*
- ➲ *I will never trust anyone again.*
- ➲ *Everything will forever be bad for me.*
- ➲ *It's either good or bad, yes or no, there's nothing in-between.*
- ➲ *All the world and all people are scary.*
- ➲ *Everything is my fault.*
- ➲ *I'll never be normal.*
- ➲ *I should have been able to stop it.*

- ➲ *I should have known better.*
- ➲ *I can't trust anyone again.*
- ➲ *I'll never be safe again.*
- ➲ *My life is destroyed.*
- ➲ *I've destroyed my family.*
- ➲ *I'll never get over this.*
- ➲ *The world will always be unsafe.*

Ask: Does that thought make you (or, an individual) feel good or sad/bad? Does it help or harm you? Do you like or dislike the thought? Is it true, accurate, and helpful? Or, is it false, negative, and harmful? How do you know?

Unhealthy perspectives should also be identified and discuss, and may include:

- ➲ Guilt, self-blame and personal responsibility
- ➲ Shame and negative attributes
- ➲ Inability to trust (individuals or anyone)
- ➲ Assumptions regarding the causes of or reasons for the trauma events
- ➲ Assumptions regarding offender motives, thoughts, beliefs, and feelings
- ➲ Negative self-beliefs and perceptions
- ➲ Assumptions regarding others' thoughts, feelings, and beliefs

CORRECT harmful thinking by generating alternative thoughts that are more helpful and accurate. Take the list of unhealthy thoughts and replace them with helpful ones.

Examples: For every negative thought, let's make a list of what you (a person) could think instead. What could you (a person) tell yourself instead of "I am stupid"?

IDENTIFY various positive words, phrases, or statements the person can use, think, and repeat in order to combat negative thoughts. Words such as *peace, rest, strength, courage, and love* might be chosen to repeat in one's head or phrases such as, *"I can do this"* or *"I will try and not give up,"* or *"If I'm scared, I know what to do."*

THINKING

■ Goals

➲ To identify the difference between thoughts and feelings

➲ To acknowledge the existence of inner thoughts

➲ To understand the relationship between thoughts, feelings, and behavior

➲ To expose wrong (inaccurate/unhealthy) thoughts and correct/replace them

Name		Program Location	

Tasks (some optional, depending on person/situation)	Date Completed	Notes
Explain the difference between "thoughts" and "feelings" (giving examples, using matching game, thought bubbles, stories...)		
Present the thinking process, including: ➲ That we have inner thoughts (internal dialog) ➲ What we think: positive vs negative thoughts ➲ What influences what we think? (experiences)		
Increase awareness by asking: What might a person be thinking when _____ happens? or What might people be thinking if they are feeling _____?		
Teach the Cognitive Triangle: How our Thoughts affect our Feelings, which lead to our Behavior (give examples, practice, discuss options, and role play)		
Review common inaccurate/harmful thinking		
Identify ways to respond to negative internal messages with accurate/helpful thoughts		
Other:		

Note: If asking, "What might *you* think (feel or do) if _____ happened?" the scenarios should address every day, general situations and not trauma-related topics. If the person is hesitant or unwilling to respond when asked personally, ask in a general way, "What might *a person* think (feel or do) if _____ happens?"

80 MATCHING THOUGHTS AND FEELINGS 1

Age	All	Setting	Group	Trauma Recovery	Thinking

Purpose	To help distinguish between thoughts and feelings and to identify the feelings associated with various thoughts.
Overview	Using thought statements, the individual chooses corresponding emotions.

Approximate Time	5-10 minutes		Supplies Needed	Worksheet and pen

■ Activity Explained

➲ The facilitator instructs, *"What we think and what we feel are two different things, though related. In fact, what we think about something will affect how we feel about it. In this activity you will be asked to identify what emotion people have with certain thoughts. You will be asked to match which thoughts you think go with which feelings."*

➲ The facilitator may give the copied worksheet to the individual to complete or may choose to read each statement verbally. Additional thoughts could be added.

■ Reflection

Did you learn anything new about thoughts and emotions today? If so, what?

■ Variations

Activity may be verbal or written. Activity may be used individually or in groups.

If reading or language is difficult, sustained attention may be challenging. With young children, faces or caricatures could be used to depict the various emotions. The facilitator should read or make a statement, then ask the individual to point to the face he/she believes best depicts the emotion that accompanies the statement.

■ Concerns

Activity may need to be tailored to be more age and culturally appropriate.

MATCHING THOUGHTS AND FEELINGS

Here is a list of various THOUGHTS and FEELINGS. Match the thoughts with the feelings by placing the Feelings letter (on the right) next to the line in front of the Thoughts (on the left). You can use some of the Feelings more than once or not at all.

	Thoughts	Feelings
	I'm so stupid.	A. Proud
	I am good at music.	B. Sad
	I can't do anything right.	C. Embarrassed
	People don't treat me right.	D. Happy
	The teacher doesn't like me.	E. Bored
	I get picked first for soccer.	F. Angry
	I wish school was more enjoyable.	G. Shy
	I don't like meeting new people in public.	H. Ashamed
	I feel awkward or clumsy.	I. Surprised
	I don't like talking in front of people.	J. Anxious
	I like myself.	K. Jealous
	I wish I was taller.	
	My birthday party was unexpected.	
	She did better than me.	
	He shouldn't have done that to me!	
	Add More Thoughts	**Feelings**

81 WHAT I THINK WHEN...

Age	All	Setting	Group	Trauma Recovery	Thinking

Purpose	To identify how our emotions influence our actions.
Overview	Individuals will answer prompts about what they are thinking when they take certain actions, such as hitting or saying mean things to others.

Approximate Time	10 minutes

Supplies Needed	Worksheet and pen

■ Activity Explained

- ○ The facilitator should give an example of what they are thinking when they perform a certain action, such as, *I go for a walk when I think... that the weather looks good, or I give presents to people when I think... that they would really love something.*
- ○ The facilitator might need to assist the person in completing the first few questions on the worksheet.
- ○ The individual should fill out the worksheet, writing what their thoughts are when they take certain actions.

■ Reflection

How does our thinking help us decide what we will do? Do we ever do something without thinking about it first? What have you learned about thoughts and actions, and their relationship to each other?

■ Variations

Activity may be used verbally or written, individually or in a group setting.

■ Concerns

The worksheet may need to be adapted according to age, culture, and setting since all of the prompts may not be applicable to everyone (i.e. siblings, school, homework, etc.).

WHAT I DO WHEN I THINK...

I find a place to be alone when I think

I don't do my homework when I think

I act silly when I think

I hit my brother/sister when I think

I share my things with friends when I think

I say mean things to others when I think

I brag about things I can do when I think

I disrupt others in class/groups when I think

I give presents to people when I think

I tell other kids that I don't want to be their friend when I think

I take extra cookies or food when I think

I say things that aren't true when I think

I go for a walk when I think

I crawl in bed and get under the blankets when I think

I like to listen to music and sing out loud when I think

I argue with my mom/dad when I think

I cut school when I think

I gossip about people when I think

I run away when I think

I draw lots of doodles (scribbles) when I think

82 WHAT I WOULD THINK 'IF'

Age	All	Setting	Group	Trauma Recovery	Thinking

Purpose	To identify one's thinking in response to various scenarios.
Overview	Given a list of many different situations, the individual is instructed to share what he/she might think in those circumstances.

Approximate Time	10-20 minutes

Supplies Needed	Worksheet and pen

■ Activity Explained

⊃ Facilitator explains, *"In this activity we want to examine what and how we think. You will be asked to write and/or share what you might THINK (what might be going through your head) during different situations."*

⊃ The individual writes responses for all scenarios. If using the verbal variation, responses are shared aloud one by one.

■ Reflection

What affects our thinking? In what circumstances might your answers change? Was it hard to write what you might THINK instead of what you might FEEL?

■ Variations

Activity may be verbal or written. Activity may be used individually or in groups.

The same exercise is used for identifying emotions. If done together, the difference between thoughts and feelings should be discussed.

■ Concerns

The worksheet may need to be adapted to be more age and culturally appropriate.

WHAT I WOULD THINK IF...

If I was given a surprise birthday party

If I flunked a math test

If a good friend died

If someone tried to kidnap me

If I got the highest score on a test at school

If a dog jumped out of the bushes and growled

If I was accused of doing something wrong that I didn't do

If my friend saw my parent drunk

If I wet my pants

If I was leaving on a trip

If my parents were fighting

. If my mom was crying

If someone touched my private parts

 If no one was around and there was nothing to do

If my friend was missing

If my parents treated my brother/sister better than me

If my cell phone was taken away

If I told a lie and got caught

 If I let someone down and didn't do what I said I would

If I was in a car accident

If I was invited to go to a special event

If the teacher announced the test was cancelled

. If I tried and tried, but couldn't do something

If I fell and was hurt

83 GUESSING THOUGHTS

Age	All	Setting	Group	Trauma Recovery	Thinking

Purpose	To identify possible thoughts based on given expressions.
Overview	Using a variety of pictures or drawings of people's faces, the individual is asked to guess what the person might be thinking. (Refer to *Guessing Feelings* activity under FEELING.)

Approximate Time	10-20 minutes

Supplies Needed	Large blank paper, glue, scissors, pencils, and old magazines or picture books

◼ Activity Explained

- ⊃ The facilitator and individual cut out a variety of faces from old magazines, newspapers, or other sources and makes a collage of the various faces.
- ⊃ The individual shares what the people in the photos/drawing might be thinking, *"What do you think this person might be thinking?"*
- ⊃ The facilitator asks: *"Why do you think the person might be thinking that thought?"*

◼ Reflection

What does it mean to "read someone's mind"? Is it possible? What can happen when we think we know what another person is thinking? Is it easier to guess feels or thoughts? Why?

◼ Variations

Activity may be used individually or in groups. If done in a group, each individual can create his/her own page of faces, or the group can collaboratively make one big collage.

The same exercise with faces/drawings is used for guessing emotions. If done together, the difference between thoughts and feelings is briefly presented.

If preferred, this activity can be done without making a collage. The facilitator could flip through photos, drawings or magazines, stopping at various photos and ask, "What do you think this person might be thinking?"

◼ Concerns

If used in a group setting, monitor participation so that no one controls the activity, other participants, the outcomes, or the discussion.

84 BEFORE AND NOW

Age	All	Setting	Group	Trauma Recovery	Thinking

Purpose	To focus on how our thoughts can change, replacing negative, harmful thoughts with healthier ones.
Overview	The individual fills out the worksheet reflecting on negative thoughts they have had (or currently have) and how they have been (or can be) replaced with better, more positive ones.

Approximate Time	10-20 minutes

Supplies Needed	Worksheet and pen and pencil

■ Activity Explained

⮑ The facilitator explains to the individual that we often believe many negative and harmful thoughts which need to be replaced with healthier, more positive ones. The facilitator shares examples (from the worksheet or personal experience).

⮑ Together, the facilitator and individual(s) make a list of negative thoughts, either from people in general or from their own experience.

⮑ The individual completes the worksheet, which encourages the replacement of negative thoughts and shares/ discusses it with the facilitator.

■ Reflection

Which thoughts were the hardest to change? Which thoughts still need to change? What has helped you replace harmful, negative thoughts with healthier, positive ones?

■ Variations

The worksheet can be filled out individually and brought to session.

Activity may be used individually or in groups. Children can do a modified version of this activity.

■ Concerns

This activity could be done in a *general or a personal way*, inviting personal reflection or asking what negative thoughts *a person* might have and how he/she could think differently. We focus on general negative thinking, however, and not on trauma experiences unless the person chooses to do so.

BEFORE AND NOW

List some of the negative thoughts and beliefs people have and then some new thoughts they could use to replace those harmful ones. If you prefer, you could write down some of the negative thoughts and beliefs that you've had and what they are now (or what they are now and how you'd like them to change.)

Example

Before, I used to think (believe) that I'm ugly.	Now I know (believe or think) that I am pretty in some ways.
Before, I used to think (believe) that:	Now I know (believe or think) that:

If you want to discuss some trauma-related thoughts, add them here.

Example

Before, I used to think (believe) that no one would want to be with me if they knew what happened.	Now I know (believe or think) that I'm not a bad person just because something bad happened to me.
Before, I used to think (believe) that what happened was my fault.	Now I know (believe or think) that the person who used and abused me is the one that's to blame, not me.
Before, I used to think (believe) that:	Now I know (believe or think) that:

85 RESPONSES

Age	All	Setting	Group	Trauma Recovery	Thinking

Purpose	To present information on common, unhealthy responses people have to abuse/trauma.
Overview	The individual learns about victims' possible responses, which may help later during the trauma narrative when the person explains their own responses, thoughts, feelings, and behaviors to what happened.

Approximate Time	15-30 minutes

Supplies Needed	Worksheet and pen and pencil

■ Activity Explained

⮑ The individual learns about various unhelpful responses to abuse as the facilitators presents the information.

■ Reflection

Why and how do people minimize, rationalize, deny, block, recanted, and/or mislabel their abuse? If these are unhealthy responses, what would a healthy one be?

■ Variations

Activity may be verbal or written.

Activity may be used individually or in groups.

■ Concerns

This activity should be discontinued if the individual has a strong emotional reaction to the information, perhaps due to intense guilt and shame.

RESPONSES TO ABUSE

Those who have experienced a trauma, such as abuse or exploitation, often develop many unhealthy responses.

Here are some examples of how people respond:

- ⮑ I *minimized* the abuse. I told myself, "It wasn't that bad." "It was only a few times." "It wasn't full intercourse."
- ⮑ I *rationalized* the abuse. I told myself, "My dad was lonely." "My mom was stressed out." "We were poor."
- ⮑ I tended to *deny* that the abuse really happened. I told myself, "You made it up." "It didn't really happen, you just imagined it." "You remember it wrong."
- ⮑ I *blocked* the abuse from my memory. I forgot that it happened or dissociated.
- ⮑ I told someone about the abuse, but then took it back (*recanted*), saying, "I made it up" because I didn't like what happened after telling them about it.
- ⮑ I *mislabeled* the abuse, thinking it was "just strict discipline," or "just being overly affectionate" rather than admitting it was abuse.

Notes

Minimized	
Rationalized	
Denied	
Blocked	
Recanted	
Mislabeled	

86 COGNITIVE TRIANGLE

Age	All	Setting	Group	Trauma Recovery	Thinking

Purpose	To understand the connection between thoughts, feelings, and behavior.
Overview	Individual will go through generic and personal scenarios to understand how their thoughts can affect how they feel and behave.

Approximate Time	30-60 minutes

Supplies Needed	Cognitive Triangle visual, whiteboard/ blackboard, pen/pencil and paper

■ Activity Explained

⮕ The facilitator introduces the Cognitive Triangle by writing thoughts at the top of a triangle, feelings in the bottom right, and behaviors in the bottom left with Thoughts ▸ Feelings ▸ Behavior. The facilitator explains that our thoughts, feelings, and behaviors are all connected, and that they will use scenarios to explore the relationship between them.

⮕ The facilitator first uses a generic example of walking down the street and approaching a friend. The facilitator asks the individual to answer questions about the scenario as he/she reads it, using *negative* thoughts, feelings, and behaviors.

I was walking down the street and saw a friend walking my way. I said, "Hello" and they didn't respond. What do you think I thought when my friend didn't say hello to me? (pause for responses*). How would thinking that make me feel? (pause for response**). So, if I felt _____, how would I behave the next time I saw that friend? (pause for response***) In this example, because my friend didn't say hello to me, I thought____, which made me feel____, so I behaved by doing _____.

*Possible scenarios might include that the person is: rude, distracted, hurting, angry, or mad at me.

** Possible feelings might include hurt, angry, concerned, frustrated, and worried.

*** Possible behaviors might include walk on by and ignore them, stop and talk, yell in anger, hit...

⮕ The facilitator goes through the scenario again, but this time the individual will fill in the thoughts, feelings, and behaviors with *positive* responses.

Now let's walk through that example again, but with a different thought. What if I was walking down the street and saw a friend coming my way and said, "Hello," but they didn't say anything back. Instead of thinking they are angry with me or that they are a mean person, what if I thought something might be wrong or they might be going through a hard situation, and because of that I felt concerned and empathetic towards them? With this new feeling, do you think I would behave differently? (pause for response) I might ask my friend how they are doing the next time I see them or ask if I can do anything to help instead of being angry or sad that they didn't greet me.

➲ The individual thinks of an example from their life of something that happened, what they thought about it (what they told themselves), and how that thought affected their feelings and behavior. The individual writes the situation in the middle of the triangle and then fills out what they thought, how they felt, and what behavior resulted.

➲ The individual then uses the same personal scenario but replaces their original thought with a different thought and indicates how that would change how they felt and how they behaved.

➲ The facilitator reviews the Cognitive Triangle and discusses that our thoughts affect our feelings, which affect our behavior, and that by changing how we think about a situation, we can change how we feel and behave towards it.

■ Reflection

What scenario did you use? What were your original thoughts, feelings, and behavior? What did you change your thought to? How did that affect your feelings and behavior? How might you use this diagram to help you in the future? What was helpful about this activity? What did you learn or like?

■ Variations

Activity may be completed individually or in groups.

The individuals can draw the cognitive triangle themselves to take with them.

If possible, it is helpful if the facilitator can act out the scenario with the individual.

If preferred, the facilitator can create their own scenarios or use a scenario from the individual's life.

■ Concerns

The facilitator should explain that everyone has negative thoughts, but most important is how we let those thoughts affect our feelings, behaviors, and relationships with others.

■ Story

I get it now. What I think about something that's happened is what determines how I act. My problem is that I've always thought the worse about things. Now that I'm aware, I hope to change my negative thinking. I realize that I've created a lot of problems by my own negative thoughts and beliefs.

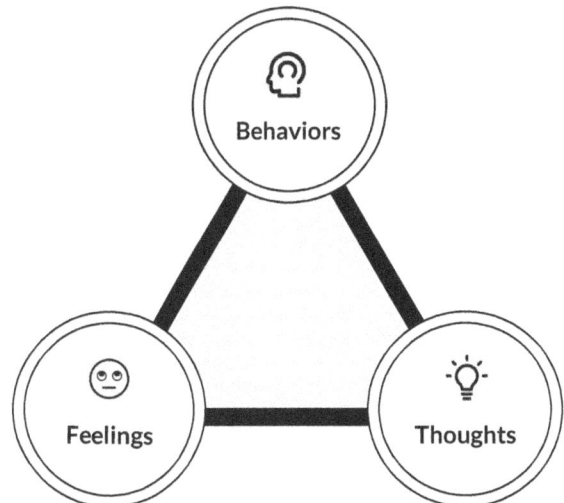

87 THOUGHTS, FEELINGS AND BEHAVIORS (IDENTIFICATION)

Age	All	Setting	Group	Trauma Recovery	Thinking

Purpose	To understand the difference between thoughts, feelings, and behaviors, as well as body language.
Overview	Individuals are given a list of words to label as either thoughts, feelings, or behaviors.

Approximate Time	5-10 minutes	**Supplies Needed**	Worksheet and pen

■ Activity Explained

- ➲ The facilitator explains the difference between thoughts, feelings, and behaviors to the individual or group.
- ➲ The individual writes a "T" next to words on their sheet that are THOUGHTS, write an "F" next to the words they think are FEELINGS, and write a "B" next to the words that are BEHAVIORS.

■ Reflection

How did you decide which words were what? Which words were "obvious," and which were more difficult to determine? Let's think of more examples and add them to the list.

■ Variations

Activity may be used individually or in groups.

Activity may be verbal or written. If activity is conducted verbally, the facilitator should say a word and have the individual or group decide what category it belongs in (thoughts, feelings, or behaviors).

■ Concerns

If needed, the facilitator can do the first few along with the individual or group to aid in understanding.

THOUGHTS - FEELINGS - BEHAVIORS (IDENTIFICATION) WORKSHEET

What is the difference between thoughts, feelings, and behaviors?

Thoughts are what are in our head. What we think about something, such as "I don't like that."

Feelings are in our heart. How we feel about something, such as "I'm mad."

Behaviors are what we do. How we behave or act on our thoughts and feelings, such as take a walk.

- ➪ Put a T next to words that are THOUGHTS.
- ➪ Put a F next to the words that are FEELINGS.
- ➪ Put B next to the words that are BEHAVIORS.

	Happy		Afraid
	Walking		Brave
	I am hungry		Talking to someone
	He likes to eat		Excited
	Sad		Safe
	Scared		Scream
	Drawing		Embarrassed
	She's my friend		Sing
	Angry		Bored
	Reading		Why did I?
	I am short		I wish I could
	Pushing		Sleep
	Hitting		Kick the ball
	He's mad at her		Get dressed
	Crying		Brush my teeth
	Lonely		Curious
	Playing		Nervous
	Anxious (worried)		Confident
	I am to blame		I am smart
	It's my fault		Smiling

Add your own examples:

88 THOUGHTS – FEELINGS – BEHAVIORS (PRACTICE)

Age	All	Setting	Group	Trauma Recovery	Thinking

Purpose	To understand the difference between thoughts, feelings, and behaviors.
Overview	Individuals are given images and asked to identify possible thoughts, feelings, and behaviors for them.

Approximate Time	10-15 minutes

Supplies Needed	Worksheet and pen

■ Activity Explained

➲ The facilitator explains the difference between thoughts, feelings, and behaviors, and then shows the worksheet pictures, indicating which image represents each of those.

➲ The individual is then asked to write possible thoughts, feelings, and behaviors that might accompany each picture on the left. If time allows, encourage the person to write both a negative and a positive example.

■ Reflection

How did you decide what the person in the picture might be thinking, feeling, and what they might do? Which were easier and which were more difficult to guess?

For children, as with youth and adults, it is important to provide opportunities for personal application with such questions as *What can you do differently next time you are thinking bad things about yourself or others? How might this help next time you have a negative thought?*

■ Variations

Activity may be used individually or in groups. If in groups, the facilitator should show the images to the whole group. Activity may be verbal or written.

Encourage doing the activity several times with various possible thoughts leading to different feelings and behaviors. Thoughts ▸ Feelings ▸ Behavior

■ Concerns

Remind participant(s) that there are no right or wrong answers.

THOUGHTS – FEELINGS – BEHAVIORS (PRACTICE) WORKSHEET

On the right side are three pictures which represent our Thoughts, Feelings and Behaviors. Write what you think the person in the picture on the left might be thinking, feeling and what they might do (how they might behave). If you want, you could do it two times for each picture, giving a positive and then a negative example.

If you experienced: _____ *(describe each picture on the left),* **what might you THINK, FEEL and DO?**

(For example: I might describe the first drawing as "Didn't get what I wanted", then I might write THINK: "No one listens to me!", FEEL: angry, hurt and rejected, DO: go throw rocks in the pond OR go tell a safe friend or adult.)

Think _____

_____

Feel _____

_____

Do _____

_____

Think _____

_____

Feel _____

_____

Do _____

_____

Think _____

_____

Feel _____

_____

Do _____

_____

89 BAD THOUGHTS – GOOD THOUGHTS

Age	All	Setting	Group	Trauma Recovery	Thinking

Purpose	To identify both good and bad thoughts we have about ourselves.
Overview	Given a list of possible negative and positive statements about oneself, the individual is instructed to indicate which ones he/she currently thinks or has thought in the past.

Approximate Time	5-10 minutes	**Supplies Needed**	Worksheet and pen

■ Activity Explained

- ⊃ The facilitator explains that we often think bad thoughts about ourselves, but that we should try to replace them with more positive, helpful ones.
- ⊃ Facilitator gives the person the worksheet and asks the person to put a check next to those statements they've thought about themselves, either now or in the past.
- ⊃ The facilitator discusses the responses with the individual, seeking to elicit additional insightful information about his/her thought processes and any patterns (i.e. mostly all negative or mostly negative in one particular section.)

■ Reflection

Were most of your responses positive or negative? Were most of your negative/positive thoughts in a specific section (self, looks, past)? What, if anything, did you learn about yourself from doing this activity? What have you learned about replacing negative thoughts with positive ones? How do you feel about your thoughts/responses?

■ Variations

Activity may be used individually or in groups.

If the facilitator determines that the individual/group is ready, ask them to think of more examples of statements under each section.

■ Concerns

It may be triggering to talk in-depth about the negative thoughts. The facilitator should be encouraging throughout the entire activity. If most answers are negative, future sessions should address how to increase positive self-talk and perspectives.

BAD THOUGHTS/GOOD THOUGHTS WORKSHEET

▌Here is a list of the "BAD" things I tell myself:

About My Abilities
- ❑ I can't do anything very well.
- ❑ I'm not very smart.
- ❑ I'm not as good as other people.
- ❑ I'm clumsy.
- ❑ _____

About My Looks
- ❑ I'm not good looking.
- ❑ I look funny.
- ❑ I'm fat.
- ❑ I'm too skinny.
- ❑ I have big ears/nose.
- ❑ _____
- ❑ _____

About My Past and Future
- ❑ I'll never get over this.
- ❑ It was my fault.
- ❑ I'm no good.
- ❑ I'm stupid.
- ❑ My future is ruined.
- ❑ There's no hope for the future.
- ❑ _____
- ❑ _____

▌Here is a list of the "GOOD" things I tell myself:

About My Abilities
- ❑ I can do some things well.
- ❑ I'm smart.
- ❑ I can figure things out.
- ❑ I'm good at _____
- ❑ _____

About My Looks
- ❑ I'm not bad looking.
- ❑ I look okay.
- ❑ I'm just right.
- ❑ I'm pretty.
- ❑ I have a nice smile.
- ❑ _____
- ❑ _____

About My Past and Future
- ❑ I'll get over this.
- ❑ It wasn't my fault.
- ❑ I'm a good person.
- ❑ I'm going to survive and thrive.
- ❑ My future is open to possibilities.
- ❑ I have hope for the future.
- ❑ _____
- ❑ _____

90 WRONG THINKING: ABUSE SCENARIOS

Age	All	Setting	Group	Trauma Recovery	Thinking

Purpose	To identify unhealthy thinking and discuss ways to address it.
Overview	Various scenarios are given that include examples of unhealthy thinking (related to abuse), which are to be identified and labeled, followed by a discussion of ways to combat these negative thoughts.

Approximate Time	15-20 minutes	**Supplies Needed**	List of scenarios (or develop a list using different trauma situations common to your setting)

■ Activity Explained

➲ The facilitator or participant(s) take turns expressively reading various scenarios or statements. After each one, discuss how to help the person (in the scenario) change his/her wrong thinking of self-blame, distrust, shame, etc., to more a healthy perspective.

➲ The facilitator presents information on "wrong thinking."

Unhealthy Perspectives are often related to:

- ■ Blame and responsibility—*It's my fault.*

- ■ Shame and stigma—*I am a bad person.*

- ■ Changes in trust/generalization of mistrust—*I can't trust anyone ever again.*

- ■ Assumptions regarding the causes, the offender, or trauma events—*He was lonely. My outfit caused it. Bad things always happen to me.*

- ■ Negative self-perceptions (body image, value, personal safety, etc.)—*I'm ugly, worthless, and unsafe.*

➲ Now, the facilitator takes the participant(s) back to each scenario to discuss which of the above unhealthy perspectives are used. Ask questions such as *What did the person believe in this story? What were they thinking? Feeling? What was their unhealthy perspective?*

■ Reflection

If appropriate and not re-traumatizing (and if the person or group is willing), allow them to discuss their own examples of wrong thinking. The leader could ask: *What are some examples of your own unhealthy thoughts? Do you identify with any of the scenarios/statements we read? Which of the list of unhealthy perspectives do you do?*

■ Variations

Activity may be used individually or in groups.

■ Concerns

Since this activity is abuse focused, it may not be appropriate for many because it might be too painful or re-traumatizing. Be aware that discussing personal examples may also be too difficult for some. If so, keep the discussion and examples at a *general*, not *personal* level.

WRONG THINKING: ABUSE SCENARIOS WORKSHEET

The counselor, group facilitator, or participant(s) may choose to take turns reading or acting out the following scenarios. Afterward, ask questions and discuss how to help the person (in the scenario) change his/her wrong thinking of self-blame, distrust, shame, etc., to healthier perspectives.

- ⮑ It's all my fault. Jimmy and I have been going out now for about three months. I told him I wasn't ready for sex, but he kept pressuring me. Last Friday, after we'd gone to the movie with some friends, he took me home, but stopped by the park first, saying he wanted to go for a walk. When we got near this area behind some rocks, he pushed me down and forced me to have sex with him. I asked him to stop, but he just ignored me. I felt horrible. I shouldn't have gone to the movies. I shouldn't have worn a skirt that night. I should have yelled louder. I should have fought harder. It's all my fault.

- ⮑ When that dirty old man touched me where he shouldn't have, I should have screamed. But I froze, not knowing what to do. I should have told Mom. But I didn't want to tell anyone because it was my fault for going to the store without permission.

- ⮑ Everything always goes wrong with me. I can't seem to do anything right. He's been abusing me every week since I can remember. Every time I hope it won't happen again, but it does. It seems that I'm jinxed. If something bad is going to happen, it'll happen to me.

- ⮑ I ruined my family because I told about what was happening. I kept it in for so long, but I just couldn't take it anymore. Now, I've destroyed my family.

- ⮑ I'll never get over this. I'll never be normal again. My life is destroyed.

- ⮑ After what happened to me, I know I can't trust anyone ever again. NO ONE!

- ⮑ There must have been something I could have done to stop what was happening. Maybe I wasn't smart enough to figure it out. I should have known better.

- ⮑ It's so horrible, disgusting, filthy, nauseating, and repulsive. I can't tell anyone about it.

Now, go back to each scenario and write which of the above unhealthy perspectives are being used.

Examples of Unhelpful Thinking *(negative thoughts or cognitive distortions)*

"I should have been able to stop it."

"I should have known better."

"I can't trust anyone again."

"I'll never to safe again."

"My life is destroyed."

"I've destroyed my family."

"I'll never get over this."

"The world is unsafe."

"I'll never be normal.

91 COMBATING NEGATIVE SELF-TALK

Age	All	Setting	Group	Trauma Recovery	Thinking

Purpose	To stop negative self-talk by identifying unhealthy thoughts and replacing them with positive thoughts.
Overview	The person creates a list of negative thoughts and combats them with healthier thoughts.

Approximate Time	15-30 minutes

Supplies Needed	Worksheet or blank paper and pen

Activity Explained

- The individual makes a list of negative thoughts (if needed, refer to The Lies activity)
- The individual then generates a list of positive thoughts to replace each of the negative thoughts (with the help of the facilitator, if needed).
- The facilitator and individual discuss strategies to replace the negative thoughts with the new, healthier ones.

Reflection

Which of these thoughts might be the most challenging to replace? What might you do to increase the chances that you will actually replace the negative thoughts with the positive ones when they come to mind?

Variations

Activity may be combined with the Before and Now activity to identify which thoughts have been replaced and which the individual is still working on replacing or has difficulty believing.

For children, simplify the words and explanations. Make sure words are developmentally, culturally, and contextually appropriate.

Concerns

If the person struggles to identify negative thoughts, refer to the activity "The Lies" for an extensive list of examples. The negative thoughts can be about anything and are not just related to trauma experiences.

COMBATTING NEGATIVE SELF-TALK

Our negative thoughts, which are generally distorted and incorrect, need to be corrected. The more we allow them room in our thinking, the more ingrained they become. First, we need to identify and expose them. It's difficult to fight against an unknown enemy, so let's make a list of our many negative, internal messages.

After exposing the unhelpful thoughts, we need to identify healthier ones. When we realize we are thinking the negative self-thoughts, we must immediately remind ourselves to repeat the more helpful ones.

For this exercise, write down what negative thoughts you often have about yourself and your life, then write what you should tell yourself in order to fight those hurtful thoughts.

Negative Thoughts About Myself and My Life	Better Thoughts About Myself and My Life

92 EIGHT NEGATIVE THINKING HABITS

Age	Youth & Adults	Setting	Group	Trauma Recovery	Thinking

Purpose	To educate the individual on negative thinking patterns and have them identify which they use/have used.
Overview	The facilitator will teach the individual/group about negative thought patterns and invite students to identify the ones they use most often.

Approximate Time	15-30 minutes	**Supplies Needed**	Information sheet for the facilitator

Activity Explained

- ➲ The facilitator presents information on the Eight Negative Thinking Habits, explaining, and giving examples.
- ➲ The facilitator asks the individual which habits they use most, giving personal examples.
- ➲ The facilitator reminds the individual that the first step to correcting negative thinking habits is to be aware that they exist. Other activities focus on Good Thinking Habits and also on Thought Replacement.

Reflection

Do you have any questions about the Eight Negative Thinking Habits? Which ones do you use most? Why do you think you use that particular thought pattern? What feelings do the different thought patterns trigger? What have you learned through this?

Variations

Activity may be used individually or in groups. The group/individuals may verbally share their own thought patterns but are allowed to pass (not share) if desired. Copies of the information could be given to participant(s) or simply read aloud by the facilitator.

Activity may be verbal or written. The facilitator may teach the individual or group about the Eight Negative Thinking Habits verbally, by having individual/group read them, or by using extra materials (poster, whiteboard, etc.) to teach.

Concerns

Some individuals may need assistance understanding and recognizing their own thought patterns.

EIGHT NEGATIVE THINKING HABITS

1.   Categorizing and Labeling

Every time I make a mistake, I tell myself I'm stupid. When I forget something, I'm a horrible person. I have all sorts of negative words and labels for myself.

2.   Everything Always

Everything will always be bad. Life is hard and harder and that's the way it is.

3.   No-Gray Areas

It's either "yes" or "no," there's no in-between. It has to be "this" or "that," there's no flexibility. Even if I make a little mistake, that's it, I'm a total failure.

4.   Tragedy Thinking

The worst possible thing that could happen is going to happen. Everything will be terrible, horrible, and a disaster.

5.   Mind Reading

I know what everyone is thinking. Why bother trying anything new, everyone thinks I'm a loser*, so it won't work. (*to blame, stupid, weak, ugly...)

6.   Contrary Thinking

What you're saying makes sense BUT... That might work BUT...

When someone give a compliment or says something encouraging, I'm thinking about all the ways it's not true or worse, what negative motives they have for saying something nice to me.

7.   Assuming the (Negative) Outcome

I know what's going to happen (and it's not going to be good). Nothing can or will work out for me. If I try this new thing, it won't work.

8.   Not Me

Good and positive things only happen to others, not me. I can't expect happy things in life because that doesn't happen to me, only to other people.

The Negative Thinking Patterns I use most are:

93 CHALLENGING NEGATIVE THOUGHTS

Age	Youth & Adults	Setting	Group	Trauma Recovery	Thinking

Purpose	To promote objective thinking by asking questions about the individual's thoughts and beliefs.
Overview	The individual learns three questions to ask about their negative thoughts in order to gain new perspectives.

Approximate Time	20 minutes

Supplies Needed	Worksheet and pen

■ Activity Explained

- ➲ The facilitator explains to the individual that it is important to evaluate reoccurring thoughts by asking ourselves three questions. By doing this, we can gain a new perspective and determine if a thought is positive or negative.
- ➲ The facilitator shares these three questions:

    - ▪ Do I believe _____ (reoccurring self-talk) is true?

    - ▪ If _____ (reoccurring self-talk) is true, what does that mean?

    - ▪ If _____ (reoccurring self-talk) is not true, what (better, healthier thought) should I think instead?

- ➲ The facilitator and individual work through these questions together using a general example (or one of the individual's recurring negative thoughts).,.

■ Reflection

How might you use these questions to challenge your negative thoughts? What thoughts are easier for you to challenge? What thoughts are more difficult to challenge?

■ Variations

This is somewhat similar to *Combating Negative Self-Talk* in which the individual is asked to think of positive responses to combat identified negative thoughts and beliefs.

■ Concerns

The focus is on challenging the individual's thoughts about themselves, not about others.

94 LIES

Age	All	Setting	Group	Trauma Recovery	Thinking

Purpose	To identify negative statements that many victims believe about themselves and their situation.
Overview	A long list of possible negative statements representing unhealthy thinking or wrong beliefs (cognitive distortions) is presented. Participant(s) may/may not choose to personally identify which they have thought.

Approximate Time	10-20 minutes

Supplies Needed	Worksheet and pen

■ Activity Explained

➲ The facilitator explains that after a negative or traumatic event, we often develop negative thoughts and beliefs (cognitive distortions), most of which are lies (not true).

➲ The facilitator and participant(s) generate a list of these "lies" then review the following list together, adding any newly identified lies.

➲ If appropriate, the individual may choose to indicate which "lies" they have personally thought/believed.

■ Reflection

Why do you think people develop these negative thoughts after a horrible event? When did/do you experience these thoughts? What made you think these thoughts? How will you recognize a thought as a lie the next time you think it? How can a person get rid of these lies?

■ Variations

Activity may be done individually or in a group, with participant(s) choosing the amount of personal disclosure they are comfortable sharing.

■ Concerns

The facilitator should clearly indicate that these thoughts are false and unhealthy, as some victims may still question if they are true.

■ Story

When given this list, a support group of exploited women marked how many of these lies they believed. Two of the women checked every one of the lies and the rest of the group marked most of them. Someone commented, *"It's like someone's in my head and knows exactly what I'm thinking."*

THE MANY LIES OF TRAUMA AND VICTIMIZATION

Read this list and check the things you have thought (or still think) about yourself. .

- ❏ I'm worthless.
- ❏ I'm a nobody.
- ❏ I'm a horrible person (a prostitute, liar, thief, addict...).
- ❏ I don't deserve anything good to happen to me.
- ❏ This is as good as it gets.
- ❏ It's all my fault.
- ❏ I can't trust anyone.
- ❏ No one will help or can help.
- ❏ No one cares.
- ❏ I can't do anything right.
- ❏ I chose this life.
- ❏ I can't make any good decisions.
- ❏ I'll never change.
- ❏ God doesn't exist.
- ❏ God is impotent (can't help).
- ❏ God doesn't care (won't help).
- ❏ Life won't or can't get any better.
- ❏ My "pimp" really does love me.
- ❏ My feelings don't matter.
- ❏ Good things won't happen to me.

- ❏ I am to blame.
- ❏ I should have tried harder.
- ❏ I should have known better.
- ❏ I must not let things bother me.
- ❏ I must hide or ignore my feelings.
- ❏ I'll never be good for anything.
- ❏ All I'm good at/for is sex.
- ❏ I've got to take care of others.
- ❏ I can't trust myself.
- ❏ I am a bad person (unworthy, shamed).
- ❏ I'm so stupid.
- ❏ People use and abuse me, even those who say they love or care about me.
- ❏ I must be tough and not let things bother me.
- ❏ Love hurts.
- ❏ This is what I deserve.
- ❏ It's helpless (the situation).
- ❏ I'm helpless.
- ❏ I'm hopeless.
- ❏ This is as good as it gets.
- ❏ This IS my life

Add to the list

- ❏ Other:
- ❏ Other:
- ❏ Other:
- ❏ Other:

95 THOUGHT STOPPING AND REPLACEMENT

Age	All	Setting	Group	Trauma Recovery	Thinking

Purpose	To give individuals tools to stop and replace negative/wrong thinking.
Overview	The facilitator teaches the individual or group about thought stopping and thought replacement methods.

Approximate Time	20 minutes		**Supplies Needed**	None

■ Activity Explained

➲ The facilitator asks the participant(s) to identify and list a variety of negative thoughts (either general ones or from personal experience). The facilitator then explains ways to stop or help control the negative thoughts.

➲ The facilitator asks participant(s) to close their eyes and think a negative thought (preferably general, such as *"I'm stupid"* or *"Most things that go wrong are my fault"*). After approximately 20 seconds, the facilitator claps his/her hands together and yells *STOP!* Repeat this several times using the same or a variety of negative self-talk. The goal is to interrupt the unpleasant thought.

➲ Next, the facilitator gives participant(s) a rubber band to wear on their wrist then asks them to once again identify and focus on a negative thought. Individuals are told to pull and snap the rubber band after 20 seconds or whenever they realize they are dwelling on negative self-talk. Repeat this exercise several times, inviting them to decide when to pull and snap the rubber band.

➲ The facilitator encourages participant(s) to continually practice these two techniques and also to identify any other methods which might help stop negative self-talk from continually intruding on their thinking.

➲ *Once the individual becomes aware of and able to practice Thought Stopping, the facilitator teaches ideas for Thought Replacement. Participant(s) are asked to identify a happy memory, positive thought, pleasant image or to choose an encouraging word or phrase to use to replace the negative thoughts. Individuals should practice the thought stopping techniques again, but this time, immediately focus on what they have chosen to use for their replacement image, place, word, phrase, thought. Utilizing the relaxation activities ("A Peaceful Place" and "My Safe Place") may be beneficial for the thought replacement exercise, as the activities encourage the detailed imagery of calming, positive places.*

Reflection

What do you think will work best for you? Yelling STOP! Or snapping the rubber band? Do you have other ideas to help you re-focus your negative thinking? Why is thought-stopping and thought replacement needed?

Variations

Activity may be used individually or in groups. Thought stopping and thought replacement may be presented separately or together.

Concerns

Those who have a history of self-harm should not use a physical technique for this exercise.

Techniques must be appropriate and beneficial, not harmful, for the individual.

96 POSITIVE THINKING HABITS

Age	All	Setting	Group	Trauma Recovery	Thinking

Purpose	To introduce positive thinking habits as a strategy for combating negative thought patterns.
Overview	The facilitator explains and gives examples of good thinking habits, encouraging the individual to use them.

Approximate Time	10-20 minutes

Supplies Needed	Information sheet (for facilitator)

■ Activity Explained

- ⮞ The facilitator presents and explains the following information on *Positive Thinking Habits*, providing examples.
- ⮞ The facilitator asks the individual to identify which positive thinking habit they use most or are likely to use.
- ⮞ The facilitator reminds the individual that an important step to stopping negative thinking habits is to be aware that they exist and focus on replacing them with positive thinking habits.

■ Reflection

Which habit do you use the most or which habit would you like to use?

■ Variations

This activity may be used individually or in groups.

This activity can be paired with the *Combating Negative Self-Talk* activity and/or the *Before and Now* activity as the person seeks to identify positive or healthy thoughts.

■ Concerns

The content needs to be developmentally and culturally appropriate.

POSITIVE THINKING HABITS

1.   Kind Thinking

Every time I make a mistake, I tell myself I'm learning. When I forget something, I'm normal. I try and be gracious to myself. Instead of using negative words I try to be more kind to myself.

2.   Possibility Thinking

There are possibilities in every aspect of life. Rather than thinking only bad will ever happen, I now know that there are infinite possibilities in life. I choose to focus on the possibilities and not the impossibilities.

3.   Yes – Gray Areas

When I'm tempted to think that everything is either "yes" or "no," and that there's no in-between, I remember that there are a lot of "gray areas" in life. I want to be flexible and adaptable, open to other ideas and options, not just a "black and white" thinker.

4.   Gratitude

When someone gives me a compliment or says something encouraging, instead of thinking it's not true, I say "thank you." I don't try to explain away the positive or disregard it but accept it with gratitude. I want to be thankful for the good and not just focus on the bad in my life.

5.   Hopeful Thinking

I'm hopeful that things will get better. Things can work out for me. If I try this new thing, it might work.

6.   Why Not Me

Good and positive things can happen to me too. I can't expect everything in life to be perfect and great, but I can expect that I'll have some good.

The Positive Thinking Habits I want to use are:

_____

_____

_____

- ✓ **Sharing**
- ✓ **Evaluating**
- ✓ **Sharing Again**
- ✓ **Sharing More**

STEP 5

SHARING

SHARING

■ Overall Goal

⊃ To provide an opportunity for the person to share and process their trauma experiences.

■ Components Of Sharing

Sharing

⊃ The individual shares his/her trauma stories with the facilitator/counselor.

Evaluating

⊃ The facilitator identifies any unhealthy thoughts, feelings, and beliefs and asks questions about them.

⊃ The individual corrects the harmful (maladaptive) thoughts, feelings, and beliefs.

Sharing Again

⊃ The individual shares his/her revised story with a chosen, emotionally safe individual.

Sharing More

⊃ The facilitator enquires about any potential trauma caused by the individual to others and encourages the person to share this as well.

■ Overview

Sharing is possible when there is a safe therapeutic environment to share about one's abuse/trauma experience(s). As the individual shares his/her personal trauma story, it loses its sting and healing progresses more quickly. We help the person integrate their trauma as part of and not the totality of their life's story.

While individuals may tell their story earlier, it may be less therapeutically beneficial because it may be shared incompletely, for shock value, to make the person appear better or worse, or to see how much the listener can handle. It is viewed as less therapeutically helpful when shared before the foundational trauma recovery steps, with the accompanying TRACTs, are completed. Therefore, we do not encourage the sharing of one's story until the previous trauma activities are completed.

When one's story is shared, we want the person to feel safe and comfortable with the counselor and those around them (CARING); to understand the effects of trauma and abuse on people (the normalization and validation of LEARNING-Trauma); to know how to calm oneself when anxious (LEARNING-Relaxation); to be able to understand and have the words to describe feelings and thoughts, and to recognize unhelpful thinking patterns (FEELING and THINKING).

We believe that the telling of one's story after these steps are worked through provides for greater healing from the trauma. Any story shared before this point may be helpful, but is more likely to be incomplete, ill-focused, or unhealthy.

SHARING

Which trauma story to tell when there are multiple?

Many victims have experienced multiple traumas, ongoing trauma, complex trauma, and/or developmental trauma. Victims of human trafficking—especially sexual exploitation and prostitution—have undergone a multiplicity of traumatic events which often includes abuse, violence, deprivation, threats, physical injury, forced abortion, drugs, sexual assault, betrayal, control, and more.

Which of these many traumas does the person share? The first or the last? The least of the worst? The answer is *it depends*, because the person chooses which trauma story to tell.

Victims of multiple traumas sometimes prefer to begin by sharing a smaller, less vulnerable trauma story as an attempt to feel less overwhelmed and more in control. From there, the individual may decide to share an event considered to be more or most traumatic. This is a progressive sharing of trauma.

Others, if ready, willing, and able, might prefer to tell the biggest or most horrible trauma first to *get it over with*. For many, telling the worst negates the need to tell all of the lesser traumatic events experienced. For others, there may be a desire to share several of their different traumatic events—perhaps related to such areas as the initial abuse, the first assault/rape, prostitution/exploitation, violence and torture, having to recruit/abuse someone else, etc.

A victim of sex trafficking (exploitation/prostitution) was asked to list her five worst traumas. They included: her first abuse, a near-death experience, an abortion, a horrible experience, and a beating by her pimp. She was then asked to put them in order of least to most traumatic and to choose where to begin. She chose the least (from the five most traumatic) and shared. She then shared the second least, then jumped to the most terrible.

The individual, not the therapist, identifies and chooses the trauma stories to share. Often the most traumatic event is not what the counselor would assume it to be. That is, a one-time initial betrayal and abuse as a child may be considered the worst trauma even in comparison to sexual exploitation with its ongoing rape, exploitation, assault, and violence.

During the SHARING step, we want to:

PREPARE the person by explaining the importance and benefits of "getting it out," or sharing one's story. If helpful, the facilitator may first read another person's trauma story as an example (with the permission of the survivor whose story it is).

ENCOURAGE the sharing of one's story in a personally chosen format.

Victims may choose to tell their trauma narrative through the following ways:

- Writing
- Music/song
- Sand play
- Story book
- Puppets
- Collage
- Poem
- Drama
- Dance
- Drawing

Sharing will need to be developmentally appropriate for the individual's age and verbal/writing abilities.

REMIND the person to use relaxation skills as needed and that negative thoughts, feelings, and reactions represent the past and not the present.

ASK the person to share his/her story while the facilitator writes it down (like dictation). Tell the person: *As you share, please give me as much information as you can remember. I wasn't there, so please, describe everything to me with as much detail as possible (or comfortable with).*

Have the person repeat their story several times throughout the process of dictation, as that will lessen the extreme emotional and physiological reactions to the event. That is, after writing part of the story, stop and say, *I'd like to read to you what I've written so far, to see if I've gotten it right and to see if there's anything you might want to change or add.* As needed, ask questions about thoughts, perceptions, self-blame, and sights, sounds, smells, colors, weather, and information about people such as ages, eye and hair color, height, weight, clothes, appearance, facial expressions, words, and any other details. It is helpful to repeat this Dictate-Stop-Read-Ask process numerous times during the process of telling one's story.

Helpful questions might include: *Could you tell me more about…? Do you remember when it happened? The date? Time of year? Season? What was the weather like that day? Cloudy, sunny, raining, windy…? Do you remember what you were wearing? What the other person was wearing? Were there any particular smells you remember or sounds? Was anyone else nearby? Any animals or things nearby? Where were you? What did the person look like? Height, weight, eye color, facial features?*

Some facilitators have found it helpful to begin by asking what happened before, during, and after the trauma event(s). Then ask such questions as: *What were you thinking (during this time)? What were you feeling? How did you react and what did you do? What happened before? Afterwards?*

Those using Trauma-Focused Cognitive Behavioral Therapy recommend implementing a book format with a beginning, middle, and end. They also use the *Ask, Listen, Repeat, Write Down* approach. **Ask** about the trauma, including details while **listening** intently to what is and is not being said. **Repeat** back what you heard, allowing the person to make any changes or additions, then **write down** the information, saying it aloud while doing it.

SHARING

■ Goal

➲ The individual shares his/her trauma stories with the facilitator/counselor.

Name		Program Location	

Tasks (some optional, depending on person/situation)	Date Completed	Notes
Read a story about someone's experience of abuse/trauma (to normalize the sharing and provide an example).		
Discuss reason and importance for creating a trauma narrative (sharing one's story).		
Have the client choose which abuse/trauma story to share (i.e. the worst, first, least, or last).		
Discuss options for storytelling in a personally chosen format: Writing, Drawing, Art, Music/song, Poem, Collage, Dance, Drama, Puppets, Sand Tray...		
Encourage use of relaxation techniques (stress reduction strategies) if anxious.		
Affirm that negative thoughts and feelings are in the past, they are not part of the present.		
Have the client tell their story using a format that was personally chosen and is age appropriate.		
Have the client tell their story in detail (dictated to and repeated by the counselor with some prompting for additional details, thoughts, feelings...). Use either the *Dictate-Stop-Read-Ask* or the *Ask, Listen, Repeat, Write Down* approach.		
Praise the client for bravely sharing their personal story of trauma and remind them that it reflects only _part_ of and not the totality of their life's story.		
If a less traumatic story was chosen, ask the person if they are ready to share another more difficult story and repeat this sharing process		

EVALUATING

■ Overall Goal

To expose any harmful thoughts and feelings in the individual's trauma narrative and assist in revising them.

■ Overview

After the individual has shared his/her trauma/abuse stories the facilitator reviews and evaluates what was shared in order to identify any unhelpful thoughts, feelings, and beliefs (thinking patterns and emotional responses) that negatively effects how the event(s) are incorporated into one's identity and world view. The individual, not the facilitator, is then encouraged to recognize and "fix" these unhealthy responses.

During the EVALUATING step, we want to:

REVIEW what was shared previously in SHARING, searching for and identifying any part of the story that reflects negative thinking (cognitive distortions) or harmful emotional responses.

The facilitator develops a list of questions to ask which assist the individual to:

IDENTIFY any unhelpful, inaccurate thoughts, beliefs or perspectives, so that the victim can...

REVISE the stories to represent more accurate and helpful perspectives on what happened.

Unhealthy perspectives were presented earlier, in THINKING, and include:

- ➲ Guilt, self-blame, and personal responsibility
- ➲ Shame and negative attributes
- ➲ Inability to trust (self or others)
- ➲ Assumptions regarding the causes of, or reasons for, the trauma events
- ➲ Assumptions regarding offender motives, thoughts, beliefs, and feelings
- ➲ Negative self-beliefs and perceptions
- ➲ Assumptions regarding others' thoughts, feelings, and beliefs

Examples of Wrong Thinking (cognitive distortions):

- ➲ *I'll never be normal*
- ➲ *I should have been able to stop it.*
- ➲ *I should have known better.*
- ➲ *I can't trust anyone again.*
- ➲ *I'll never to safe again.*
- ➲ *My life is destroyed.*

- ➲ *I've destroyed my family.*
- ➲ *I'll never get over this.*
- ➲ *The world will always be unsafe.*

EVALUATING

■ Goal

↻ To help the person evaluate and revise their story by exposing unhelpful thoughts and feelings.

Name		Program Location	

Tasks (some optional, depending on person/situation)	Date Completed	Notes
Review the person's trauma narrative and develop a list of questions to elicit identification of inaccurate, unhelpful thoughts.		
Review the story with the person, asking questions so they identify the <u>harmful thoughts</u> and feelings.		
Assist the client in developing accurate/ helpful thoughts, so that he/she "fixes" the story.		
Review and read the newly edited story again.		
Discuss with client what he/she has learned through this process.		
Praise the client for courage and growth.		
This corrected version of their story can be added to the Book About Me if the client wants.		
Other:		

SHARING AGAIN

■ Overall Goal

➲ The individual shares his/her story with another, emotionally safe individual.

■ Overview

The individual re-tells their story, which is now revised and healthier, to another person. This increases healing, brings the hidden out of darkness, and decreases shame's hold on the person.

During the SHARING AGAIN step, we want to:

ASSESS if the individual is emotionally ready to share their story with someone other than the counselor. Discussing expectations, hopes, and possible reactions is helpful in assessing and preparing the person to share again.

CHOOSE with whom to share their story. It should be an emotionally safe, close, caring person. It may be necessary to help the individual select someone with whom to share; someone capable of being supportive and encouraging. Depending on the victim's housing situation, the chosen person may be a parent, house mom, Social Worker, foster parent, residential program manager, or close friend.

Here are a few guidelines for helping choose the person. Is the person:

➲ A good listener?

➲ Caring?

➲ Capable of listening to tough stuff (uncomfortable material)?

➲ Able to listen and not get overly emotional?

➲ Able to keep focused on you and not have it become about him or her?

➲ Not judgmental, blaming, nor critical?

➲ Able to not blame themselves for what happened?

➲ Able to keep confidentiality (not tell anyone)?

➲ Supportive of you, who you are, and your healing journey?

PREPARE the chosen person for the sharing session by coaching him/her on how best to respond and what to say and not say. Help the person understand what responses are helpful: giving praise and encouragement during and after the session, such as *Thank you for sharing with me; You are brave to share this; You're amazing; or I'm so glad you're sharing this.*

Help the person understand what responses are not helpful: crying uncontrollably, getting mad, focusing on self, making statements such as *Why didn't you tell me sooner? What were you thinking?! Or You should have told someone!*

SHARE the trauma/abuse story (the revised, corrected version). The victim shares about their trauma experiences by reading their story, telling it, or presenting it in their initial self-chosen way (music, drama, poem).

DEBRIEF with the victim afterward. *How did you feel sharing it with someone else? How did it go for you? What thoughts and feelings did you have before, during, and after?*

If needed and possible, also have a debrief session with the person chosen to hear the victim's story, asking him/her similar questions.

SHARING AGAIN

■ Goal

⊃ To decrease hidden shame and increase healing by sharing the trauma story with another safe person.

Name		Program Location	

Tasks (some optional, depending on person/situation)	Date Completed	Notes
Assess client's readiness to share his/her story with someone other than the counselor.		
Client identifies a supportive person with whom to share their personal abuse/trauma story.		
Assess the support person's readiness to hear the client's trauma story and prepare (coach) the person in how best to respond.		
Prepare client to share their trauma story, discussing expectations and possible reactions of the chosen person.		
Encourage the use of relaxation techniques (anxiety reduction strategies) as needed.		
Client shares their (revised, corrected) trauma story with the support person.		
Acknowledge both parties with gratitude.		
Debrief the experience with client.		
Debrief the experience with support person (if desired/possible).		
Other:		

SHARING MORE

■ Overall Goal

The facilitator asks about any potential trauma caused <u>by</u> the individual to others and encourages the individual to share this as well.

■ Overview

The individual is encouraged to reveal instances where he/she may have traumatized someone else; where they were the offender. Like before, this increases healing, brings the hidden out of darkness, and decreases shame's hold on the person.

The primary focus of all trauma counseling is healing from trauma experienced by the victim. The counseling provides opportunities for the person to share about the traumatic, abusive things that have happened or been done to him/her. The emphasis is on healing from their own trauma experiences. In this section, however, we focus on what the person may have done to others whether in anger, while under control or coercion, or for other reasons.

In working with the sexually exploited (victims of human trafficking), many have shared of horrible things they did to others (either by coercion or in anger).

Examples include:

- ➲ Having to hold someone down while they were being raped/abused/tortured.
- ➲ Having to watch someone be raped, hurt, tortured, or killed.
- ➲ Being forced to commit violence, sexual or abusive acts on others.
- ➲ Doing abusive, traumatizing things to others (not by force).
- ➲ Enjoying and participating in the abusive activities.

Refer to the activity *What I Did – Sharing More* for additional examples and an activity worksheet. This helps make the unspeakable things become 'speakable' and can normalize the victim's response to the experience: *I'm not the only one who's done these terrible things to others.*

During the SHARING MORE step, we want to:

PREPARE the individual by explaining the importance and benefits of *getting it out*. Use the activity worksheet, *What I Did – Sharing More*, to help explain the process. It also provides a checklist of possible activities the individual may have done to others which can help normalize the victim's response to the incident(s).

REMIND the individual to use the relaxation techniques learned earlier as needed, and that negative self-talk and feelings need to be exposed and addressed.

ENCOURAGE sharing in a personally chosen way, then...

ASK the individual to share this part of their story with as much details as possible by dictating it to the counselor, using either the *Dictate-Stop-Read-Ask or the Ask, Listen, Repeat, Write Down* approach.

REPEAT the sharing of any other stories of trauma done to others. If there are many, ask the individual to name the five worst, then choose from those.

EVALUATE the trauma narratives, identifying unhealthy thoughts and feelings.

REVISE any inaccurate or harmful thoughts and feelings, allowing the client to determine the changes.

SHARE AGAIN with another person (optional according to the individual, the culture and context).

SHARING MORE

■ Goal

⊃ To decrease hidden shame and increase healing by sharing the trauma story with another safe person.

Name		Program Location	

Tasks (some optional, depending on person/situation)	Date Completed	Notes
SHARING MORE		
If/when the person is willing, encourage the sharing of what they may have done to cause trauma to others.		
Reiterate the importance of sharing this part of their trauma story. Of getting it out rather than keeping it in.		
Encourage the use of relaxation techniques (anxiety reduction strategies) if anxious.		
Have the client tell their story in a personally chosen way that is age appropriate.		
If appropriate, have the client tell their story in detail (dictated to and repeated by the counselor with some prompting for additional details, thoughts, feelings...). Use either the *Dictate-Stop-Read-Ask* or the *Ask, Listen, Repeat, Write Down* approach.		
Praise the client for sharing this part of their story.		
If there are numerous events in which the person was the offender or contributed to others' trauma, repeat this sharing process for each incident if needed.		
SHARING MORE: EVALUATING		
Review the person's trauma narrative and develop a list of questions to elicit identification of inaccurate, unhelpful thoughts.		
Review the story with the person, asking questions so they identify the harmful thoughts and feelings.		

Tasks (some optional, depending on person/situation)	Date Completed	Notes
Assist the client in developing accurate/helpful thoughts, so that he/she "fixes" the story.		
Review and read the newly edited story again.		
Discuss with client about what he/she has learned through this process.		
SHARING MORE - AGAIN (optional but recommended)		
Assess client's readiness to share this part of his/her story with someone other than the counselor.		
Client identifies a supportive person with whom to share his/her story.		
Assess the support person's readiness to hear this part of the client's story and prepare (coach) the person in how best to respond.		
Prepare client to share this part of his/her story, discussing expectations and possible reactions of the chosen person.		
Encourage the use of relaxation techniques (anxiety reduction strategies) as needed.		
Client shares their (revised, corrected) story with the support person.		
Acknowledge both parties with gratitude.		
Debrief the sharing experience with client, praising the client for courage and growth.		
Debrief the sharing experience with support person (if desired/possible).		
Other:		

97 TELLING MY STORY

Age	All	Setting	Individual	Trauma Recovery	SHARING-Sharing

Purpose	To provide a framework for individuals to tell their abuse story.
Overview	The individual works through a worksheet that has him/her tell the details of their trauma experience.

Approximate Time	10-45 minutes

Supplies Needed	Worksheet and pen

■ Activity Explained

- ➲ The facilitator explains the importance of sharing one's story.
- ➲ The individual works through the checklist, outlining their personal trauma story.

■ Reflection

How do you feel after having shared your story? Was it harder or easier than you thought it would be? What worried you most? What did you learn from sharing it with a trustworthy person?

■ Variations

Activity may be verbal if needed (due to age or language concerns). For victims of trauma other than abuse, this form can be adapted or used as a starting point for creating one based on the experience of the individual and those you serve.

■ Concerns

Activity may be triggering and take some time to complete. Remind the person that they can take their time and should stop and use the relaxation skills learned when needed.

■ Story

A survivor of multiple sexual abuse was hesitant to share her story. She said later that it was this worksheet that helped and guided her to get it out and tell it.

TELLING MY ABUSE STORY

Telling your trauma story, or getting it out in the open, is key in the healing process. By completing the checklists and questions below, you'll share your story. The long-held pain will decrease, and hope will grow. (*Although your heart might resist doing this story-telling, you are encouraged to complete it for <u>each</u> abusive relationship you experienced.*)

■ My Story

When I was ___ years old, I was (type of abuse) _____ by my (relationship,) _____, (name) _____.
It happened most of the time in/at (locations) _____ and _____.

I experienced: *(check all that apply)*

❑   physical   ❑   emotional/verbal abuse

❑   sexual   ❑   neglect

It happened this often:

❑   once   ❑   once a month

❑   daily   ❑   unpredictable but about _____# times

❑   every week

Most often, it happened (time of day, certain day of week) _____

The abuse went on for _____#

❑   years   ❑   weeks

❑   months   ❑   days

Who else was in the area (house, building) when you were being abused?

_____.

I think _____ knew that something was going on.

This person (name), _____, saw something going on and knew about the abuse.

I think the abuser may have (or did) hurt others (names of others) _____, _____.

Write or describe what happened, giving as much detail as possible. Use additional paper as needed.

This is what happened:

_____

My Reaction

Fight – Flight/Flee — Freeze *(Check all that apply)*

- ❑ I still believe I could/should have responded differently.
- ❑ I have carried much guilt and shame from believing that I didn't respond as I should have.
- ❑ Now I know that it wasn't wrong or shameful to freeze.
- ❑ Now I know that it is common to comply.
- ❑ I didn't react because I didn't know it was wrong.
- ❑ I didn't react because I thought I didn't have a choice.
- ❑ Other:

My Thoughts and Beliefs *(Refer to Responses activity)*

- ❑ I realize that I've tended to _____(minimize, rationalize, deny, blocked, mislabel) what happened to me.

When the abuse happened, I thought:

_____

_____

This is what I was told or what I understood (spoken or implied):

_____

_____

I believed most everything that was implied or told to me BUT not anymore.

- ❑ I still believe some of what I was told or implied to me about what happened.
- ❑ I still believe most of what I was told or implied to me about what happened.

Keeping Silent?

When the abuse happened I told someone (disclosed):

- ❑ right away
- ❑ much later
- ❑ never

- ❑ now is the first time
- ❑ someone else told

I kept silent (didn't tell anyone) because: (shame, survival, scared, guilt, etc.)

_____

_____

My feelings about the abuse - *I felt or still feel*:

- ❑ Angry
- ❑ Anxious, worried
- ❑ Aroused
- ❑ Betrayed
- ❑ Blamed
- ❑ Confused (Ambivalent)
- ❑ Deceived
- ❑ Dirty
- ❑ Embarrassed
- ❑ Excited
- ❑ Guilty
- ❑ Helpless
- ❑ Hopeless/Depressed
- ❑ Loved
- ❑ Numb
- ❑ Powerless
- ❑ Sad
- ❑ Scared, fearful
- ❑ Shame
- ❑ Sneaky
- ❑ Special
- ❑ Stuck
- ❑ Stupid
- ❑ Other: _____

Where I Direct My Anger

- ❑ I still blame myself.
- ❑ I tend to excuse the abuser more than me.
- ❑ I tend to direct my anger at myself.
- ❑ I need to redirect my anger at the abuser.
- ❑ I need to not be so hard on myself.
- ❑ I need to forgive myself.
- ❑ I am angry at_____ (God, parent, law enforcement, teacher, etc.).

What We Think

These are the LIES I believe: (Refer to *The Lies* activity)

_____

_____

Here's what I did to deal with what happened: (Refer to information presented earlier on *Behavioral Responses* or activity *How I Coped*)

_____

_____

What I Did

- ❑ I've done some things that have hurt others.
- ❑ I still feel ashamed about what I did.
- ❑ I wish I could undo it all.

Now looking back, I think I did those things to others...

- ❑ To numb the pain I felt.
- ❑ To survive, cope.
- ❑ Because I had such rage inside.
- ❑ To hurt others like I felt hurt.
- ❑ Because I didn't know it was wrong.
- ❑ Because I was threatened, forced, or coerced into doing them.
- ❑ Other: _____

I've had these feelings toward the abuser:

✓ (check) = before the abuse   X (letter X) = during the abuse   0 (number 0) = now

- ❑ Love
- ❑ Hatred
- ❑ Pity
- ❑ Betrayal

- ❑ Friendship
- ❑ Anger
- ❑ Compassion
- ❑ Other:

Forgiveness

- ❑ I refuse to forgive those who hurt me.
- ❑ I refuse to forgive those who didn't protect or help me.
- ❑ I want to forgive those who hurt me, but it's hard.
- ❑ I will forgive but I won't forget nor trust the

people again.

- ❑ I do not want reconciliation with the offender(s).
- ❑ I need to forgive myself.
- ❑ __ Other: _____

These are the people, places, things, and events that still *trigger* painful memories:

_____

_____

- ❑ I will strive to remember and do those things that help me to heal. And, I will seek to avoid those things that make me feel worse.

- ❑ I will seek help from others (friends, family and/or professionals) to help in this healing journey.

These are the people, places, things, and events that still *trigger* painful memories:

_____

_____

I want to... (check all that apply)

- ❑ Move on
- ❑ Get the pain out
- ❑ Get counseling
- ❑ Turn to God
- ❑ Stop using
- ❑ Toughen up

- ❑ Tell someone
- ❑ Cry and scream
- ❑ Share my story
- ❑ Report what happened
- ❑ Help others like me
- ❑ Forget it ever happened

- ❑ Feel better
- ❑ Get rid of my intense anger
- ❑ Get rid of my sex addiction
- ❑ Forgive
- ❑ Other:

- ❑ I don't want what happened to me to determine my future possibilities. I will pursue my future plans, dreams, and goals.
- ❑ I will share my story with someone else.

Here are some of my **future plans, hopes and dreams:**

98 SHARING MY ABUSE STORY CHECKLISTS

Age	All	Setting	Individual	Trauma Recovery	SHARING-Sharing

Purpose	To provide a framework for individuals to tell their story.
Overview	The individual completes a checklist that addresses details of their abuse experience. **Note**: This is similar to the previous activity, Telling My Story, but includes more detailed checklists. The facilitator selects or adapts either one of these activities but does not use both.

Approximate Time	15-45 minutes

Supplies Needed	Worksheet and pen

■ Activity Explained

- ➲ The facilitator explains the importance of sharing one's story.
- ➲ The individual works through the checklist, providing detailed information about their personal story of abuse.

■ Reflection

How do you feel after sharing your story? Was it harder or easier than you thought it would be? What worried you most? What did you learn from sharing with a trustworthy person?

■ Variations

Activity may be verbal if needed (due to age or language concerns). For victims of trauma other than abuse, this form can be adapted or used as a starting point for creating one based on the experience of the individual and those you serve.

■ Concerns

Activity may be very triggering and take some time to complete. Remind the person that they can take their time should stop and use the relaxation skills learned when needed.

■ Story

Many have shared that this checklist helped them to finally tell their story. It provides the words, thoughts, feelings, explanations, ideas, concerns, and responses of the abused. They just need to check those that apply to them.

SHARING MY ABUSE STORY

I was first abused when I was _____ years old, It went on for _____ (months/years/#times) _____

I was _____ years old when it happened again. It went for _____ (months/years/#times) _____

The Abuser(s) was/were: *Put a check next to those that apply*

❑ A father
❑ An uncle
❑ A grandfather
❑ A brother
❑ A cousin
❑ A teacher
❑ A coach
❑ A youth pastor

❑ A friend's parent
❑ A parent's friend
❑ A neighbor
❑ A mom
❑ A sister
❑ An aunt
❑ A grandmother
❑ A stranger

❑ A boyfriend
❑ Step-father
❑ Step-mother
❑ Step-brother
❑ Step-sister
❑ Friend
❑ Other:

Where it happened: *Put a check next to those that apply*

❑ At home in the house
❑ At home in a bedroom
❑ At home in bathroom
❑ At home in the attic
❑ At home in basement
❑ At church

❑ At work
❑ In a car/vehicle/boat
❑ At school
❑ At a friend's house
❑ At a relative's house
❑ At a park or in woods

❑ Underground (shelter, culvert, sewer pipe)
❑ Public building
❑ Pool/Jacuzzi
❑ Tent
❑ Other:

The Abuse involved: *Put a check next to those that apply*

❑ Fondling and touching
❑ Rape
❑ Sodomy (anal sex)
❑ Being hit and/or hurt
❑ Violence

❑ Object penetration
❑ Oral sex
❑ Pornography
❑ Being sold for sex
❑ Being filmed watching sex/

porn
❑ Masturbation
❑ Sex with animals
❑ Parading around
❑ Other:

When I was being abused, I remember:

Sights	Sounds	Touch	Tastes	Smells

These are some things I remember from when the abuse first happened (use additional paper as needed)

When it happened, my reaction was to:

❑ Fight

❑ Flee

❑ Freeze (most common)

When the abuse happened: Check all that apply

❑ I didn't know it was wrong.

❑ I knew it was wrong.

❑ I thought it was wrong but wasn't sure.

❑ I enjoyed the attention and/or feelings).

❑ I thought it was normal or what families do.

❑ I wanted it to stop but didn't know how.

❑ I didn't know what to do or who to talk to.

❑ I didn't want to tell anyone.

❑ I thought I was supposed to do it.

❑ Other:

When it happened, I told (disclosed):

- ❑ right away
- ❑ much later
- ❑ never
- ❑ someone else told

I kept silent (didn't tell anyone) because: *(check as many as apply)*

- ❑ I was afraid for my safety.
- ❑ I was afraid of what others would think.
- ❑ I was afraid no one would believe me.
- ❑ I was afraid for my younger siblings.
- ❑ I was afraid for my family.
- ❑ I was afraid I'd get in trouble.
- ❑ I was ashamed.
- ❑ I felt it was my fault.
- ❑ I enjoyed it and didn't want it to stop.
- ❑ I was dependent on abuser (financially, emotionally).
- ❑ Other:

I felt: *Check those that apply*

❑ Scared	❑ Angry	❑ Betrayed	❑ Dirty
❑ To blame	❑ Sad	❑ Embarrassed	❑ Stupid
❑ Shame	❑ Helpless	❑ Special	❑ Like a slut/whore
❑ Deceived	❑ Hopeless	❑ Loved	❑ Worried
❑ Guilty	❑ Confused	❑ Excited	❑ Other:

My reactions were: *Check those that apply*

❑ Froze	❑ Mad at parent(s)	❑ Said I lied	❑ Wished I'd never told
❑ Blamed myself	❑ Mad at God	❑ Pretended it didn't	❑ Other:
❑ Didn't tell anyone (right away)	❑ Mad at abuser	❑ happen	❑ Other:
❑ Hated myself	❑ Felt unsafe	❑ Minimized it ("It's not that bad")	

Here's some things I've done since having been abused: *Check those that apply*

- ❏ Lie
- ❏ Cheat
- ❏ Steal
- ❏ Vandalize
- ❏ Run away
- ❏ Drink alcohol a lot
- ❏ Drugs
- ❏ Depression

- ❏ 'Crazy" or bizarre behavior
- ❏ Prostitution
- ❏ Cutting self
- ❏ Addictions
- ❏ Eating problems
- ❏ Compulsive behavior

- ❏ Gotten tougher
- ❏ Gotten weaker
- ❏ Become aggressive
- ❏ Low self esteem
- ❏ Don't trust any more
- ❏ Gotten depressed
- ❏ Get sick often

- ❏ Physical Problems
- ❏ Suicidal
- ❏ Loner
- ❏ Promiscuity
- ❏ Dissociate
- ❏ Bully others

When I feel anger about what happened

It is usually directed at: (rank each person using each number only once. 1=most of the anger / 2=much of the anger / 3=some anger / 4=less anger / 5=little anger)

Abuser	
Parent	
Self	
God	
Police/Law/Enforcement/Other:	

My feelings about the abuser are:

Love	
Hate	
Pity	
Betrayal	
Friendship	
Affection	
Anger	

These are some of my TRIGGERS, the people, places, or things that remind me of what happened and make me angry, anxious, or sad:

_____

_____

Here's what makes me feel worse: *(use additional paper as needed)*

_____

_____

Here's what makes me feel better: *(use additional paper as needed)*

I want to: *Circle those that apply*

❑ Move on.

❑ Get the pain out.

❑ Get counseling.

❑ Turn to God.

❑ Stop using.

❑ Toughen up.

❑ Tell someone.

❑ Cry and scream.

❑ Share my story.

❑ Report what happened.

❑ Help others like me.

❑ Forget it ever happened.

❑ Feel better.

❑ Get rid of my intense anger.

❑ Get rid of my sex addiction.

❑ Forgive.

❑ Other:

99 REMEMBERING THE PLACE

Age	All	Setting	Individual	Trauma Recovery	SHARING-Sharing

Purpose	To identify the places where the trauma took place.
Overview	Individual identifies those places in which their abuse/trauma was experienced and how they feel in those or similar places. **Note:** This information is included in the previous two activities and should only be used if previous activities are not being used for the individual.

Approximate Time	10 minutes

Supplies Needed	Worksheet and pen

■ Activity Explained

- ➲ The facilitator reviews places where trauma/abuse can occur.
- ➲ The individual identifies the locations where abuse/trauma most often happened to them, using the checklist on the worksheet.
- ➲ The individual identifies where and when they feel overwhelmed and triggered, using the checklist on the worksheet.

■ Reflection

What do you do when you have to go to or near where you were traumatized? What happens when you have to go somewhere that reminds you of that place? Where is somewhere you feel safe?

■ Variations

Activity may be verbal or written. Activity may be used individually or in groups.

■ Concerns

Individuals may be triggered by sharing their experience.

REMEMBERING THE PLACE

The traumatic event I experienced happened at:

- ❏ My home
- ❏ My school/work
- ❏ My neighborhood or community
- ❏ In a vehicle
- ❏ In a new, unfamiliar place
- ❏ Other:_____

Where my Abuse/Trauma happened: *(check as many as apply)*

- ❏ At home
- ❏ In a bedroom
- ❏ At home bathroom
- ❏ In the attic
- ❏ In basement
- ❏ In church/synagogue
- ❏ At work
- ❏ In a car/vehicle/boat
- ❏ At school
- ❏ At a friend's house
- ❏ At a relative's house
- ❏ At a park or woods
- ❏ Underground (shelter, culvert, sewer pipe)
- ❏ Public building
- ❏ Pool/Jacuzzi
- ❏ Tent
- ❏ Other _____

Most often I was abused in/at (location):

- ❏ My home
- ❏ My school/work
- ❏ My neighborhood
- ❏ In a bedroom / living room / bathroom / kitchen / closet / other_____

I feel overwhelmed when...

- ❏ I get triggered with bad memories when I'm back in that place again.
- ❏ I get triggered with bad memories when I'm in places similar to where I was primarily abused.
- ❏ I can go there now and not feel too anxious, angry, sad, or self-condemning.
- ❏ I still avoid the place or places that are similar to where I was abused.
- ❏ I feel _____ when I'm back in that place or in a similar type of place.

100 ABUSE SENTENCE COMPLETION

Age	All	Setting	Individual	Trauma Recovery	SHARING-Sharing

Purpose	To share about and to identify thoughts and feelings related to past abuse.
Overview	The individual completes sentences that relate to his/her trauma story.

Approximate Time	10-20 minutes		Supplies Needed	Worksheet and pen

■ Activity Explained

⊃ The facilitator explains that the individual will be sharing about their abuse/trauma by completing sentences.

⊃ The facilitator shares their own example and shows how to finish one or two sentences from the worksheet before the individual begins. (For example, #16. "If only _____," may elicit a response, "I'd worked harder."

⊃ The individual completes the sentences on the worksheet, thinking specifically about their personal trauma story.

■ Reflection

How do you feel after writing down your thoughts and feelings? Was this harder or easier than you thought it would be?

■ Variations

Activity may be verbal or written.

■ Concerns

Individuals may find it triggering to think about their trauma and may need assistance in writing down their responses.

SENTENCE COMPLETION

I wish the abuse/trauma
_____

When I think about the abuse/trauma I
_____

The offender
_____

I felt
_____

Sometimes I get
_____

When the trauma was happening, I'd tell myself
_____

My Dad
_____

My Mom
_____

My brother (s)/sister (s)
_____

My children
_____

No one knew
_____

The abuse/trauma was a
_____

I wondered
_____

Why couldn't
_____

If only
_____

The trauma made me feel like
_____

When she/he looked at me
_____

I would dream
_____

Even today
_____

God
_____

I was only
_____

How could I
_____

I wanted so much
_____

Where was
_____

The pain
_____

101 FIGHT, FLIGHT, OR FREEZE SHARING

Age	All	Setting	Individual	Trauma Recovery	SHARING-Sharing

Purpose	To share and to process the person's initial responses to trauma/abuse.
Overview	Individuals identify their Fight, Flight, or Freeze response to trauma.

Approximate Time	10-15 minutes		Supplies Needed	Worksheet and pen

■ Activity Explained

⮑ The facilitator reviews Fight, Flight, or Freeze responses with the individual (refer to the chapter Understanding Trauma and also to Fight, Flight, or Freeze activity)

⮑ The person completes the worksheet and then discusses/shares it with the facilitator.

■ Reflection

If you could go back and change how you responded to your abuse/trauma, what do you wish you could have done differently? Let's talk about what you checked, especially about what you still think and feel about how you or your body responded to the trauma.

■ Variations

Activity may be verbal or written.

■ Concerns

Individuals may be triggered by thinking about their traumatic experience.

■ Story

When victims realize that freezing is a normal response to danger, that they didn't choose how they responded, but that their body's survival instinct took over, they express great relief and feeling lighter (less burdened by guilt and shame).

FIGHT, FLIGHT, OR FREEZE

If needed, review the information on *Fight, Flight, or Freeze* (under LEARNING), then complete the following:

When the abuse/trauma happened, my reaction was to:

- ❑ Fight
- ❑ Flee
- ❑ Freeze
- ❑ Comply (thinking there was no other option)

(Check those that apply)

- ❑ I have carried much guilt and shame from believing that I didn't respond right.
- ❑ I still believe I could or should have responded differently.
- ❑ I wish I fought back (screamed louder, kicked harder, etc.).
- ❑ At first, I felt ashamed because I froze, but now I know that it wasn't wrong. It was a normal response.
- ❑ I complied because I felt I had no choice.
- ❑ I complied because I was scared.
- ❑ I complied because I thought it was "normal" or okay.
- ❑ Other: _____
- ❑ Other: _____

If you could go back and change how you responded, what do you wish you could have done differently?

_____

_____

Let's talk about what you checked, especially about what you still think and feel about how you or your body responded to the situation.

_____

102 FORGIVING

Age	All	Setting	Individual	Trauma Recovery	SHARING-Sharing

Purpose	To teach about forgiveness and its importance in healing from trauma.
Overview	The individual learns about what forgiveness is (and isn't), and decides what they want to do.

Approximate Time	15 minutes

Supplies Needed	Worksheet and pen

■ Activity Explained

⮑ The facilitator explains what forgiveness is and isn't, and why it is important part of the healing process, using the worksheet and any other materials (Scripture, stories, or examples.)

⮑ The individual indicates on the checklist what he/she will do in response to what happened to him/her.

■ Reflection

What does it look like to forgive someone? What makes it difficult to forgive others? How do you know when you're ready to forgive someone? How does one forgive themselves? What happens if you refuse to forgive someone?

■ Variations

Activity may be verbal or written.

■ Concerns

Individual may be triggered by reflecting upon those who have hurt him/her.

The facilitator may need to assist the person through the steps to forgiveness.

■ Story

What joy is shared by those who are able to forgive both themselves and others. They tell of feeling happier, lighter, better, freer, and more excited about the future.

WHAT FORGIVENESS IS (AND ISN'T)

Forgiveness is choosing to release the hurt and the desire for revenge. It's a choice, not a feeling. This means that you consciously make the decision to pardon the offender, even when you don't feel like it. It is making up your mind to release something and then daily facing the challenges of living out that decision. It doesn't depend on your fluctuating emotions. You willingly say, "I forgive," with no timeline or pressure for your heart to catch up.

When we don't forgive, we are the ones who suffer. When we hang on to hate, we become bitter. A victim of exploitation summed it up beautifully, "Unforgiveness is like drinking poison and expecting the other person to die."

Forgiveness IS...

- An attempt to let go of past hurts and anger.
- A decision not to let the past determine the future.
- A powerful way to neutralize volatile emotions.
- A choice.
- A step toward becoming more compassionate.
- An amazing way to move forward.
- Necessary.

Forgiveness is NOT...

- Condoning the behavior.
- Forgetting what happened.
- Restoring trust in the person.
- Agreeing to reconcile.
- Doing the person a favor.
- Easy.

My Response

- ☐ I refuse to forgive those who hurt me.
- ☐ I refuse to forgive those who didn't protect or help me (parent, others).
- ☐ I want to forgive those who hurt me, but it's hard.
- ☐ I will forgive, but I won't forget or trust the people again.
- ☐ I do not want reconciliation with the offender(s).
- ☐ I know I need to forgive myself, but it's hard to do.
- ☐ I choose to forgive the abuser.
- ☐ I choose to forgive those involved who didn't help.
- ☐ I choose to forgive myself.

103 SHARING AGAIN – WITH ANOTHER PERSON

Age	All	Setting	Individual	Trauma Recovery	SHARING- Sharing Again

Purpose	To help the individual identify with whom to share their story.
Overview	This activity stresses the importance of sharing one's trauma story with another person. It uses a checklist to help the individual decide who might be best to hear their trauma narrative.

Approximate Time	10-20 minutes

Supplies Needed	Worksheet and pen

■ Activity Explained

- ➲ The facilitator explains that it is important in the healing process to share one's trauma story with someone else (other than the person in the counselor role).
- ➲ The individual identifies a person with whom they might want to share their trauma story.
- ➲ The individual goes through the checklist to see whether the person they are considering would be appropriate.

■ Reflection

Would this person be the appropriate individual to hear your story? Is there anyone else you might like to invite to hear your story? How do you think sharing your story again might be helpful?

■ Variations

Activity may be verbal or written.

■ Concerns

Individuals may have a hard time identifying someone in their life that they feel safe sharing their story with.

SHARING AGAIN – WITH ANOTHER PERSON

We begin by sharing our stories with our counselor. But we do not stop there. For our emotional healing we must share our stories with someone else.

Trauma research confirms that telling your story to one or more people assists in healing and can bring a sense of closure. Before you take this brave step and share your story with someone you trust, you'll want to make sure the person is safe—that he or she is emotionally safe for you.

People have chosen: a parent, house or foster mom, sibling, close friend, teacher, neighbor, co-worker, pastor, youth leader, dorm leader, coach, relative, and others.

WHO are you considering:		

Here are a few guidelines for helping you choose the person with whom to share your story.

Is the person:

- ❑ A good listener?
- ❑ Caring?
- ❑ Capable of listening to tough stuff?
- ❑ Able to listen and not get overly emotional?
- ❑ Able to keep focused on you and not have it become about him or her?
- ❑ Not judgmental, blaming, nor critical?
- ❑ Able to not blame themselves for what happened?
- ❑ Able to keep confidentiality (not tell anyone)?
- ❑ Supportive of you, who you are, and your healing journey?

If you are unsure about the answers for the person you are thinking about, you might want to reconsider and choose a different person. Sharing your story is hard enough without feeling like you need to take care of the person, worry about confidentiality, or their reaction.

I am sharing my story with: *(name)*	
Relationship: *(friend, family, mentor)*	
Date shared	

104 HOW I COPED

Age	All	Setting	Individual	Trauma Recovery	SHARING-Sharing

Purpose	To identify unhealthy and negative responses to trauma.
Overview	The individual reads through and completes a checklist of unhealthy coping strategies to identify which ones they have used in the past or still use.

Approximate Time	10-20 minutes	Supplies Needed	Worksheet and pen

■ Activity Explained

- ➲ The facilitator explains what coping skills are and shares examples.
- ➲ The individual goes through the checklist on the worksheet and checks the coping skills that they have used or still use.

■ Reflection

Which of these coping skills have you used in the past, but no longer use? Which of these coping skills do you still use?

■ Variations

Activity may be verbal or written.

■ Concerns

Individuals may be triggered by or ashamed of some of their coping mechanisms.

■ Story

Now, after learning so much about what happened, I realized that what I was doing was just my way of trying to deal with everything and how bad I felt. It helps to know that that is normal.

HOW I COPED: UNHEALTHY RESPONSES AND DESTRUCTIVE BEHAVIORS

Victims develop coping skills in an attempt to deal with the internal pain of the trauma they experienced.. Unfortunately, many of these are unhealthy or self-destructive. Whether the coping behavior is to deal with the negative thoughts, to deaden the pain, or to distract from intrusive events, not all coping mechanisms are good for us.

The following statements represent harmful behaviors often used by trauma victims. Some behaviors may be in the past, while some are continued on long after healing has begun, often becoming bad habits. Check the methods that you used to cope with your negative thoughts and feelings after the trauma.

In an attempt to deal with the internal pain of the abuse:

- ❏ I've lied, cheated, and manipulated others.
- ❏ I've stolen.
- ❏ I've vandalized property or things.
- ❏ I ran away.
- ❏ I have abused alcohol.
- ❏ I've used illegal or other drugs (inhalants or other chemicals).
- ❏ I've been depressed and sad for long amounts of time.
- ❏ Some people said I was crazy or had bizarre behavior.
- ❏ I became promiscuous and slept with a lot of people.
- ❏ I've cut myself or engaged in other acts of self-harm or self-mutilation.
- ❏ I've developed addictions.
- ❏ I've had eating problems or disorders.
- ❏ I've had compulsive behavior.
- ❏ I've acted tough, defiant, and rebellious.
- ❏ I've been aggressive and bullied others.
- ❏ I've been passive and weak.
- ❏ I can be quite impulsive.
- ❏ I've had times when I hated myself and had low self-esteem.
- ❏ I've had problems with trusting others and with being overly suspicious.
- ❏ I've had problems getting along with others.

- ❑ Sometimes I became too clingy or indiscriminate in relationships.
- ❑ I've had lots of problems with anger or my temper.
- ❑ I developed some sexual addictions: pornography, masturbation, or similar.
- ❑ I've had problems with boundaries (co-dependency).
- ❑ It has been hard for me to take care of myself (self-protection, self-care).
- ❑ I get sick frequently and/or have had multiple physical problems.
- ❑ I've had suicidal behaviors, thoughts, and attempts.
- ❑ I've had anxiety or panic attacks.
- ❑ I dissociate (tune out, have out-of-body experiences, and/or lose time).
- ❑ I've developed imaginary friends.
- ❑ I've had school problems (academic and/or achievement).
- ❑ I've had trouble making friends and fitting in (social problems).
- ❑ I've had problems getting close to people (attachment, bonding).
- ❑ I like to help others perhaps more than normal (rescuing others, caretaking).
- ❑ I like to be invisible, to withdraw from others, and be detached.
- ❑ I sabotage success and expect failure.
- ❑ I've been an overachiever, perfectionist.
- ❑ I've developed some strange habits.
- ❑ I've exercised way too much (excessive exercising).
- ❑ Other: _____

105 WHAT I DID – SHARING MORE

Age	All	Setting	Individual	Trauma Recovery	SHARING-Sharing More

Purpose	To process through the negative behaviors/patterns the individual might have engaged in during their trauma experience.
Overview	The individual reviews a checklist identifying actions that victims have taken to victimize or negatively affect others.

Approximate Time	15-45 minutes

Supplies Needed	Worksheet and pen

■ Activity Explained

➲ The facilitator explains why it is important to share about any trauma the person may have caused to others (refer to the worksheet explaining its importance).

➲ The individual completes the checklist about what they did and why or, if too re-traumatizing, reviews the list with the facilitator who may ask *Have you done any of those?*

➲ Allow time for emotions to surface, tears to flow, anger to release, etc.

■ Reflection

How do you feel about sharing what you may have done to others? Was it helpful to learn about some of the reasons why victims hurt others? How was it helpful? What are you going to do to make amends? What steps are you going to take to forgive yourself?

■ Variations

Activity may be verbal or written. Extra care and time should be taken if the facilitator takes the individual through the activity verbally.

■ Concerns

Activity can be very difficult for individuals experiencing deep feelings of regret and remorse.

■ Story

For many, what they did is so overwhelmingly shameful that they do not want anyone, ever, to know about it. But those who have shared liken it to having a fatal brain tumor or malignant cancerous growth removed.

WHAT I DID

When we talk about trauma, we usually talk about what was done or what happened to victims. But as you heal, you must also look at the deep, dark, shameful areas where you yourself may have caused trauma or harm *to others*. While this can be excruciating and difficult, it is needed for healing and recovery. As you share your trauma story, you must include the good, the bad, and the ugly. Otherwise, it is like a malignant growth where surgeons remove only part, but not all of it. Unless you get it all out and tell your entire abuse story, there will still be shame, guilt, and remorse festering inside.

Some of the "shameful" things you did were your way of coping or surviving what was happening to you. While some of these you knew were wrong, you did other things because you didn't know they were wrong. You may have engaged in some activities because you were forced, threatened, coerced, or scammed into doing them.

Whatever the reason, you may have participated in activities you are painfully ashamed of. In response, you may want to forget the memories, block them out, erase them, or pretend they didn't really happen. So, you live with deep remorse and regret, wanting to keep the memories buried and locked away. This is understandable, but unhealthy.

You may need to confess what you did to someone, ask forgiveness from the person(s) you hurt, make amends, attempt reconciliation, and/or seek professional or legal advice.

Full healing cannot take place without you facing what you have done. If this is too difficult to face now, skip over it, but do come back and finish this section when you feel ready. Don't keep it hidden in the dark, where it will continue to cause you harm. Bring it into the light and receive freedom from its death-hold grip on you.

What I Think about What I Did

- ❏ I've done some things that have hurt others.
- ❏ I still feel ashamed about it.
- ❏ I wish I could undo it all.

Now looking back, I think I did those things:

- ❏ To numb the pain I felt inside.
- ❏ To survive, cope.
- ❏ Because I had such rage inside.
- ❏ To hurt others like I felt hurt.
- ❏ Because I didn't know it was wrong.
- ❏ Because I was threatened, forced, or coerced into doing them.
- ❏ Other:

What I Did

Place a check next to those things you did or in which you were a participant. This list is not complete, so please add other areas in which you may have caused harm or trauma to others.

- ❑ Lied to family or a close friend.

- ❑ Lied to the police, judge, social worker, etc.

- ❑ Stolen.

- ❑ Recruited someone to provide sex for someone else.

- ❑ Beaten someone up (fists, kicks, etc.); physically assaulted or injured someone.

- ❑ Killed an animal.

- ❑ Killed or helped someone kill another person.

- ❑ Coerced someone into hurting someone else.

- ❑ Held someone down while others raped or beat her or him.

- ❑ Sexually abused others.

- ❑ Injured someone with an object: knife, belt, bottle, stick, whip, etc.

- ❑ Given drugs to others.

- ❑ Sold drugs.

- ❑ Put foreign objects inside someone's body (mouth, anus, vagina, ears).

- ❑ Participated in a group/gang illegal activity (stealing, rape, physical assault, etc.).

- ❑ Forced a child to do something to or for you (sexual or otherwise).

- ❑ Talked someone into doing something they clearly didn't want to do.

- ❑ Vandalized or destroyed someone else's property or possession.

- ❑ Other:

- ❑ Other:

What I Need to Do

- ❑ Confess to someone what I did.

- ❑ Ask forgiveness and/or seek reconciliation with the person.

- ❑ Make amends; provide compensation to the person.

- ❑ Seek professional help (therapy, legal advice, or other).

- ✓ **Free**
- ✓ **Safe**
- ✓ **Well**

STEP 6

LIVING

LIVING: FREE, SAFE, AND WELL

■ Overall Goal

To live free of fear, with a sense of safety and with future goals. To minimize the risk of future victimization by decreasing trauma reminders, increasing self-confidence, and empowering personal goals.

■ Overview

- ➲ **LIVING FREE:** We identify any ongoing trauma avoidance areas and develop plans to minimize or eliminate them.
- ➲ **LIVING SAFE:** We seek to increase the individual's personal sense of safety and safety skills.
- ➲ **LIVING WELL:** We encourage the rekindling of dreams, volunteer involvement, setting future goals, and celebrating accomplishments.

Living Free:

We want the person to...

IDENTIFY any ongoing triggers, harmless trauma reminders (fears) and avoidance areas that continue even after sharing one's trauma story. These may include specific people, places, things, events and also smells, sights, sounds, tastes, tactile reminders and more.

DEVELOP a plan for decreasing the negative responses to these (usually through gradual exposure or desensitization).

IMPLEMENT and monitor the plan

Living Safe:

We want the person to...

CREATE a list of common, potentially dangerous situations. As personal safety skills of prevention and protection are introduced, return to discuss what one could do in each situation. Examples may include being home alone, last remaining passenger on the bus, physical or sexual assault, social expectations, dangerous neighborhood, bad dating or friendship situation, and many others.

LEARN personal safety skills of prevention and protection.

These skills may include:

- ➲ Assertiveness training
- ➲ Reading danger signals, listening to gut instincts; intuition
- ➲ Identifying safe people and places
- ➲ Getting help
- ➲ Developing a What If... safety plan (what to do, where to go, who to call)

- ⊃ Prevention strategies
- ⊃ Self-Defense skills
- ⊃ Boundaries (emotional and physical)
- ⊃ Knowing your rights
- ⊃ Other topics as identified

FOSTER problem-solving, values clarification, and decision-making skills through the use of a variety of role play formats using real life scenarios.

PRACTICE role-playing real life situations, which allows us to:

- ⊃ Rehearse, practice, and be prepared when/if the person is in a variety of difficult, unexpected, or uncomfortable situations.
- ⊃ Explore different scenarios/outcomes for various situations.
- ⊃ Develop problem solving skills.
- ⊃ Clarify what we believe and value.
- ⊃ Develop thinking, problem solving, and empathy skills.
- ⊃ Evaluate what influences our decisions.

DEVELOP a Personal Safety Plan stating what to do, where to go, and who to contact when/if feeling unsafe (emotionally and/or physically).

Living Well:

We encourage the person to...

REKINDLE past dreams which may have been abandoned due to the trauma and evaluate which dream to pursue.

VOLUNTEER in some capacity. This confirms their ability to contribute amidst feelings of inadequacy. Helping others redirects our attention from ourselves to others and provides an opportunity to contribute to the well-being of others.

Volunteering Examples:

- ⊃ volunteer at a crisis center
- ⊃ work with neighborhood children
- ⊃ teach crafts at a former brothel
- ⊃ do street outreach
- ⊃ serve at an animal shelter
- ⊃ volunteer at a detention center
- ⊃ work with a church youth group
- ⊃ share your story
- ⊃ become an advocate
- ⊃ serve at a homeless shelter
- ⊃ serve at a family center

SHARE their story, but only if they choose to do so. One may want to share his/her personal journey, which can bring hope to others and healing for oneself. They may want to share more generally, such as, "I went through some tough things" or the facilitator can ask, *"What advice would you give to others who have gone through what you have? What (if anything) would you like to do to help others or to share with others?"*

SET future goals (educational, vocational, emotional, etc.) and develop realistic plans to accomplish them. Include hobbies, activities, and other desired extracurricular pursuits. While some goals may already be in process (usually educational and vocational), holistic goals (mental, emotional, social, spiritual and physical) should be identified as well.

COMPLETE any post-tests or measures required or desired for the counseling process (to determine client growth, counseling, and/or program effectiveness). Evaluate the counseling process together. Finish the "Book About Me" with pages that include one's future goals, hopes, and dreams.

CELEBRATE the completion of the counseling process with a debriefing or with a closure event (for example, award a certificate or a treat). Inform the person that future setbacks are normal and that they can return to visit you if/when needed.

LIVING FREE: We identify any trauma avoidance areas (anxieties and phobias) and develop plans to minimize/eliminate them.

LIVING SAFE: We seek to increase the individual's personal sense of safety and safety skills.

LIVING WELL: We encourage the rekindling of dreams, volunteer involvement, setting future goals, and celebrating accomplishments.

Name		Program Location	

Tasks (some optional, depending on person/situation)	Date Completed	Notes
Living FREE (of avoidance areas, triggers, and fears)		
Identify trauma avoidance areas (anxiety producing reminders).		
Develop and implement a plan for each area.		
Living SAFE (protection, prevention, and planning)		
Teach personal rights *(if not done earlier)*.		
Teach personal safety skills (refer to earlier list).		
Teach problem solving, decision-making and value-clarification skills (best done through the use of various role play formats).		
Practice Role plays, utilizing various possible real-life scenarios.		
Make a Personal Safety Plan: what to do, where to go, who to contact if/when feeling unsafe.		
LIVING WELL (future planning and end of counseling)		
Identify previous dreams/plans and which to rekindle and pursue.		
Review and read the newly edited story again.		

Tasks (some optional, depending on person/situation)	Date Completed	Notes
Discuss potential for helping others (*if appropriate*) and implement when possible.		
Set holistic goals for the future (mental, emotional, social, physical, spiritual), as well as education/vocation/recreation goals.		
Complete any final assessments (post-test measures, evaluation).		
Complete "Book About Me" (including the Safely Plan, Future Goals, Hopes and Dreams).		
Acknowledge completion of counseling (certificate, celebration).		
Other:		

LIVING: FREE

106 FACING MY TRIGGERS

Age	All	Setting	Individual	Trauma Recovery	LIVING - Free

Purpose	To help individuals identify triggering situations.
Overview	Individuals identify specific sights, smells, sounds, tastes, etc. that accompany the memories of their trauma experience.

Approximate Time	15-25 minutes

Supplies Needed	Worksheet and pen

■ Activity Explained

- ⊃ The facilitator explains what a "'trigger" is and gives examples.
- ⊃ The individual writes memories related to their abuse, thinking through the five senses. What sights, sounds, touches, tastes, and smells are related to their trauma?
- ⊃ The individual selects those triggers that still create overwhelming emotional responses and makes a smaller list of those people, places, things, events, emotions, or behaviors that still trigger the individual, or activate unhealthy responses.
- ⊃ The individual identifies which triggers keep them from normal daily activities or places that could be safe.

■ Reflection

Reflection should focus on the biological and emotional reactions that take place when individuals are triggered. Individuals are encouraged to reflect on their reactions to their triggers and how they can overcome those reactions.

■ Variations

Activity may be adapted for groups as long as participants are not forced to share.

Activity may be verbal but written is preferred.

■ Concerns

Activity may be emotionally overwhelming, thus needs to be conducted slowly and with close support from the facilitator.

MY TRIGGERS—LINGERING, NEGATIVE MEMORIES

Many of our trauma memories developed into *triggers*, or instant reminders of what happened. These can bring unpleasant thoughts, feelings, and reactions, or they can lead to a flashback, in which the trauma event is experienced, once again, as if it were recurring. Some have shared...

- *I get sick to my stomach whenever I smell that certain aftershave cologne.*

- *A man walked down the street with a particular kind of hat on, and I lost it. I didn't remember until then that the abuser wore the same kind of hat.*

- *If my partner touches me a certain way, I freeze and start to panic.*

- *Sometimes it's still hard for me to look a blond-haired, blue-eyed person in the eyes.*

- *I hate red curtains, futons, wood floors, or holes in the wall!*

- *Loud music and diesel trucks set me off.*

- *Dreams are my trigger—when I have a nightmare about him or what happened.*

There are certain people, places, events, and things, as well as certain sights, sounds, tastes, touches, and smells that can trigger our negative trauma memories. Identifying them can be a challenge, but well worth the effort. It's hard to fight a ghost you can't see. Recognizing these intruders enables us to develop defensive and offensive strategies to help in our healing.

■ Memories

Write down any memories related to the abuse, in the following areas.

When I experienced the trauma, I remember:

Sights: _____ (bright paint/wallpaper, dark room, trees outside, old clothes)

_____

Sounds: _____ (dog barking, music playing, loud breathing, teapot whistling)

_____

Touch: _____ (soft baby blanket, facial hair, rough hands, wet skin)

_____

Tastes: _____ (blood, coffee, saliva, semen

_____

Smells: _____ (aftershave, vomit, sweat, garlic)

_____

■ My Triggers

What people, places, things, events, emotions, or behaviors still activate unhealthy responses?

Using the memories listed previously (sights, sounds, touches, tastes, and smells), make another list of those specific people, places, things, dreams, events, and/or behaviors that trigger negative reactions.

107 OVERCOMING MY FEARS PLAN

Age	All	Setting	Individual	Trauma Recovery	LIVING - Free

Purpose	To identify the steps to overcome the lingering fears left from trauma.
Overview	The facilitator assists the individual in developing a plan towards defeating triggers and fears that continue even after the trauma narrative has been shared.

Approximate Time	15-25 minutes

Supplies Needed	Worksheet and pen

■ Activity Explained

- ⊃ The individual identifies the people, places, and things that still cause overwhelming feelings of fear or anxiety (refer to the previous activity).
- ⊃ The facilitator assists the individual in creating a goal and a step-by step plan that will aid the individual in overcoming their fears. The facilitator may need to provide additional guidance and ideas in developing the action plans for minimizing the trauma triggers.
- ⊃ The facilitator reminds the person to engage in relaxation activities before implementing their plan in order to reduce anxiety. The facilitator also encourages reflection on how to emotionally prepare to slowly face and overcome fears/anxieties.
- ⊃ The facilitator and individual should repeat the creation of a goal and a step-by-step plan for all of the individual's remaining fears/anxieties.

■ Reflection

What are your biggest fears related to this activity? What relaxation skills would be most helpful as you prepare? What thought stopping or thought replacement skills will you use? What else would be helpful?

■ Variations

For younger children, the process of overcoming triggers could be adapted into a game if appropriate.

Concerns

The individual determines when to begin and at what pace. If the individual wants to discontinue, they may do so, although the facilitator may ask them if they can tolerate another fifteen seconds. If they say no, do not continue. The activity may be attempted again later.

OVERCOMING MY FEARS

In the last activity, you identified the sights, sounds, smells, touch, and tastes connected with your trauma. Although they are reminders, and might trigger an emotional response, most do not interfere with your daily life. There may be some, however, that cause an intense emotional reaction, so much so that you avoid the person, places, or things. These have developed into ongoing fears which may be:

- ➲ Riding in a car after an accident.
- ➲ Going in a particular room or place where the abuse happened.
- ➲ Taking a shower.
- ➲ Seeing a dog.
- ➲ Shopping at the market.

What people, places, things, or events still cause you overwhelming feelings of fear? List them here.

_____

_____

_____

_____

Now, with the help of the facilitator, develop a plan for overcoming each fear, one at a time.

The final step to reach the goal is that it no longer elicits overwhelming fear, creates avoidance and "ruins your day". The first step is something you could possibly tolerate now. For example:

FEAR: Of dogs

Why: During the abuse, a dog was barking loudly outside and every time I hear a dog barking, I feel like I'm right back in the abuse situation.

GOAL: To be able to be around dogs without freaking out; to be able to pet and/or play with a dog again.

Step 1: Look at photos of various dogs; identify the one most similar to the original dog (if known).

Step 2: Look out a window at a real dog.

Step 3: Watch a video of a dog playing.

Step 4: Stand near a dog on a leash.

Step 5: Pet a dog on a leash.

Step 6: Pet a dog.

Step 7: Play fetch with a dog.

FEAR
_____

What Happened
_____

_____

GOAL
_____

_____

STEPS:

(develop a practical plan, including details)

108 - OVERCOMING MY FEARS PRACTICE

Age	All	Setting	Individual	Trauma Recovery	LIVING - Free

Purpose	To take steps toward overcoming the lingering fears left from trauma.
Overview	The facilitator assists the individual in taking steps to defeat triggers and fears that continue even after the trauma narrative has been shared. Implement the *Overcoming My Fears Plan* developed previously.

Approximate Time	To be determined by previous plan		**Supplies Needed**	To be determined by previous plan

■ Activity Explained

- ➲ The facilitator assists the individual in completing their step-by-step plan to overcome their fears/anxieties, one at a time.
- ➲ The individual determines when to begin and at what pace. If the individual wants to discontinue, they may do so, although the facilitator may ask them if they can tolerate another fifteen seconds. If they say no, do not continue. The activity may be attempted again later.
- ➲ Some steps of the plan may need to be done repeatedly before the individual can move on the next step.
- ➲ The facilitator should provide repeated encouragement and continuous reflection on the feelings that arise at each step of the plan, focusing on how to overcome them.

■ Reflection

You're doing great. You did it! How do you feel after having completed that step? What were you thinking as you did that step? What were you telling yourself?

■ Variations

Implementing the plans may be done with the facilitator or with another, informed adult, such as a parent or house mom.

■ Concerns

As already mentioned, plans should proceed at the individual's pace though encouragement to continue may frequently be needed.

■ Story

For some, once they have overcome one trigger, others lose their power. Once one trigger was defeated, others also surrendered.

LIVING: SAFE

LIVING

109 WHAT HELPS? WHAT HARMS?

Age	All	Setting	Individual	Trauma Recovery	LIVING - Safe

Purpose	To identify what helps and what hinders the person's emotional healing. To maximize and encourage those things which help and minimize those things which harm.
Overview	The individual identifies the people, places, things, and activities that help or harm their healing journey.

Approximate Time	10-20 minutes

Supplies Needed	Worksheet or paper and pen

◼ Activity Explained

⊃ The individual identifies the things that help them grow and heal from their past negative experiences. These may be people, places, things, attitudes, personality traits, beliefs, or activities. The facilitator encourages focusing on these helpful and healing people, places, and things, and provides other examples as needed (refer to worksheet).

⊃ The individual is also asked to identify the people, places, or things that hinder or harm their healing journey and is encouraged to avoid them whenever possible.

◼ Reflection

How can you increase your use of those things that help you grow? What steps do you need to take to avoid things that harm you?

◼ Variations

Activity may be verbal or written. The individual may complete the worksheet individually and bring it to the session.

◼ Concerns

This information should not be gathered when the individual is in crisis.

WHAT HELPS? WHAT HARMS HEALING?

Name		Date	

Make a list of those things that ***HELP*** and those things that ***HARM*** your growth and healing. These may be people, places, events, things, activities, or beliefs you have about the world, yourself, addictions, spiritual faith, relationships, or personality characteristics.

People, Places, Things and Activities that HELP	People, Places, Things and Activities that HARM
Examples: my faith in God, my determination and perseverance, my love of music, supportive friends.	*Examples: my feelings of family obligation, thinking the problem is my fault, no money for therapy.*

110 WHO TO CONTACT

Age	All	Setting	Group	Trauma Recovery	LIVING - Safe

Purpose	Individuals identify people they can safely turn to for help or assistance when they are in need.
Overview	Individuals identify safe people in their life who they can ask for help. and create a document of contact information for helpful emergency contacts.

Approximate Time	10-20 minutes		Supplies Needed	Phone or paper and pen

■ Activity Explained

- ⮑ The individual is encouraged to identify the people in their life who they feel safe contacting.

- ⮑ Participants identify friends, family, or people at school and in their community who they feel comfortable contacting in times of needs. Participants write down the names and phone numbers of these people.

- ⮑ Participants are encouraged to have this list readily available and to use it when discouraged, self-condemning, in crisis, or in need of support or help.

■ Reflection

What about this person makes you feel safe with them? In what situations would it benefit you to contact one of these individuals?

■ Variations

The list may be programmed into the person's phone, but a written copy should also be placed in the person's information file.

Activity may be done individually or in groups.

■ Concerns

Participants may not be able to identify people to list in each category but ask that they write at least one contact down.

WHO TO CONTACT

If I need help, here's who I'll contact:

School			
Name		Phone	
Name		Phone	
Name		Phone	
Community			
Name		Phone	
Name		Phone	
Name		Phone	
Family			
Name		Phone	
Name		Phone	
Name		Phone	
OTHER (social worker, counselor, caseworker)			
Name		Phone	
Name		Phone	
Name		Phone	

OTHER
If case of an emergency, I will call _____ (emergency number for my country/region)
If I need immediate medical or psychological care, I could contact this hospital or clinic:

Name		Phone	

111 CONFRONTING MY ABUSER

Age	All	Setting	Individual	Trauma Recovery	LIVING - Safe

Purpose	To encourage the individual to consider whether or not to confront one's abuser, and what one would do and say if they did.
Overview	The individual is asked to clarify their thoughts and decisions regarding if/when to confront their abuser.

Approximate Time	20-30 minutes

Supplies Needed	Worksheet and pen

■ Activity Explained

- ➲ The individual communicates their desires for if/when they confront their abuser.
- ➲ The individual identifies what they would like to do and say and addresses any limitations or concerns, as well as the if, when, where, and who they would want to be there.
- ➲ The individual names what they will do if/when they start to feel overwhelmed among other scenarios.

■ Reflection

Would you ever want to confront the person(s) that hurt you? What would you do or say if you could? Do you feel ready to confront him/her now? If not, how do you think you will know when you're ready? If you feel ready, when, where, and how would you do it?

■ Variations

Activity may be verbal or written.

■ Concerns

For this activity individuals are encouraged to think about and plan what they would want to say to the person that harmed them, even if they do not want or feel ready to confront the person. Encourage the individual to do this activity even if the person is dead, lives far away, or is unknown.

■ Story

One woman who was raped as a child said she wouldn't know where to find the person who hurt her but still completed the exercise. She later shared, *I didn't think I needed to do this but, wow, it was so healing for me to think about what I would tell the person if I could.*

CONFRONTATION PLAN

If I decide to communicate with and confront the person who harmed me, I would do and say the following:
If the person who harmed me denies or minimizes what happened, I will:
If the person blames me (or says I remember it wrong), I will:
If the person gets angry and starts yelling, I will:
If the person asks for forgiveness, I will:
If I start feeling overwhelmed or confused, I will:
If the person wants to have future contact or a different level of relationship, I will:
When it's over, I want to:

If/When I communicate with the person who harmed me, it will be:

❑ In a letter   ❑ In person   ❑ On the phone

If/When we meet in person, I want it to be:

Where		When	

Who I want to be there with me:

112 WRITING A LETTER

Age	All	Setting	Individual	Trauma Recovery	LIVING - Safe

Purpose	To express desired thoughts and feelings to the offender or a non-offending caregiver about the trauma in order to process the experience.
Overview	The individual writes a letter to their offender or non-offending caregiver in order to process and express what they think and feel, whether or not the letter is sent.

Approximate Time	20-30 minutes	**Supplies Needed**	Worksheet and pen

■ Activity Explained

➲ The individual writes a letter using the prompts provided on the worksheet, deciding what they would like to communicate.

➲ The facilitator guides the process by asking what else they would like to communicate in order to express the many thoughts and emotions surrounding the trauma.

➲ The individual decides whether or not to send the letter.

■ Reflection

Is there anything else you would like to say or that you want the person to hear? Do you want to send it? Why or why not?

■ Variations

Activity could be done verbally rather than in written form, especially if the person clearly knows they will not be sending it.

■ Concerns

The prompts should be tailored to match the trauma experience of the individual.

The facilitator may need to assist in the writing process.

WRITING A LETTER

To:

❏ Offender   ❏ Non-offending Caregiver (parent)

Their Name		Date	

Here are some ideas of what to include in your letter:

(You choose what you want to include and in what order.)

- ➲ How I feel about writing this letter
- ➲ What I thought about you before, during, and after what happened
- ➲ What you did or didn't do
- ➲ What you said or didn't say
- ➲ What I wish you'd known or done differently
- ➲ What I wish I'd known or done differently
- ➲ What I liked and didn't like about you
- ➲ How I feel about you
- ➲ What I'd like to happen now
- ➲ What I wish was different
- ➲ What I want/don't want regarding our relationship
- ➲ What I'd like the future to look like
- ➲ Anything else?

113 MY LETTER TO YOU

Age	All	Setting	Individual	Trauma Recovery	LIVING - Safe

Purpose	To communicate the individual's thoughts and feelings about his/her trauma experience in a letter.
Overview	Whether it is sent or not, writing a letter encourages the person to communicate what happened and how they feel about what happened. The intended recipient can be anyone and may be a friend or foe, abuser or defender, or parent or perpetrator. Getting out long-held thoughts and emotions helps the person live free, feeling safer.

Approximate Time	10-30 minutes

Supplies Needed	Blank paper and pen

■ Activity Explained

⮑ *My Letter* to You is best used after the individual has shared his/her story (*Trauma Narrative*). Some will find this exercise difficult and may need some coaching as to what to include in the letter. This activity helps the individual communicate to people who were directly and indirectly involved in their trauma experience.

⮑ The person chooses who to write the letter to and whether or not it will be sent. The letter could even be written to someone who is now deceased. The goal is for the person to have the opportunity to communicate long-held emotions, questions, beliefs and thoughts, and/or to share about their trauma story if desired.

⮑ The individual chooses what they want to write, which might include:

- What you thought or believed and how you felt/feel about what happened.
- How you reacted, what you did, and/or how it affected you.
- What you wish was different and/or what you would do over.
- What you've learned and how you've grown.

⮑ Once the letter is completed, the facilitator and individual discuss the pros and cons of whether or not to send the letter.

■ Reflection

How did it feel to write this letter? Would it be helpful for you to send this letter? Is there anything else or anyone else you'd like to write?

■ Variations

There is great flexibility in this exercise. The individual may want to write several letters to different people reflecting various aspects of their reactions, thoughts, and feelings about what happened.

■ Concerns

The individual must be emotionally ready and have adequately processed their trauma before engaging in this activity.

114 DEVELOPING ROLE PLAY TOPICS

Age	All	Setting	Group	Trauma Recovery	LIVING - Safe

Purpose	To stimulate creative thinking, build self-esteem, and foster relationships between group members.
Overview	Individuals role play about situations they may or may not have experienced or may experience in the future.

Approximate Time	10-20 minutes

Supplies Needed	None

■ Activity Explained

➲ The facilitator reminds group members before they begin that they are not to make negative comments or to put down others' ideas or suggestions. The facilitator then asks the group for role play ideas, writing all ideas down, no matter how crazy it may seem.

➲ The group should first decide on an idea related to everyday life and determine the *who, what, when, and where* of the role play.

➲ The group can then choose a deeper, more emotional topic and also determine the *who, what, when, and where* of the role play.

■ Reflection

Are there any other role play situations common in your country or that may be applicable to your life?

■ Variations

Groups may choose to enact the role plays after developing them or save them for a later activity.

This activity may also be done one-on-one with an individual and a facilitator.

■ Concerns

When beginning the use of role plays, it is suggested that topics be safe, with low vulnerability and emotional risk. Everyday situations should be used before any that relate to trauma. For example, group members could role play the dilemma of choosing which vocational program to enter (beauty or culinary school) before enacting a role play about confronting those that harmed them.

DEVELOPING A LIST OF TOPICS

Participants will role play situations they may or may not have experienced or may experience in the future. When generating a list, the topics do not all need to be from group members' experiences. They may come from any viable life situation. Topic ideas can be generated by the facilitator beforehand or with the participants.

When developing the list with the group, remind members not to make negative comments or put down others' ideas or suggestions. While brainstorming ideas, it is important to generate and write down as many ideas as possible, providing a non-critical environment and an acceptance of all ideas, even seemingly crazy ones because they often spark other creative and useful ideas.

When beginning the use of role plays, it is suggested that selected topics be safe with low vulnerability and emotional risk. Everyday situations could be used before using role plays around trauma and abuse. For example, group members could role play the dilemma of choosing which vocational program to enter (beauty or culinary school) before enacting a role play about confronting an abuser or reintegration with family, community or culture.

Everyday Topics

Topics which focus on everyday life might include:

- ⮂ Whether or not to share one's belongings with others.
- ⮂ Which vocational program to do.
- ⮂ Whether to watch television or do homework.
- ⮂ Whether to tell the truth or lie—so as not to hurt someone's feelings.
- ⮂ Whether or not to cut one's hair, get ears pierced, wear make-up, etc.
- ⮂ Whether or not to eat a meal or skip it.
- ⮂ Whether or not to go visit one's family.
- ⮂ Other (peer pressure, lying, how to spend personal time, what clothes to wear, relationships with family and friends, etc.)

Deeper Issues

Topics which deal with deeper issues might include:

- ⮂ What to do when asked out by a boy who knows about you.
- ⮂ What to do when someone puts you down.
- ⮂ What to do when approached sexually.
- ⮂ What to do when you're out of work and you are approached for sex work.
- ⮂ What to do about your unsupportive family.
- ⮂ What to do if pregnant.
- ⮂ How to earn money.
- ⮂ Other (drug use, dating, sex, religion, cultural challenges, family relationships, confronting an abuser, etc.)

ROLE PLAY TOPIC EXAMPLES

■ Issue: vocational choice

People Involved: Tah, age 15, and her counselor (or friend)

Situation: Tah is confused and not sure whether or not she wants to go to the beauty school or the cooking school. The deadline to make a decision is tomorrow

Time and Place: counseling room

■ Issue: cultural reintegration

People Involved: Trena, age 17, living at a restoration home and her house Mom

Situation: When Trena was waiting for the van today, she went in to a store and a man said something derogatory to her (said she was a filthy prostitute)

Time and Place: store in city

■ Issue: Peer Pressure

People Involved: Tak and her friend Sue, both age 13

Situation: Sue tells Tak that she can join a special group if she does her homework and lies to the teacher

Time and Place: after school

■ Issue: Personal Independence versus responsibility to family

People Involved: Sun, age 12, and her aunt

Situation: The aunt tells Sun that her family needs more money and that she should leave school and go to work

Time and Place: during a home visit

■ Issue: Pregnancy

People Involved: Two 16-year-old girls

Situation: One of the girls thinks she might be pregnant and decides to talk with the other who is considered more "experienced"

Time and Place: ----

■ Issue: Drugs

People Involved: Two young girls

Situation: The girls are talking about whether or not it is okay to use drugs.

Time and Place: ---

Issue: Family relationships

People Involved: Trah, age 9, and Srey, age 13, both sold into prostitution by their mothers

Situation: Trah is asking Srey about all of her feelings, both good and bad, about her mother

Time and Place: restoration program

■ Issue: Lying

People Involved: Girl, age 9, and House Mom

Situation: The girl lost the necklace she borrowed from the House Mom and is tempted to lie and say that someone stole it.

Time and Place: restoration program

■ Issue: Family

People Involved: Girl, age 14, and her mother (who knew about her being sold by her neighbor)

Situation: Mother asks the girls to return to sex work to make money for the family

Time and Place: phone call

115 ROLE PLAY DEBRIEF QUESTIONS

For The Facilitator	Setting	Individual	Trauma Recovery	LIVING - Safe

Purpose	To assist facilitators by providing lists of possible questions to use after leading a role play exercise.
Overview	Numerous questions are given facilitators to ask participants after engaging in role plays.

Approximate Time	10-45 minutes (depending on length of debrief time after a role play activity)	Supplies Needed	Worksheet

■ Activity Explained

- ➲ The facilitator reviews the various lists of role play debrief questions. It is helpful to make a copy.
- ➲ The facilitator selects those most relevant to the role play being used.
- ➲ Afterwards, the facilitator may want to indicate which questions were best suited for the group and/or which were already asked, in preparation for using them again.

■ Reflection

The following questions are those that could be used under REFLECTION for the various role play activities.

■ Variations

Encourage facilitators to make their own list of questions, more relevant to their participants and situation.

■ Concerns

Select and/or adapt questions so that they are both age and culturally appropriate for the participant group.

DISCUSSING/DEBRIEFING THE ROLE PLAYS

Here are several lists of questions which can be asked after each role play to discuss or debrief the experience. Select which questions are best suited for the group. Select and/or adapt questions according to what is age-appropriate for the participant group.

■ QUESTIONS for Post Role Play Discussion

- ➲ What alternatives did the player(s) consider?
- ➲ Can you think of some alternatives that were not considered?
- ➲ What would be the probable consequences of the line of action that was being taken?
- ➲ What risks were involved?
- ➲ What would you consider a positive outcome at this point?
- ➲ Would both characters consider this a satisfactory outcome?
- ➲ Did the role play focus on the problem, the communication, or the personalities of the individuals?
- ➲ What are some of the influences that may have affected the individuals' perspectives?
- ➲ Could you identify and assumptions or hidden messages?
- ➲ What was the nature of the relationship? Mentor/teacher? Peer? Parent? Subordinate?

■ PROCESS and CONTENT

- ➲ What could be the final outcome of that role play? Any predictions?
- ➲ What are some of the other possible options or approaches?
- ➲ What might be some of the consequences of different outcomes?
- ➲ How was the communication between the members in the role play?
- ➲ How would you describe the relationship between group members?
- ➲ How could the communication have been improved?
- ➲ What wasn't being said (but implied)? Any hidden agendas?

■ THOUGHTS and FEELINGS

- ➲ What did you THINK about the role play?
- ➲ How did you FEEL watching it or being a part of it?
- ➲ With whom did you identify and why?
- ➲ Have you experienced that yourself? When and where?
- ➲ What made you feel uncomfortable and why?
- ➲ What do you wish would have been different? Why?

■ VALUES and BELIEFS – Choosing and Doing

1. Identifying Preferences:

What do I really like?

What do I want?

What can make me happy?

2. Identifying Influences:

What influences have led me to these preferences?

How much of my choices are determined by parents, peers, media, culture?

How freely have I chosen?

3. Identifying Alternatives:

What are the possible alternatives to this choice?

Have I given sufficient thought to them?

4. Identifying Consequences:

What are the probable and possible consequences for each option?

Am I willing to risk the consequences?

Are the consequences socially beneficial or harmful?

5. Actions:

Am I able to act on the choices I have made?

How do my actions reflect my choice?

6. Patterning:

Do my actions reflect a continuing commitment to this choice?

How can I change the patterns of my life so that this choice is continually reflected in my actions?

116 SITUATIONS AND CHARADES

Age	All	Setting	Group	Trauma Recovery	LIVING - Safe

Purpose	To familiarize group members with body language and non-verbal cues.
Overview	The group develops a list of dilemmas or emotional situations and writes them down on cards. Individual group members select a card and then act out the situation (without using words) while the rest of the group members guess what is happening.

Approximate Time	20minutes	**Supplies Needed**	Paper (cards) and pens

■ Activity Explained

⇨ Group members write emotional situations (good or bad, negative or positive) on paper/cards. (If needed, refer to list of scenarios generated in *Developing Role Play Topics*, presented earlier)

⇨ Each individual chooses a card without showing others and takes turns acting out the situation without speaking or using any words/sounds.

⇨ Other group members guess what is happening.

■ Reflection

Was the situation a negative or positive one? How did you know if the situation was good or bad? What gave the situation away? Was it hard to act out the stories? Were some easier than others? What did you learn about body language?

■ Variations

Team Game: the group is divided into two teams and only team members guess when a teammate is acting out what's on the card. If the team guesses correctly, they get a point.

One-on-one (facilitator and individual): Each person writes several of their own scenarios and acts them out for the other person to guess.

■ Concerns

Some individuals may not feel comfortable acting in front of the group. You can encourage them but make acting optional.

SITUATIONS AND CHARADES

This role play activity helps members become more aware of body language and non-verbal cues. The group develops a list of dilemmas or emotional situations and writes them down on cards. Individual group members select a card and then act out the situation (without using words) while the rest of the members guess what is happening. (This can also be done as a team game or one-on-one.)

Examples:

- You got the highest grade on a math test in school.
- You just found out you are pregnant.
- You just got rescued from working in a brothel.
- You have to go to the police to report that your bicycle got stolen.
- You are very hungry.
- You're alone and a strange man is following you.
- You're on your way to the doctor.
- You're on your way to the wedding of a friend.
- You wanted to watch a movie, but the house mom said "No."
- You are tired and want to go to sleep but must finish some tasks first.

117 - ADVICE GIVING

Age	All	Setting	Group	Trauma Recovery	LIVING - Safe

Purpose	To encourage decision-making, problem-solving, reflection on negative and positive consequences, and to empower making informed decisions.
Overview	An individual or group is given various scenarios in which they are asked to give advice and to determine the consequences of those decisions.

Approximate Time	10-30 minutes

Supplies Needed	Worksheet for facilitator's use

■ Activity Explained

- ⊃ A scenario may be read, acted out, or created (the individual or group may make up their own scenario).
- ⊃ The participants decide, then share, the advice they would give to the individual in the scenario.
- ⊃ The individuals reflect on how the advice would affect the individual and their thoughts, feelings, and beliefs. For example *What would be the consequences or possible outcome of acting on the given advice?*

■ Reflection

What do you think the person will do? What advice will he/she take? What might happen if the person took your advice? How might he/she feel? Think? What might happen if the person took different advice? How might he/she feel? Think?

■ Variations

This activity works well in group settings. The advice can be given by anyone in the group and others do not need to agree. If desired, the group can divide in two or more groups, each taking a particular advice-giving perspective to discuss or debate.

If preferred, this may become a written activity where the individual or group members write out what advice they would give rather than discussing it openly. Group discussion could follow if desired.

An empty chair or Face Circle (basic face drawn on a piece of paper) may be used as a focal point to represent the person needing advice.

■ Concerns

Scenarios may be triggering to some individuals and need to be chosen with caution.

Same-age groups (or similar maturity levels) are recommended.

ADVICE GIVING

In this role play, a story is read or created in which someone is in need of advice.

- ⮑ Examples are given below, but please create additional scenarios relevant to your culture and context.
- ⮑ An empty chair or the Face Circle (basic face drawn on a piece of paper) could be used as a point of focus.
- ⮑ An individual, group, or designated sub-groups can be the advice giver.
- ⮑ Discussion afterwards should focus on how the different advice, if taken, could affect the thoughts, feelings, and beliefs of the person and what the possible consequences might be.

▮ Questions to consider:

What do you think the person will do?

What advice will he/she take?

What might happen if the person took your advice?

How would he/she feel? Think?

What might happen if the person took different advice?

How would he/she feel? Think?

▮ Examples

- ⮑ Shay, 16 years, is pregnant and doesn't know what to do.
- ⮑ Tak, 10 years, doesn't like the Social Worker (Program Director) at all.
- ⮑ Mina, 14 years, can go back home if she wants. But not sure she wants to leave.
- ⮑ Bap, 18 years, is invited to a party with a new friend.
- ⮑ Luna's father is beating her mother and her younger sister.
- ⮑ Joe, 12 years, is encouraged to take drugs by his friends.
- ⮑ Nina, 13 years, is being told to have sex with her boyfriend.

118 - FACE INTERVIEW

Age	All	Setting	Group	Trauma Recovery	LIVING - Safe

Purpose	To build communication and interviewing skills while learning about how others think
Overview	An individual or group interviews another individual or group who are answering as if they were playing the role of another person.

Approximate Time	15-20 minutes		**Supplies Needed**	

■ Activity Explained

Note: Refer to additional information provided elsewhere on *Developing Role Play Topics, Role Play Scenarios, and Role Play Debrief Questions* before conducting this activity.

- ➲ The facilitator draws a large circle face on a whiteboard or piece of paper and identifies WHO the face is.
- ➲ An individual or half the group will then pretend to be the WHO person and answer questions as the other individual or group interview them.

■ Reflection

Debrief the activity (refer to *Role Play Debrief Questions*) by asking such questions as: *How did you like this activity? What would you do differently? Did the person being interviewed seem realistic?*

■ Variations

Questions or statements can be made to the WHO (an empty chair or drawing of a face) without anyone answering. (see Story below.)

■ Concerns

Facilitators should be sure to pick a WHO person that would be familiar to all present or create one that individuals can relate to.

■ Story

This has been used with groups of young girls who had been sexually abused, used, and sold. Using just a face drawn on a piece of paper, the girls were instructed to ask questions or make statements to the person who was labeled: *The One Who Hurt You* (pimp, parent, neighbor, trafficker). At first, only a few talked, but slowly, more and more participated, *Why did you do what you did? You are a bad person. You only care about money. Were you abused as a child? Did you hurt others? You should go to jail.* One by one, most began to participate, expressing long-held questions, emotions, and thoughts.

FACE INTERVIEW

For this role play the leader draws a large circle face on a whiteboard or piece of paper and identifies WHO the face is. Individual(s) (one, three or half of the group) can be asked to answer for the identified person, while the rest of the group members ask questions, as if interviewing the person. The person (WHO) can be anyone (even a group member) or famous, be from any time in history or the present and have a positive or negative reputation.

■ The steps involve:

- ➲ Decide WHO will be interviewed.
- ➲ Develop a list of questions (or allow the interview to unfold).
- ➲ Invite one or more participants to answer the interview questions and everyone else to ask the questions. Or, divide into two groups with one being interviewed and one answering.
- ➲ Group members do not need to coordinate their answers and are free to answer spontaneously even if they represent different perspectives.

■ Examples

- ➲ **WHO:** Sonri, an 18-year-old former prostituted girl, now working as a restaurant cook
- ➲ **WHO:** Brad Pitt, a famous movie actor
- ➲ **WHO:** Pol Pot, a leader who allowed the torture and killing of millions of Cambodians in the 1970s or Adolf Hitler, who allowed the torture and killing of millions during World War II
- ➲ **WHO:** former President Obama of the USA
- ➲ **WHO:** AJ, a man who sells women and girls for sex (pimp, trafficker)
- ➲ **WHO:** Joe, a teenager addicted to pornography
- ➲ **WHO:** Teresa, a worried mother
- ➲ **WHO:** Marie, a recently raped young woman
- ➲ **WHO:** Sam, a middle-aged man who frequently buys prostitution services
- ➲ **WHO:** John, an investment banker and financial analyst expert

■ Possible Interview Questions

- ➲ How did you get started?
- ➲ Did you go to school? What did you study?
- ➲ Where did you grow up and what was your family like?
- ➲ What do you do for fun? (What did you do for fun?)
- ➲ Who influenced you?
- ➲ Would you consider yourself to be a good or a bad person?
- ➲ If you could live your life over, what would you do differently?
- ➲ Do you have any regrets about things you've done in your life?

119 WHAT WOULD YOU DO?

Age	All	Setting	Group	Trauma Recovery	LIVING - Safe

Purpose	The goal of this activity is to encourage participants to problem solve while also clarifying their values.
Overview	This activity provides a variety of situations and then asks *What would you do?*

Approximate Time	20-45 minutes

Supplies Needed	Scenarios

◼ Activity Explained

- ➲ The facilitator reads a situation to the participant(s) then asks, "What would you do if this was you?"
- ➲ The individual or group member shares what they would do if they were in the given situation. Sharing can take place in large or small sub-groups. Group members should take turns sharing their responses.
- ➲ Participants and facilitator may ask questions about why people chose to take certain actions in each scenario but may not criticize or condemn another's answer. Repeat process for as many scenarios as desired (from those provided or create your own, culturally relevant ones).

◼ Reflection

Discuss the values that are questioned in each scenario. For example, Scenario 1 deals with honesty, encouraging participants to think about honesty after they respond to *What would you do?* Other scenarios address issues such as abortion, violent discipline, integrity, etc. Encourage participants to think more deeply about their thoughts and feelings about these issues rather than give short, quick answers.

◼ Variations

Activity may be used individually or in groups. Activity may be conducted verbally or written.

◼ Concerns

Choose scenarios that are age and culturally appropriate and not re-traumatizing.

WHAT WOULD YOU DO?

- ⮥ Your father owes money to a neighbor who comes to your house asking to speak to your father. Your father tells you to tell the neighbor that he is not home, even though he is in the back of the house. What would you do and why?
- ⮥ A popular girl steals something and you get blamed. What would you do and why?
- ⮥ A 16-year-old boy likes a 16-year-old-girl but is too shy to tell her. What should he do?
- ⮥ A father has no money to buy food for his family. His neighbor told him that he could find a job in the city for his 12-year-old daughter (but the father knows the neighbor has sold other children to brothels). What should he do?
- ⮥ The teacher asks you to help correct a test. When you correct your friend's test you see that she got several answers wrong and you could change them without the teacher knowing. What would you do?
- ⮥ Anna found out she is pregnant and knows that her parents will throw her out of the house. Her friend told her about getting an abortion. What would you do or how would you advise her?
- ⮥ You meet a boy and like him. Your family has said they do not want you to date someone of that race, faith, or nationality. What should you do?
- ⮥ You can't find a job, feel pressure to send money home, and are offered a job at a strip club. What would you do?
- ⮥ You overhear your parents say that your mom has cancer and only three months to live, but they don't want any of the children to know. What would you do?
- ⮥ You're supposed to meet with the director but forgot the meeting because you were talking with a friend. You missed your last meeting as well and the director was mad. What do you do or say?
- ⮥ You're at the store and see a woman hitting her young child. What would you do?
- ⮥ You would like to work with a classmate on a project. How do you ask?
- ⮥ You stop by a few neighbors' homes to ask if they have seen your bike. What do you say?
- ⮥ You see some friends playing a game down the street and would like to play with them. What do you do?
- ⮥ Someone accuses you of cheating on a test when you didn't. What would you do and say?
- ⮥ You did your chore, but someone made a mess and the caregiver doesn't believe you when you say you did it.
- ⮥ You bought something at the store and when you get home you realize it is broken.

120 MY *"WHAT I'D DO"* PLAN

| Age | All | Setting | Group | Trauma Recovery | LIVING - Safe |

| Purpose | To encourage participants to decide in advance how they would respond in various difficult situations. |
| Overview | Participants identify their preferred actions and reactions when in challenging situations. |

| Approximate Time | 30 minutes |

| Supplies Needed | Worksheet and pen |

◼ Activity Explained

- ➲ The participant(s) is given various scenarios and asked how they might best respond to the situation.
- ➲ The participant identifies their desired response for each of the given scenarios.
- ➲ If time allows, it is beneficial to identify various possible responses to the scenarios, increasing the person's thinking, processing, problem-solving, and decision-making abilities.
- ➲ The participant shares answers with the facilitator and they discuss other possible ideas and plans.

◼ Reflection

Have you or anyone you know experienced this or a similar situation before? What might a person do in that situation (what are the various possible options)? What do you hope you will do in that scenario? Are you satisfied with your answers? Are there any situations where you wish you would respond differently? What is the likelihood that you will actually respond in the way you wrote? What might help increase the chances that you will do what you'd like to do in that situation?

◼ Variations

Activity may be verbal or written.

Activity can be done with individuals or with groups, large or small. In groups, sharing answers should be optional with only follow-up questions, not criticism, allowed.

◼ Concerns

Individuals may need assistance answering some of the prompts.

Facilitator may need to help the person revise and improved their plan if the identified solution would be harmful to the person.

MY "WHAT I'D DO" PLAN

■ *Here's what I'll do IF...*

Someone misunderstood what I said:

_____

_____

Someone starts to touch me without my permission:

_____

_____

Someone lies to me or about me:

_____

_____

Someone doesn't believe me:

_____

_____

Someone steals something from me:

_____

_____

Someone talks bad about a friend or family member:

_____

_____

Someone ignores me or is rude to me:

_____

_____

Someone bullies me:

_____

_____

A person forces me to have sex:

_____

_____

Someone _____

_____

_____

121 FINISHING THE STORY

Age	All	Setting	Group	Trauma Recovery	LIVING - Safe

Purpose	To build communication and creative-thinking skills while problem-solving and exploring different options and endings to various stories.
Overview	An unfinished scenario is read aloud and participant(s) decide or act out how they think the story should or could end.

Approximate Time	10-30 minutes

Supplies Needed	None

■ Activity Explained

Note: Refer to additional information provided in *Developing Role Play Topics, Role Play Scenarios, and Role Play Debrief Questions* before conducting this activity.

- ⮑ The facilitator reads or tells a story with a dilemma but stops before any resolution has been made or options for action are given.
- ⮑ The individuals are then asked to share their thoughts or role play the story, developing their own ending.
- ⮑ Each story may be done several times, allowing different endings and versions with both positive and negative outcomes to emerge.
- ⮑ Discuss what makes the stories positive or negative and what might change a situation from one to the other.

■ Reflection

What made you take the story in that direction? How could you have ended it differently? What are other possible endings to the story? What would be a sad or harmful ending? What would be a positive, happy ending?

■ Variations

Instead of a role play that develops and evolves, the group may verbally brainstorm how the story might end. The members may share ideas, options, and alternatives for finishing the story, then discuss.

■ Concerns

Stories used need to be age and culturally appropriate.

"FINISHING THE STORY" ROLE PLAY

Read or tell a story with a dilemma and stop before any resolution has been decided or any final action has been taken. Participants are then asked to role play the story, developing their own ending to the story. Each story or scenario could be enacted several times, allowing different endings and versions to emerge. Encourage both positive and negative endings and discuss how the ending might be different given different circumstances.

■ Example Stories

(refer also to list of scenarios generated in *Developing Role Play Topics*.)

Chay is a 12-year-old girl wondering if she should go to work at the local brothel in order to make money for her poor family.

Bopni is a 15-year-old-girl whose mother is sick and whose father has no work.

Mia is a 16-year-old girl working in the brothels who meets a nice man at the grocery store. She wonders if she should tell him about her life, hoping that he might be able to help her escape.

Joni is an 18-year-old boy who finds a job in nearby country but is unsure if it is legitimate.

Charley is a 34-year-old married man and father of three children. He just lost his job.

122 "DON'T BE SURPRISED"

Age	All	Setting	Group	Trauma Recovery	LIVING - Safe

Purpose	To demonstrate empathy and normalize the emotions and feelings experienced by a trauma victim.
Overview	The individual reads the poem *Don't Be Surprised* and relates it to their own experience.

Approximate Time	5-15 minutes		**Supplies Needed**	Poem

■ Activity Explained

- ➲ The facilitator should give a copy of *Don't Be Surprised* to the participant(s)
- ➲ Those present take turns reading the poem, one stanza each.
- ➲ After reading, debrief the thoughts and feelings. The facilitator should ask the individual if they have experienced any similar thoughts or feelings as what was shared.

■ Reflection

Have you ever wondered some these things too? Which ones stand out to you? How did you feel and what did you think as we read this? What did you like or not like about the poem?

■ Variations

One stanza may be read at a time, then questions asked before moving on to read the next.

The people, places and things listed may need to be changed in order to reflect more accurately the cultural context. For example, instead of: "miss your boyfriend," "the Life" and "friends," put, "miss your Madam," "miss the attention," "miss a favorite customer," and/or "miss the familiar place."

■ Concerns

Some of the material in the stanzas may be triggering to individuals.

■ Story

This has been used in a support group for sexually exploited women who reviewed and discussed only one section each week.

When shared with a group of program directors from restoration homes for the sexually exploited in North America, they asked, *"Can we make a big copy of this and put it up on the wall in the recovery home?"*

I wholeheartedly replied, *YES!*

DON'T BE SURPRISED (WRITTEN BY BC JOHNSON, 2010)

■ Don't be surprised if you...

Feel strange and out of place

Think this new place and people are too good to be true

Think that it won't last—that it couldn't last

Are waiting for something bad to happen

■ Don't be surprised if you...

Don't trust the people here

Don't know what and who to believe

Feel confused about knowing who's safe and not safe

Are waiting for someone to hit or hurt you

■ Don't be surprised if you...

Miss the familiar

Miss your boyfriend

Miss "The Life"

Miss your friends (wife-in-laws)

■ Don't be surprised if you...

Feel scared and unsure about the future

Don't know what you want to do

Don't know where to start

Have a hard time making decisions for yourself

■ Don't be surprised if you...

Feel like a nobody

Feel insecure

Feel like you deserve bad things to happen to you

Feel bad about yourself

■ Don't be surprised if you...

Have nightmares

Have flashbacks

Feel anxious and have panic attacks

Feel depressed

■ Don't be surprised if you...

Have a hard time trusting people for awhile

Are not sure who to trust

Are not sure how to trust

Are not sure when to trust

■ Don't be surprised if you...

(add to the lists)

■ Don't be surprised... it's NORMAL!

123 JUST BECAUSE

Age	All	Setting	Group	Trauma Recovery	LIVING - Safe

Purpose	To develop empathy and to normalize one's personal response to the traumatic experience.
Overview	The individual reads the poem *Just Because* and relates it to their own experience.

Approximate Time	15 minutes

Supplies Needed	Poem

■ Activity Explained

- ➲ The facilitator should give a copy of Just Because to the participant(s)
- ➲ Those present take turns read reading the poem, one stanza each.
- ➲ After reading, debrief the thoughts and feelings. The facilitator should ask the individual if they have experienced any similarities with what was shared.

■ Reflection

Have you ever wondered some these things too? Which ones stand out to you? How did you feel and what did you think as we read this? What did you like or not like about the poem?

■ Variations

One stanza may be read at a time, then questions asked before moving on to read the next.

The people, places and things listed may need to be changed in order to reflect more accurately the cultural context. For example, instead of: "miss your boyfriend," "miss the Life" and "friends," put "miss your Madam," "miss the attention," "miss a favorite customer," and/or "miss the familiar place."

■ Concerns

Some of the material in the stanzas may be triggering to individuals.

■ Story

Like, Don't Be Surprised, this has also been displayed in restoration program facilities.

JUST BECAUSE (WRITTEN BY BC JOHNSON, 2010)

■ **Just because...**

You miss him, doesn't mean you should go back to be with him.

You miss "The Life," doesn't mean you should return.

You miss the good parts doesn't mean you should forget the many bad parts.

■ **Just because...**

You think you'd be better off just going back to "The Life," doesn't mean you should.

You think you'll never fit in anywhere else, doesn't mean you should stop trying.

You think you don't deserve anything good, doesn't mean you don't.

■ **Just because...**

You feel like life won't get better, doesn't mean it won't.

You feel like a nobody, doesn't mean you are.

You feel like giving up trying, doesn't mean you should.

■ **Just because...**

You are overwhelmed now doesn't mean you will always be.

You are scared now doesn't mean you will always be afraid.

You don't know what the future holds, doesn't mean you should give up.

■ **Just because...**

You don't like your new life at times, doesn't mean you should give it up.

You learned to distrust people doesn't mean you should never trust ever again.

You were told no one can love you like he does, doesn't mean it is true.

■ **Just because...**

You are scared, doesn't mean you shouldn't try.

You are confused, doesn't mean you should give up.

You don't know what real love it, doesn't mean you can't experience it, because you can

You CAN make it through this.

You ARE strong—look at what you've already survived (and that was MUCH harder than this)!

You DO have value and worth.

　　DON'T GIVE IN.　　　*DON'T GIVE UP.*

*But **IF you fall**, get back up, however long it takes. Keep walking away from "The Life" and the lies it shouts into your head and heart, saying that you can't change. Because you CAN. It may be hard at times, but it IS possible!*

LIVING: WELL

LIVING

HEALTHY COMPARISONS

Please complete this *Healthy Comparisons* rating form. Rate yourself in the various areas using the scale below. Select a number rating how you felt right after the trauma(s) and then how you feel now. Write a few words to describe yourself at those two times.

Rating Scale: 0 – 5

- 0 = none
- 1 = rarely, horrible
- 2 = low, occasionally, bad
- 3 = medium, regularly, fair

- 4 = frequent, good
- 5 = all-the-time, great
- DNA = Does Not Apply

Area How was/is your...?		Right after the Trauma(s)		Now
Self-blame *0-5 = none - always*	5	Felt guilty all the time	2	Rare thoughts of guilt
Self-esteem *1-5 = horrible – great*				
School achievement or work performance *0-5 = 0 = DNA, 1-5 = horrible - great*				
Self-blame *0-5 = none - always*				
Ability to concentrate *1-5 = horrible – great*				
Have support, help *0-5 = none – All the Time*				
Worry about what others would think/believe? *1-5 - rarely – All the Time*				
Worry about your future? *1-5 - rarely –All the Time*				
Feel Alone and/or Misunderstood *1-5 - rarely – All the Time*				
Other:				

125 A HEALTHY ME

Age	All	Setting	Group	Trauma Recovery	LIVING - Well

Purpose	To identify what it would look like to be emotionally healthy.
Overview	The individual thinks and writes about what it would look like for them to be healthy.

Approximate Time	5-30 minutes (depends on if given as homework or discussed)	Supplies Needed	Worksheet and pen

■ Activity Explained

- ◌ The individual writes down what they want to look like, how they want to feel, and who they want to be.

  Example: *A healthy me is happy (not depressed) and content with life; has a good self-esteem; doesn't get uptight over little things; is comfortable in social settings; communicates effectively with my spouse and children; is positive (not a nag).*

- ◌ The facilitator encourages the individual to focus on positive outcomes rather than on problem situations. Because it is written rather than discussed, it helps the individual to clearly articulate where they want to be and encourages a focus on a positive future.

■ Reflection

What actions would you need to take to move towards this healthier version of you?

What help or encouragement do you need in order to achieve this healthier version of yourself?

■ Variations

This written exercise is best completed independently and brought to the session.

■ Concerns

The focus should stay positive and not cause the individual to think negatively of themselves.

THE HEALTHY ME

■ Directions:

List the traits or characteristics that would reflect what a *Healthy* You would look like. That is, who do you want to be and what do you want to do?

If needed, for comparison, you could list those areas you consider to be weaknesses (or unhealthy) and use them to define what a *Healthy* You would look like.

For example, you might write:

- ➲ *A healthy me is not depressed; has good self-esteem; is able to express anger; is able to forgive myself.*
- ➲ *A healthy me is happy (not depressed) and content with life; has a good self-esteem; doesn't get uptight over little things; is comfortable in social settings; communicates effectively with my spouse and children; is positive (not a nag).*

■ A Healthy Me...

126 I FEEL BETTER WHEN...

Age	All	Setting	Group	Trauma Recovery	LIVING - Well

Purpose	To foster self-esteem, positive feelings, and combat discouragement.
Overview	A personalized list is made to help the individual identify enjoyable activities. They are encouraged to refer to and engage in these activities, especially when feeling discouraged.

Approximate Time	10-20 minutes

Supplies Needed	Worksheet and pen

■ Activity Explained

⮱ The individual identifies and makes a list of those things that bring them positive feelings and enjoyment; such as going for a walk, reading a novel, taking a refreshing shower, baking homemade bread, exercising, painting, playing guitar, or singing. These are the activities that make them feel good about themselves and life. (Refer to the list created in *Calming Activities*.)

⮱ The facilitator explains that when discouraged or depressed, we often forget what we like doing, especially when many of our previously enjoyable activities have lost their appeal.

⮱ The facilitator instructs the individual to engage in the activities on their list whenever they begin to experience negative thoughts or feelings.

■ Reflection

Are some of the activities on your list easy and convenient to do, or do they require planning, time, and/or money? Please continue to add to the list. Can you think of any more people, places, things, or experiences that encourage you or make you feel better?

■ Variations

Activity may be completed individually and brought to the session.

■ Concerns

It is best if the list is made when the individual is not currently experiencing depression. If, however, is it made during a difficult time, the facilitator may need to help the person identify helpful, enjoyable activities. This activity will generally not be effective for the severely depressed.

LIFE IS BETTER WHEN I...

■ Directions:

Here's an incomplete list of activities that people have shared were helpful when they were feeling down or discouraged. Make your own list, but first check the items listed here which you find helpful.

- ➲ go for a walk
- ➲ read a novel
- ➲ take a shower
- ➲ draw a picture

- ➲ go running
- ➲ cook
- ➲ play guitar
- ➲ eat

- ➲ sing
- ➲ go swimming
- ➲ take a nap

Here are some things I can do that have helped me to feel better when I'm down and discouraged:

1 -

2 -

3 -

4 -

5 -

6 -

7 -

8 -

9 -

10 -

127 WHAT WOULD YOU GRAB?

Age	All	Setting	Group	Trauma Recovery	LIVING - Well

Purpose	To identify and clarify what we value and why.
Overview	Individuals are asked to think and share about three things they would grab if their house was on fire.

Approximate Time	10 minutes

Supplies Needed	None

■ Activity Explained

- ➲ The individuals are asked to think about their response to the following question:

    If the house you are staying in was on fire and you could only grab three (3) things, what would they be and WHY?

- ➲ The individuals are asked to share what they would grab and why they chose those specific items.
- ➲ Participants are encouraged to ask each other questions to stimulate the clarification of values.

■ Reflection

What sort of value do the chosen items have for you? Monetary? Personal?

What other items would be hard to leave behind besides these three?

What items would you choose not to take with you Are they replaceable?

■ Variations

Activity may be used individually or in groups. If activity is conducted one-one-one, the facilitator should share what items he/she would take and why.

Activity may be written if desired.

■ Concerns

You may personalize and contextualize the question by asking, *If the center was on fire, or If your bedroom caught fire...*

128 SETTING GOALS

Age	All	Setting	Individual	Trauma Recovery	LIVING - Well

Purpose	To identify personal goals and determine steps to achieve them.
Overview	The individual identifies desired goals and then determines the steps needed to accomplish them. This promotes healing, self-efficacy, and empowerment.

Approximate Time	15-30 minutes

Supplies Needed	Worksheet and pen

■ Activity Explained

- ⊃ The facilitator presents the purpose of personal goal setting.
- ⊃ The facilitator instructs how to identify goals and how to reach them – the when, where, how, why details
- ⊃ The facilitator provides several specific examples relevant to the person and his/her situation.
- ⊃ The facilitator assists the individual, as needed, in completing the *Personal Goals* worksheet and developing a plan for implementation and accountability (finding someone who will ask how they are doing in reaching the goals).

■ Reflection

What made you choose these specific goals?

Are they realistic and attainable or do you think it will be easy to become discouraged and give up?

How can you start working towards these goals?

What will help you to keep on going when feeling overwhelmed or discouraged?

■ Variations

Activity may be completed individually and brought to the session.

■ Concerns

The individual may need assistance in identifying and making realistic goals, writing them down, knowing how to implement them, and selecting an accountability person.

■ Story

Goals are seldom accomplished unless a specific, detailed plan has been documented stating how to attain them.

SETTING PERSONAL GOALS

A personal goal is like a dream or wish—except it is attainable. A goal can be achieved if we figure out the steps needed to reach it. It might take hard work, focus, and intentional actions, but it can be reached.

In order for goals to be helpful, they must be written AND specific. Once an overall goal is identified, steps must be developed that include the *what, when, where, how and how often*. It is also helpful to have a person help us by checking in and asking whether or not we are doing what we planned to do in order to accomplish our goals. You may use extra paper and make other categories as needed.

Example: *If my overall fitness goal is to get in shape, I must be specific in how it will be accomplished. I might decide to walk three time a week on Monday, Wednesdays, and Fridays from 7-7:45 a.m. around our neighborhood, AND I exercise two times each week on a bicycle on Tuesday and Thursdays from 5:30-6:00 p.m.*

Area Overall Goal Specific Details: What, When, Where, How, and How Often

Example: Feelings

1). In order to communicate more opening, I will go through the long list of emotions every night and check those I felt during that day. 2). When I'm feeling a strong emotion, I will share about it with a safe person before the end of the day.

Family	Friends
Finances	Food
Fitness	Fun
Feelings	Future

129 FUTURE HOPES AND DREAMS

Age	All	Setting	Group	Trauma Recovery	LIVING - Well

Purpose	To stimulate and motivate positive, hopeful thinking about the person's future.
Overview	The individual answers questions about their future hopes and dreams.

Approximate Time	10-15 minutes

Supplies Needed	Worksheet and pen

■ Activity Explained

- ⮑ The individual writes down or verbally shares his/her answers to incomplete sentences asking about his/her hopes and dreams for the future.

■ Reflection

What steps can you take to fulfill these hopes and dreams?

Which ones are meant to stay as dreams?

Which ones are mean to be pursued and accomplished?

■ Variations

Activity may be verbal or written. Activity may be used individually or in groups.

An optional drawing may be made to represent any hope or dream.

■ Concerns

Activity may be verbal or written. Activity may be used individually or in groups.

An optional drawing may be made to represent any hope or dream.

MY FUTURE HOPES AND PLANS

Someday, I would like to
_____

I would like to study
_____

I would like to help
_____

I would like to meet
_____

I would like to finish
_____

I would like to go
_____

I would like a job doing
_____

I would hope to marry someone who
_____

I would like to get better at
_____

If I could do anything, I would
_____

If I have children, I would
_____

My dream is to one day
_____

_____

I plan to
_____

_____

■ A Drawing about my Future Hopes and Plans

(Optional: use this space to draw something that represents your future)

130 I AM PROUD

Age	All	Setting	Group	Trauma Recovery	LIVING - Well

Purpose	To encourage self-reflection and build self-esteem.
Overview	The individual answers questions about actions or decisions that they are proud of.

Approximate Time	15 minutes		Supplies Needed	Worksheet and pen

■ Activity Explained

⊃   The individual responds to questions about times they were proud of themselves.

■ Reflection

Was it hard or easy to think of answers to the statements?

Why did these moments/actions make you proud?

Who else would be proud of you for these moments/actions?

Add to the statements when you remember other proud moments.

■ Variations

Activity may be used individually or in groups. Sharing and reflection may need to change if activity is used in a group setting. Items can be changed or adapted according to age group, culture, and setting.

■ Concerns

The individual may need assistance in identifying positive actions of which they are proud.

I AM PROUD

I am proud that I tried (something new)

_____

I am proud that I stopped (bad habit)

_____

I am proud that I finished (a big project)

_____

I am proud that I didn't

_____

I am proud that, on my own, I can

_____

I am proud that when I'm scared I

_____

I was proud that even when the other kids did

_____

I am proud that in school I

_____

I am proud that when the teacher

_____

I am proud that I take good care of

_____

I am proud that I don't need

_____

I am proud that I made

_____

I am proud that I take care of my body

_____

I am proud that I helped

_____

I am proud that I

_____

131 MAKING DECISIONS

Age	All	Setting	Group	Trauma Recovery	LIVING - Well

Purpose	To develop a framework to aid in making beneficial and well-considered decisions.
Overview	The individual chooses a problem or dilemma they are facing then follows a series of steps to help decide the best course of action and what they should do to implement it.

Approximate Time	10-20 minutes

Supplies Needed	Worksheet and pen

■ Activity Explained

- ➲ The individual chooses a problem or dilemma they are currently facing and identifies various solutions or desired outcomes.
- ➲ The individual considers the pros and cons of each possible solution and the risks.
- ➲ The individual identifies the most desirable outcome and the choice(s) they are going to make.

■ Reflection

Did you ask yourself all of the questions?

Did you find them helpful in making your decision?

What was most helpful in this decision-making process?

What specific steps do you now need to make to follow up on your decision?

■ Variations

Activity may be verbal or written.

■ Concerns

The facilitator may need to help guide the individual toward realistic solutions.

MAKING DECISIONS

■ Decision-Making Steps

- ➲ Identify and clarify the dilemma.
- ➲ Recognize the various options available and generate a list of possible resolutions.
- ➲ Consider the positive and negative aspects of each possible solution or decision.
- ➲ Consider the consequences or possible outcomes of each solution or decision.
- ➲ Eliminate unhealthy or harm-producing choices.
- ➲ Choose the solution deemed most beneficial overall.
- ➲ Make the decision and a plan for implementing it.

■ My Decision-Making Process

What is the problem I am facing or the decision I need to make?

(Identify and clarify the dilemma.)

What are all of the possible choices, decisions, or solutions that could be made with my dilemma?

(Recognize the various options available and generate a list of possible resolutions.)

Taking each identified possible solution, what are the strengths and weaknesses of each?

(Consider the positive and negative aspects of each possible solution or decision.)

Taking each identified possible solution, what would be the consequences or outcomes of each?

(Consider the consequences and outcomes of each possible solution or decision.)

Which solutions aren't good for me or others? Get rid of those.

(Eliminate unhealthy or harm-producing choices.)

Which solutions are good for me and others and would lead to a positive, helpful outcome? Choose one.

(Choose the solution deemed most beneficial overall.)

_____

This is my decision. I want to finalize, confirm, share, and act on it.

(Make the decision and a plan for implementing it.)

My Decision
_____

What I will do to make sure it gets done:

_____

132 MY PERSONAL SHIELD

Age	All	Setting	Individual	Trauma Recovery	LIVING - Well

Purpose	To identify the relationships and situations that bring strength and encouragement.
Overview	The individual is given a drawing of a personal shield and instructed to draw their family, things that give them strength, and things that make them happy.

Approximate Time	10-20 minutes

Supplies Needed	Worksheet art supplies

■ Activity Explained

- ⊃ The facilitator explains that in ancient times, warriors carried shields to protect themselves. On the shields were symbols or pictures to depict important people, places, things or events in their lives.
- ⊃ In each section of the shield, the individual draws their family, themselves or something they are proud of, something difficult that they survived, and something that makes them happy.

■ Reflection

Why do you think warriors decorated their shields in ancient times?

How can you use your paper shield, or what you put on your paper shield, to protect you?

■ Variations

Activity may be completed individually or in groups.

■ Concerns

The individual can choose who they want to be their "family" on their shield.

Remind the person that this activity is to help them recognize what brings them strength and is not about artistic ability.

MY PERSONAL SHIELD

In ancient times, warriors carried shields into battle to protect themselves. On the shields were symbols or pictures to depict important people, places, things, or events in their lives. If this were YOUR personal shield, what would you have on it? Make a drawing or symbol to represent:

- ➲ Your family (top left).
- ➲ You or something that you are proud of (top right).
- ➲ Something difficult that happened that you survived (bottom left).
- ➲ Something that gives you strength or makes you feel happy (bottom right).

133 POSITIVES: WHAT'S GOOD ABOUT ME

Age	All	Setting	Group	Trauma Recovery	LIVING - Well

Purpose	To build self-esteem and critical self-reflection skills.
Overview	The individual responds to positive prompts about themselves.

Approximate Time	10-15 minutes		**Supplies Needed**	Worksheet and pen

■ Activity Explained

- ⮑ The individual acknowledges positive descriptions of themselves by completing various prompts about what they are good at, what they like about their looks or abilities, and compliments/positive feedback they have received.

- ⮑ The individual shares and discusses this with the facilitator or group.

■ Reflection

Is there anything positive about yourself that previously was considered a weakness?

What do you enjoy most about yourself?

What do you think others enjoy most?

■ Variations

Activity may be used individually or in groups. If used in groups, individuals can write down their answers and then choose what to share and reflect with the group.

Activity may be done verbally or written.

■ Concerns

The facilitator may need to assist individuals in thinking of positive things about themselves.

POSITIVES: WHAT'S GOOD ABOUT ME

What I'm Good at:

_____

_____

What I like about my looks and/or abilities

_____

_____

What positive things my family and friends say about me:

_____

_____

Compliments I've gotten:

_____

_____

Positive comments from others (teachers, co-workers, neighbors):

_____

_____

134 WHAT I COULD DO WITHOUT

Age	All	Setting	Group	Trauma Recovery	LIVING - Well

Purpose	The purpose of this activity is to prioritize and appreciate various things in our everyday lives.
Overview	The individual makes a list of ten items they use daily, prioritizing them from most important to least important, then is asked which five they could live without.

Approximate Time	15 minutes		Supplies Needed	Worksheet and pen

■ Activity Explained

- ⮑ The individual makes a list of ten items they use daily. Items could be used during eating, sleeping, working, relaxing, fun, etc.

- ⮑ The individual ranks all ten items in order of importance, with 1 representing most important and 10 being least important.

- ⮑ The individual is instructed to delete the five lowest ranked items.

- ⮑ The facilitator asks various questions to determine personal values and priorities, and to encourage appreciation of what we do have.

■ Reflection

Why are some things more important than others?

How do you decide if one thing is more important than another?

Do you need all of these items?

What are things you use every day that you could get rid of easily?

What would it be like if you didn't have or could no longer use those items?

What would your daily life be like? How would you adapt?

■ Variations

Activity may be verbal or written. Activity may be used individually or in a group.

■ Concerns

Some individuals may not have many belongings and should be encouraged to identify objects such as toothbrush, hairbrush, fork, spoon, book, chair, bed, or notebook.

WHAT I COULD DO WITHOUT

The purpose of this activity is to help us prioritize and also appreciate various things in our everyday lives.

Write a list of 10 items that you use daily (whether for eating, sleeping, studying, working, resting, fun, etc.). After making the list, rank or prioritize them in order of importance. Number 1 is the most important item and number 10 is the least important.

Rank	Item

Now, cross off those five with the lowest ranking (#6-10).

What would it be like if you didn't have or could no longer use those items?

_____

What would your daily life be like?

_____

How would you adapt?

_____

135 WHAT I'VE LEARNED

Age	All	Setting	Group	Trauma Recovery	LIVING - Well

Purpose	To build critical thinking and self-reflecting skills while identifying resiliency factors.
Overview	The individual is asked to reflect on their strengths before, during, and after their trauma experience and how difficult experiences can help to make us stronger, better people.

Approximate Time	10-15 minutes	**Supplies Needed**	None or paper and pen

■ Activity Explained

- ➲ The facilitator leads a discussion asking the participant(s) to share about their lives and what positive qualities and strengths they have developed since their trauma experience. (Refer to Reflection questions below.)
- ➲ The individual is asked to share about positive personal characteristics and strengths they had before their trauma experience, reflect on which ones helped them through their trauma experience and to identify any new strengths developed since their trauma.

■ Reflection

Share three or more positive qualities or characteristics about yourself:

What are your greatest strengths—things you are good at doing (abilities, skills). These can be tangible, such as I am a fast runner or I know self-defense techniques, or intangible, such as, I am good at encouraging people or I can stand up for myself.

Which of these qualities and strengths did you have before your trauma experience? Were any of these helpful during or after the trauma? Which ones?

Did some of these positive qualities and strengths developed after your trauma experience? Which ones?

What new strengths and abilities do you have? What have you learned? How have you grown?

How do you think you have changed positively since your trauma experience?

■ Variations

Activity can be written or verbal individually or in a group setting. The facilitator could ask group members to share one strength from before and one strength from after their trauma experience and discuss how difficult things often make us stronger.

■ Concerns

The facilitator may need to help individual define a specific experience, as the individual may have had more than one trauma experience. As always, questions need to be adapted (simplified) with children and should be culturally relevant.

REFERENCES

- Cohen, J. A., Mannarino, A. P., and Deblinger, E. (2006). Treating trauma and traumatic grief in children and adolescents. New York: The Guilford Press.

- Cohen, J. A., Mannarino, A. P., and Deblinger, E. (2012). Trauma-Focused CBT for children and Adolescents, Treatment approaches. New York: The Guilford Press.

- National Child Traumatic Stress Network. Complex Trauma in Children and Adolescents. (2019). www.NCTSNet.org

- Cook A., Blaustein, M., Spinazzola, J., and van der Kolk, B. (2003). Complex trauma in children and adolescents: White paper. Allston, MA: National Child Traumatic Stress Network, Complex Trauma (NCTSN) Task force

- Courtois, Christine (2004), in Psychotherapy: Theory, Research, Practice, Training, Vol 41, No 4, 412-425

- Courtois, C. (2010) Understanding Complex Trauma, Complex Reactions, and Treatment Approaches, retrieved from www.giftfromwithin.org/html/cptsd-understanding-treatment.html

- Harborview Center for Sexual Assault and Traumatic Stress. The C.A.T. Project

- Herman, J. L. (1997). Trauma and recovery. New York: Basic Books.

- Johnson, R. (2012) Aftercare for Survivors of Human Trafficking. Social Work and Christianity: An International Journal, 39(4)

- Johnson, R. (2018). Journey to Hope: Overcoming Abuse. Rescue:Freedom International.

- Jonzon, E., and Lindblad, A. (2004). Disclosure, reactions, and social support: Findings from a sample of adult victims of child sexual abuse. Child Maltreatment, 9, 190–200.

- Konkel, L. (2018, January). What Are Common Symptoms of Anxiety Disorders?. Retrieved from www.everydayhealth.com/anxiety/guide/symptoms.

- Levine, P. A. (1997). Waking the tiger: Healing trauma: the innate capacity to transform overwhelming experiences. Berkeley, Calif: North Atlantic Books, p. 95-96

- Maruish, M. (2012). Essentials of Treatment Planning, John Wiley and Sons, p. 141

- Myers, J.E.B.,Berliner, L., Briere, J., Hendrix, C.T., Reid, T. and Jenny, C. (2002) The APSAC handbook on child maltreatment. Newbury Park, CA: Sage Publications, 2, p. 10.

- Merriam Webster Dictionary (2018) Trauma. www.merriam-webster.com/dictionary/trauma

- Pelcovitz, D.; Van Der Kolk, B.; Roth, S.; Mandel, F.; Kaplan, S.; Resick, P. (1997). Development of a criteria set and a structured interview for disorders of extreme stress (SIDES). Journal of traumatic stress. 10 (1), pp. 3–16.

- Schaeffer, P., Leventhal, J. M., and Asnes, A. G. (2011). Children's disclosures of sexual abuse: Learning from direct inquiry. Child Abuse and Neglect, 35, 343–352.

- Smith, D., Letourneau, E. J., Saunders, B. E., Kilpatrick, D. G., Resnick, H. S., and Best, C. L. (2000). Delay in disclosure of childhood rape: Results from a national survey. Child Abuse and Neglect, 24, 273–287.

INDEX (ALPHABETICAL)

INDEX (AGE AND SETTING)

TRACTs | TRAUMA RECOVERY ACTIVITIES

Group

Both

ABOUT THE AUTHOR

Dr. Johnson has served as trainer, counselor, consulting psychologist, clinical director and aftercare director for numerous anti-trafficking and child abuse organizations. Becca recently served as the International Program and Training Director for Rescue:Freedom International which partners with anti-trafficking programs around the world.

Dr. Johnson has been a licensed psychologist for 30 years, with a focus on "helping the hurting heal". Becca provides support, training and consultation on trauma-sensitive, trauma-focused care.

Becca has served as the Clinical Director for Engedi Refuge (USA), a residential recovery home for women victims of domestic sex trafficking, overseeing individual and group therapy. She has also been actively involved with Agape International Mission (AIM, Cambodia), having served as Director of Aftercare Programming .She continues as consulting psychologist for their Agape Restoration Center, a residential program for young girls removed from the sex trade in Cambodia and serves on their task force regarding a domestic (USA) response to sexual exploitation and recovery.

Becca consults and provides trauma recovery training both nationally and globally for those working with victims of sex abuse, human trafficking and sexual exploitation. Dr. Johnson has provided training for numerous organizations in Thailand, Cambodia, Myanmar, Laos, India, Philippines, South Korea, Taiwan, Costa Rica, Guatemala, Honduras, Nicaragua, Belize, Colombia, Bolivia, Brazil, Chile, Kenya, Uganda, Tanzania, Bulgaria, Moldovia, Romania, Germany, Spain, Italy, Greece, Cyprus, Australia, New Zealand, Canada and Great Britain.

Becca has also provided anti-human trafficking, aftercare and trauma training for Shared Hope International and many other anti-trafficking organizations and served as an Aftercare Associate with International Justice Mission (IJM). IJM previously required their global Aftercare programs to implement Dr. Johnson's user-friendly version of a well-researched trauma model with human/sex trafficking victims.

Becca has presented at numerous conferences, has developed a four-part, 45 session online training program on trauma, trauma recovery, and vicarious trauma. Dr. Johnson has also published two articles on trauma recovery for sex trafficking victims.

Dr. Becca has also authored books on helping the abused heal (*The Journey to Hope – Overcoming Abuse, 2018*), child abuse (*For Their Sake*), guilt (*Good Guilt, Bad Guilt*) and anger (*Overcoming Emotions that Destroy with Chip Ingram*) and will soon release a co-authored book (*with Jessa Dillow Crisp*) on encouraging sex trafficking survivors to Leave the Life.

FUTURE CONTRIBUTIONS

Your insights and experience are valued, especially when future additions are made to this list of trauma activities (TRACTs).

If you have any suggestions, recommendations, concerns or variations for the activities listed in this book, please send them in.

If you have additional activities helpful in trauma recovery and are willing to share, please send them as well to the contact below.

DrBeccaJohnson@gmail.com

Thank you.

www.ingramcontent.com/pod-product-compliance
Lightning Source LLC
Chambersburg PA
CBHW05045711O426
42742CB00018B/3282